D1605844

THE GREATEST ADVENTURES IN HUMAN DEVELOPMENT

THE GREATEST ADVENTURES IN HUMAN DEVELOPMENT

You Are the Hero

G. Kenneth West
Lynchburg College
Lynchburg, Virginia

ACCELERATED DEVELOPMENT
A member of the Taylor & Francis Group

USA	Publishing Office:	ACCELERATED DEVELOPMENT
		A member of the Taylor & Francis Group
		1101 Vermont Ave., N.W., Suite 200
		Washington, DC 20005
		Tel: (202) 289-2174
		Fax: (202) 289-3665
	Distribution Center:	ACCELERATED DEVELOPMENT
		A member of the Taylor & Francis Group
		1900 Frost Road, Suite 101
		Bristol, PA 19007-1598
		Tel: (215) 785-5800
		Fax: (215) 785-5515
UK		Taylor & Francis, Ltd.
		4 John Street
		London WC1N 2ET
		Tel: 071 405 2237
		Fax: 071 831 2035

THE GREATEST ADVENTURES IN HUMAN DEVELOPMENT: You Are the Hero

Copyright © 1995 Taylor & Francis. All rights reserved. Printed in the United States of America. Except as permitted under the United States Copyright Act of 1976, no part of this publication may be reproduced or distributed in any form or by any means, or stored in a database or retrieval system, without prior written permission from the publisher.

1 2 3 4 5 6 7 8 9 0 BRBR 0 9 8 7 6 5

This book was set in Times Roman by Sandra F. Watts. Technical development by Cynthia Long. Edited by Deena Williams Newman. Cover design by Michelle Fleitz. Printing and binding by Braun-Brumfield, Inc.

A CIP catalog record for this book is available from the British Library.

(∞) The paper in this publication meets the requirements of the ANSI Standard Z39.48-1984 (Permanence of Paper)

Library of Congress Cataloging-in-Publication Data

West, G. Kenneth.
    The greatest adventures in human development: you are the hero/G. Kenneth West.
        p. cm.
    Includes bibliographical references and index.

    1. Conduct of life. 2. Life change events. 3. Adjustment (Psychology) 4. Social values. I. Title.
BF637.C5W47 1995
158—dc20
                                           95-20240
                                           CIP

ISBN 1-56032-409-0 (cloth)
ISBN 1-56032-391-4 (paper)

To Patty

Even if no other great adventures had come my way,
our years together would have made my life complete.
Je t'aime.

TABLE OF CONTENTS

LIST OF FIGURES

PREFACE

Heroes in mythology knew of the great treasures that life offers. With courage and intelligence, these men and women faced the dangers and dragons of their world as they ventured across mysterious seas and continents. But gaining possession of life's treasures proved to be only half of their quest. Returning safely required insight, resolve, and at times even good fortune.

Today human beings differ little from mythical heroes. The dragons and challenges of life have changed their shapes and appearances. A few new ones may have been born. Nevertheless, modern adults still know of life's great treasures. As in the days of old, they must once again cross life's great seas to fulfill their dreams. And, once in possession, their trip home remains, at times, the most exciting yet perilous part of the voyage. In this modern era, the individual is still the hero of the greatest adventures in human development.

Throughout the generations the valuable quests in life have remained the same. Love beckons. For many, marriage and the nurturing of children fill the years with happiness and despair, victory and constant challenge. Work and careers offer opportunity and unique difficulties. And, as always, the search for the meaning of life awaits each seeker.

Fortunately, modern travelers inherit maps from those who journeyed before. Psychologists, counselors, theologians, and writers contribute important clues to guide individuals in their travels. Each chapter in this book examines one of life's greatest adventures and offers the wisdom and advice of those who know each voyage best. Although they serve only as advisors, their insights offer each reader an advantage over those who travel without direction.

In these chapters the reader will explore birth and loss, loving and leaving, growing up and growing old, children who succeed and fail, stagnant and fulfilling careers, faith and despair, crisis and transformation, and the final trials of the elderly. Also explored are the difficult travels of the poor and disadvantaged, and the possibility each reader has of making a positive difference in many of their lives.

Nothing can be more exciting than your life. No matter what challenge or crisis presently confronts you, it can become a call to marvelous quests. You are the hero of life's greatest adventures. Perhaps this book will make your passage a little easier.

ACKNOWLEDGEMENTS

Mentors alter the course of a person's life—forever. By displaying an active interest in my writing and ideas when I was a student at Wake Forest University, Betty Leighton redirected my career. We frequently met for lunch to discuss papers written simply for that occasion. As a professional writer and editor, Betty knew her craft. But more importantly, she simply loved the art of writing. All of us who came under her wing soon shared her passion.

Since those college days, Betty Leighton has contributed significantly to each of my books. Not only has she served as an editor, but also as a cheerleader and close friend. Betty is one of those people for whom words of appreciation seem feeble.

I feel no more capable of expressing my gratitude to my wife, Patty, and our children, Patrick, Emily and Dustin. Patty read each chapter many times and served as the illustrator for the book. As a doctoral student at the University of Virginia, she needed no additional demands made upon her time. But, as always, she accepted each request with enthusiasm and creativity.

As an unrelenting optimist, Patty always believes that good things are on the horizon. Fortunately, her positive expectations prove to be infectious. This book would not have been written without her support and inspiration.

Writing by necessity becomes a family affair. Our children heard frequently about the manuscript and, at times, I imagine they believed that the book had become another sibling. But despite the intrusion writing makes, they enthusiastically supported all of my efforts. In addition, the West children's daily excitement for life inspired many of these chapters.

Teaching at Lynchburg College, a small liberal arts college in the beautiful hills of Virginia, offers opportunities and pleasures that I wish everyone could experience. We know our students well and learn about their lives and struggles. The classroom becomes a second home. To my students, I owe not only an appreciation for their openness and enthusiasm, but also my boundless admiration.

Equally important are the close friendships that develop among faculty. For almost two decades, I've cherished my relationships with colleagues Ed Polloway, Pete Warren, Tom Tiller, Rosel Schewel and J. David Smith (now at the University of South Carolina). I'm most grateful for their constant encouragement. Lynchburg College provided financial support for writing and revising the manuscript. For that assistance, I'm tremendously appreciative.

Others provided encouragement. For almost a decade I've written a weekly newspaper column for the News and Daily Advance of Lynchburg. My editors Billy Cline and Cecil Mullan seem to provide that helpful, encouraging word at exactly the right moment. Their enthusiasm makes the weekly discipline even more fulfilling. At times, I'm overwhelmed by the positive reactions of the readers and citizens of this beautiful, Virginia community.

And finally, I offer a special thanks to the Hoffberger and Catalano families. Their stories, at least in part, appear in the final chapter of the book. Members of both families and their friends welcomed me into their lives with graciousness and enthusiasm. They shared insights and wisdom that will remain with me throughout my years.

I am greatly blessed in life to be paid for doing what I love to do. Teaching and writing are my passions. I've been doubly blessed to pursue these pleasures surrounded by people whom I love.

Chapter **1**

ADVENTURES AND DRAGONS

> Far better it is to dare mighty things, to win glorious triumphs, even though checked by failure, than to take rank with those poor spirits who neither enjoy much nor suffer much, because they live in the gray twilight that knows not victory or defeat.
>
> Theodore Roosevelt

Ponderings. *What are the most important challenges in your life at this moment? What major opportunities do you see unfolding in the next five years? What are your dreams for these years? What events or forces could prevent you from realizing these dreams? As you consider the lives of others, what life events do you believe bring the most meaning to people's lives? In modern society, what internal and external factors most frequently prevent people from reaching their dreams?*

I first realized my life was a great adventure when my sixth-grade teacher, Mrs. Cross, read aloud *The Odyssey* to us. I knew then that these stories were not just about men and women who lived thousands of years ago; they were about me and about you. We are the Penelopes, the Telemachuses, and the Odysseuses of our own life adventures. We are also flawed characters like Icarus and Achilles.

Like Odysseus's adventures, ours are filled with monsters, temptations, and twists of fate that can disrupt, sidetrack, and even end our voyages. But, like Odysseus and Penelope, we have within us the spirit and wits to persevere, to live vibrantly, and to take control of our lives.

This book is about the hero in each of us. It describes the "spirit within" that urges us to live passionately. It warns of dragons that may slay us and temptations that may seduce us into prematurely ending our voyages. We are the modern sojourners, though not unlike those who traveled before us—our own ancestors.

THE CALL TO ADVENTURE

A few men and women lead movements that liberate nations or oppressed people. The average person rarely knows them personally, but knows of them. They seem to respond without hesitation to inward and outward calls to free others from political or spiritual bondage. In doing so, they risk their lives and often die along the journey. Although more visible in their accomplishments and acclaim, world heroes are not greatly different from everyone else. Each person receives the call.

True, most people do not receive the summons to adventure in earth-shaking ways. In fact, we may wonder if we want to depart from the safety of our lives. Within each individual is a need for adventure but also the desire to keep everything the same. Predictability provides comfort; even when the ordinary falls short of our dreams, it is familiar and controllable.

Therefore, it is not surprising that personal calls for change and commitment are greeted with conflicting emotions. The invitation of the call may ask that we discover a mysterious part of ourselves that longs to be unleashed. Or it may require us to shed heavy psychological armor, carried from our pasts, that prevents us from facing important life challenges. We may be asked to leave familiar family patterns that are comfortable but are preventing us or our children from becoming full participants in the great adventures of life. The call will come often during our lifetimes.

No matter what the specific invitation of the call requires, it always demands that the well-known be abandoned and an odyssey into the unknown begun. There are no guarantees of safety or assurance. Of such risk taking heroes are made.

Many calls to adventure seem pleasant. They arrive when we believe we are ready for change. Sometimes we are ready, but at other times we are not. Therefore, these can be the most dangerous invitations, even though their arrival excites us. Often we are ill prepared for or even unaware of the dangers of the approaching journey. Such calls come with the advent of new love, new career possibilities, the birth of a child, or with various opportunities that present themselves during transitional periods. If we plunge headlong into an adventure that we are not prepared for, we may be overcome by the challenges that confront us. More difficult calls will follow.

More troublesome calls arrive with thunder; rarely are we ready for their force. They announce that we or those we love are not fulfilling their needs. Despite our intentions, something has gone awry in life. Such summonses occur at the most inopportune times when we feel consumed by life's other tasks.

Because we do not welcome calls that disrupt the normal flow of life, we may not understand the miraculous nature of the invitation. The miracle is that we receive an opportunity to embark on a liberating adventure, to bring a new passion for life to us and those we love.

These disruptive calls, like the god Proteus, take many forms. Depression often is the disguise, announcing that we have inner gifts not being developed. Marital disharmony declares that marriage, the hoped-for union of two spirits, can be so much more than we are experiencing. A child's psychological symptoms or school problems may set us on a quest for the liberation of our loved ones. Such calls may already be familiar to you.

These invitations frighten us. We know of the potential perils that await us, and we may even imagine disasters that will never evolve. We fear the abyss into which we must descend to meet and conquer the challenges that threaten us. Altering the course of life in midstream is no easy undertaking.

Supporters will be there to help. Teachers, therapists, friends, and spiritual mentors may direct us, but they can serve only as advisors. The future cannot be foretold, and we must frequently venture alone. Everyone has a unique voyage to undertake. The call will come. To hear it and respond requires the heart of a hero.

What is the call like? Think how on a long car trip you might drive for hours at night, and the broken lines pass by, again and again. Your mind wanders. You feel relaxed. Suddenly a thought startles you: I don't remember driving this car! You panic. You cannot recall the curves, the hills, passing cars or any judgment you just made. How did you dodge disaster? In the moment of panic you break into a cold sweat. Immediately, you consciously takes control of the wheel. Now every decision seems crucial. You travel down the same highway, yet everything is different. You have heard one of life's simpler calls.

Many who hear life's challenging calls refuse to take charge of the wheel. They wish to pretend that they are not responsible for the journey. Their need for comfort and predictability outweighs their spirit for adventure. They let go of the passion in favor of false security. They fear their challenges will overcome them; therefore, they choose to drive unconsciously into the night.

The timid of the earth will not jump into life's center ring where the action is. Instead, they remain satisfied with the sideshows. Nevertheless, most who fail to respond to the call will have full lives—lives that are filled with daily routines and pleasures, lives filled with events over which they feel little control, with criticism of those who take risks in life, with anger toward the fates whom they blame for their lot, with attempts to treat the hemorrhages of their lives with the small bandages offered by external sources.

Part of them still wishes to soar, however. They may become obsessed with lives of soap opera stars, so filled with emotion and change. Or, nurturing no passions of their own, they may vicariously feel the exhilaration of a basketball player who leaps above the rim to slam home a winning shot. Their addiction to the passion of others becomes a testimony to their own reluctance to live beyond the predictable. But also it gives hope that the gentle voice inside still beckons them. Some day they may take charge of the wheel.

But enough about those who ignore the call or who hearing it, fail to embark. This book is about heroes. This is a book about those who know the brevity of life and wish to experience their days to the fullest.

THE VOYAGES WE UNDERTAKE

The voyages undertaken in life are well-known. One's parents embarked on them, and their parents before them. The adventures take place on at least four great seas: love (marriage and the raising of children), careers, religion, and friendship/community making (the creation of a better planet for the adventures of future generations).

Psychologists frequently discuss life's greatest adventures. For example, Sigmund Freud wrote primarily of the first two opportunities, marriage and work. Alfred Adler and Rudolf Dreikurs recognized the additional searches. But despite the work of psychologists, the blessing and curse discovered by each sojourner is that no map or instructions dictate exactly which journeys to embark on or how to overcome the challenges to be faced.

For many, the entire life adventure can take place on a single sea. There are holy people, dedicated teachers, devoted spouses, caregivers, and noted humanitarians who concentrate on one life challenge. But most people travel all four. To balance these challenges in life calls for wisdom and courage. The challenges are different for each person; no two lives are the same.

Despite all the advice sought and received, voyagers must chart their own course, learn from their own meandering, and then frequently redirect their adventures. For each traveler the currents will change and the hazards may vary. Nevertheless, the opportunities presented by travel on the four seas fill life with the excitement and tragedy inherent in living.

One should not be frightened by the uncertainty of the odyssey. Most of the help one needs lies within.

THE INNER SPIRIT

I believe that man will not merely endure; he will prevail. He is immortal, not because he alone among creatures has an inexhaustible voice, but because he has a soul, a spirit capable of compassion and sacrifice and endurance.

William Faulkner

In his 1949 Nobel Prize acceptance speech, William Faulkner emphasized what humans for thousands of years have known: We each have a driving, inward spirit. This spirit is not a relic of superstition or a figment of literary imagination, but an inner force capable of guiding individuals to richer development.

Carl Rogers (1951, 1972; Figure 1.1) and Abraham Maslow (1968, 1971; Figure 1.2) built modern theories on their belief in the "self-actualizing tendency" that drives each human being toward greater development. As Rogers described, "This is the inherent tendency of the organism to develop all its capacities in ways which serve to maintain or enhance the organism" (Rogers, 1951, p. 196). Moreover, individuals have "an inherent capacity to move away from maladjustment and toward psychological health" (Corey, 1986, p. 102). When in harmony with this spirit, we live authentically, communicate clearly, know what is important, and resist goals and roles that violate our healthy growth. We can live in the present. And we can create relationships that enhance the inner growth of our loved ones.

Figure 1.1. Carl Rogers. Courtesy of The Center for Studies of the Person.

Figure 1.2.   Abraham Maslow. Courtesy of Brandeis University.

Through the ages, people have attempted to understand and describe this spiritual drive. Each generation knows its presence and feels its power. Yet each finds different ways to discuss its magnificence. For the ancient Hebrews, the spirit was described as the "wind" within an individual. At religious celebrations the spiritual community exchanged the pax of peace by kissing one another. It was thought that their breath carried the spirit and a shared kiss allowed worshippers to celebrate the gift of the spirit. Today, this mystery of the inner life is still pondered.

This spirit or force within carries a small voice, a feeling that can direct a person. Yet its quiet instructions can also be ignored. Rogers' works described, for example, how at an early age children begin to play roles that please others. They need to hear the applause of those they love. At their worst, they soon dance like puppets pulled by the strings of their loved ones and, later, by the expectations of society. As adults, they may frequently discover that they are out of touch with their own needs and desires. They are lived rather than living. They cannot distinguish between their dreams and the dreams others have for them.

Fortunately, the spirit within never dies or abandons us. When our behaviors conflict too violently with what our inner voice knows is best, we begin to develop symptoms, such as depression, insomnia, or disease. When forced to violate their inner voices, children begin to dysfunction as well. This is why family therapists consider most family crisis and symptomatic behavior to be a miracle. These knocks on the door signal that the spirit within begs to be heard. It is in crisis that human beings reach a crossroads, a second chance to be guided from within rather than from without.

In this age of science and technology, we may begin to doubt that we possess an inner spirit that is capable of directing us. Indeed, if you search for the words *spirit, self-actualization* or their equivalent in the index of most modern developmental psychology texts, you will be as unlikely to find it as you will the word *God, religion* or even *love*. What cannot be seen or measured is ignored.

By accepting this narrow understanding of life, humans are left at the mercy of outside forces. Soon they become convinced that the radical behaviorists are right, that people are no more than the combination of genetic material, their past training and current moods. People who ignore the spirit within them surrender their life travels to the expectations of society and to the authority of its guardians. Sadly, with surrender one abdicates the role of hero in one's own adventure.

Highly developed, the inward drive eventually propels one to give to others, to care about coming generations. Alfred Adler (Figure 1.3) and later Rudolf Dreikurs (Figure 1.4), theorists who made psychology accessible to the common man, called this force "social interest" or a "feeling with the whole *sub specie aeternitatis,* under the aspect of eternity. It means striving to form a community which must be thought of as everlasting" (Adler, 1964, pp. 34–35).

Erik Erikson (1964a), the famous developmental theorist, called this same developed spirit *generativity.* Generativity means giving to the next generation through our families, careers, and service. In an interview in the New York Times during his 80th year, Erikson wrote of the importance of the struggle between generativity and the self-absorption caused by one's surrender of spirited living.

> The only thing that can save us as a species is seeing how we're not thinking about future generations in the way we live. What's lacking is generativity, a generativity that will promote positive values in the lives of the next generation.
>
> Unfortunately, we set the example of greed, wanting a bigger and better everything, with no thought of what will make a better world for our great grandchildren. (1988, p. 1)

Most people feel the inward spirit, by whatever name it is known. They want to follow its call. They hear its whisper in the night. They know they are something more than an animal living without reflection or direction. Nevertheless, it is so difficult to escape the clutches of the dragons within and the dragons without. It is a challenge to follow the advice given by the well-known teacher Joseph Campbell to his students: "Follow your bliss."

Dragons along the Way

As in all great adventures, there must be dragons. We face fierce ones. Dragons are those forces within us as well as without that derail us from adventures. They trick us into accepting an unexamined life, as if that is all there is, or as if we cannot or should not change ourselves or our circumstances. When powerful dragons overcome us, their roar drowns out the driving spirit within us that still whispers "my life can be more than this."

Many dragons—the fiercest ones—live within. Some may be part of one's human nature or personal circumstance; others are born during childhood. If unchallenged, our personal challenges steal our minds, for we cannot think of

Figure 1.3. Alfred Adler. Courtesy of NASAP.

Figure 1.4.   Rudolf Dreikurs. Courtesy of NASAP.

how to change; our hearts, because we forget how passionate love can be; our eyes, because we become blind to the possibilities for change; our backbones, because we lose the courage to will to be different; and our souls, because we sacrifice our futures. The challenges from within can transform life into repetitive boredom or anxious desperation. The clock ticks onward, but we dare not leave the safety of what has been and what is. We become imprisoned because of our lack of self-confidence, vision, and courage.

External dragons change appearances from generation to generation. They are well-known societal demons that enter our lives through social acceptability. Most of them are two-headed. One head bears a friendly face that offers to help us succeed in everyday life; the other is a cynical soul-killer that convinces us that society's goals are our own. Within the clutches of the two-headed beings, sojourners may dysfunction. And worse, their children can become ill prepared to meet the great challenges in human development.

Recognition of the monsters is the first step in the hero's quest. Once known, the challenges remain formidable but less powerful.

Fear of Death: The Monster Within

"My goal in life is to be happy," respond most of my students when asked to discuss their life goals. My heart aches for them. Constant happiness can only be attained by gods, not mortals. The Buddha knew. His religious principles were based on the realization that all life is filled with suffering. We all face illness, aging, and death. Every stage of life, every relationship, comes to an end. At the conclusion of one chapter in life's journey, we must accept the death of a familiar, often cherished way of living and loving. Only when we allow the past to die can we give birth to the future.

Death is too much of a stranger to modern sojourners. Isn't it curious how some people treat terminally ill patients as if they are mystical beings? Every word the dying person utters is measured by the listener as if the meaning of life might be hidden within. The irony is that we are all terminal; we just don't know when or how we shall die.

The awareness of death can fill humans with great passion. That is, in fact, what separated mortals from the Greek gods, wrote Søren Kierkegaard, who has been called the father of existentialism by many scholars. Because the gods would never die, they could not feel as deeply the passions that humans expressed. The gods became fascinated with the lives of these unpredictable mortals. To love knowing that our love will end, to raise children realizing that they must leave our home, to contribute to this world knowing that we must depart from it, all of this creates intense feelings within us. We are the only animals who know that we are growing older and can actually anticipate our deaths; that makes life an emotional and passionate adventure.

Although past cultures helped people to integrate life and death, ours separates the two. Americans want to live forever. They are best at creating possibility and overcoming limitations. They may be weakest at accepting death as part of living, at letting go of the past. Death becomes an experience to be ignored. In fact, discussions of death are rare outside of specialized professions. Although death is the only event I will share with each reader, it is the one we may be least likely to discuss in general conversation. It is not nice to remind people within this eternal youth culture that they will grow older and actually die.

Rollo May (Figure 1.5) wrote convincingly in *Love and Will* (May, 1969) about the repression of death in our age. Indeed, an entire funeral industry thrives upon our denial. Dead people are made to look alive. Flowers cover expensive caskets that a grieving family invested in to "protect" the body of the "departed." Mourners praise those family members who shed no tears at the funerals of those with whom they shared life's adventure. "She was so strong," people remark. How frightening death must be for mourners who prefer that family members display no public grief.

My father died suddenly after a gall bladder attack. Dad was a religion professor and, ironically, a man who resented the funeral industry's habit of preying on our fear of death. Before his funeral my mother, who was still in shock, asked one of my sisters and me to fulfill the request of the funeral director to "view the body" before friends paid their final respects.

The young man in charge of Dad's body was handling his first case since graduating from mortuary school. He greeted us with that familiar voice, the one that apparently is learned in Mortuary 101. Looking down at the body, the young man inquired, "Is this the way the departed appeared in life?"

My sister and I, sensing how our father would react to this, glanced at each other and tried not to laugh. My first impulse was to say, "No, he looked a bit livelier." But the young man's response to our initial surprise caused us to feel compassion. Finally, we shared the idea that my father never smiled in the way he now appeared. The young man responded apologetically, "Could you please leave the room?" We did. And to our horror and amusement, the preserver of the dead rearranged my father's expression to look more "lifelike."

Figure 1.5.   Rollo May. Courtesy of W. W. Norton & Company.

For life's greatest adventures to be fully lived, adults must accept many deaths in life. Acceptance is difficult because our modern culture not only denies death but also prefers not to think of aging. But when we are unable to accept our final destiny, then we are less able to die each day in ways that will allow the birth of future possibilities and unexpressed parts of ourselves and others. Only through the death of the old ways of life can new experiences and relationships be born. To love well, one must die to the freedom of the single life. To enrich children's lives, one must die to the carefree days enjoyed by a childless couple. To enjoy our later years, we must die to the identity we enjoyed as parents of young children. Only in dying to the past are we prepared to give birth to the future, which will bring new challenges and adventures.

Those unwilling to die hold on to things like drowning swimmers. They hold on to money and possessions as if in the holding they somehow could avoid hearing the ticking of the biological clock. They hold on to relationships as they were in the past or are in the present, afraid of giving in to the unknown. They hold on to their image as a predictable character, even when the image they portray no longer serves them or others well. In midlife they hold on to their youth. But one can almost hear their fingernails scratching down the walls of time. People not ready to hear the call to adventure are dragged ungracefully into the future.

Don't look without for life's greatest challenges. Look within. Death can be the friend that gives passion to your life. It can empower you to refuse to settle for the ordinary, the given, the routine. Accepting death allows you to let go of one stage of life and journey into another.

SOCIETY'S TWO-HEADED DRAGONS

The Rush

Throughout this book we will look at the marvelous opportunities people have to create meaning in our fast-paced society. But along with the positive possibilities, our society also carries the seeds of potential destruction. If we remain in charge of our dreams, values, and decisions, society will become the tool that allows us to live meaningful and contributive lives. However, if we surrender our inner control, we can be swept away into a frenzied life—one filled with lists and things to do, but empty of meaning. The Rush can become our greatest challenge.

We have no time to be human. We rush down life's highway with such speed that we rarely notice our fellow sojourners or the exits that we pass along the way. As we gather momentum at every mile mark, we seem to accelerate. Indeed, we become a part of The Rush.

The Rush of this era—how we hate it; how we love it. To plunge with abandon into The Rush promises us rewards beyond the imaginations of people from most cultures. Cars, houses, condominiums, clothes, trips, prestige, and financial security are all ours! "Just think of the rewards," urges the friendly voice of the monster. "Quickly, you will own more than your parents or their parents or any generation before. To own, to possess: It's everything!"

Most modern men and women must live within The Rush. Some sell their souls for its promised treasures. The wise take only what is necessary to enrich living. One is dedicated to external rewards and position; the other is focused on love, self-growth, and the quest for discovery. For those who live life without reflection, the quiet voice within can be lost amidst the clamor of The Rush. But for those who are inwardly directed, the small voice becomes a trusted and valued guide even in their most hectic days.

In truth, today's Rush is only a "new and improved" version of The Rush that existed in the day of Ebeneezer Scrooge. A visit from the ghost of the present shows the highway of today's life. Follow along, and these scenes may seem familiar.

Speed begins before birth. We initiate the fetus into The Rush these days; the unborn need a fast start, "they" suggest. Possibly we should read Shakespeare's works or play Beethoven's sonatas to them. Parents need to rev up the engines of the unborn. After all, the preschool years that follow present hazardous challenges, with day care, gymnastics, and lessons of all kinds. Kids must succeed early because kindergarten follows. There, learning to read early is essential, and the social demands made on 5 year olds dazzle. So here come the children, ready or not, to tackle sports, violins, academics, and sex education.

When do children have time to relax and play? Certainly not in elementary school. The foundations learned here equip a child for The Rush. Those who travel slowly, because of nature or desire, find themselves in special programs. Once identified as slow, they may never muster the speed required to survive in middle schools and beyond.

Those early teen years provide no time for children to relax or think. With drugs rampant and new hormones shooting wildly, teens barely keep pace with their own emotions. But hurry! High school follows and that is when it really counts. Colleges will watch a child's every move, in and out of the classroom. A single disgruntled teacher might shift a person from the fast lane. Everything must be perfect. But despite tremendous effort, the Scholastic Achievement Test and other national tests loom at the end of one's studies like the Grim Reaper of youth. Nevertheless, preparatory S.A.T. courses may be one's salvation!

Off to college. But a person cannot think about life now. The fast lane takes you into a profession. "Major in something practical, something that will speed you to the next road mark in life," one is told. "Make contacts. Earn good grades. Graduate schools make good launching pads. For heaven's sake, avoid the liberal arts," the pragmatists advise. Liberal arts often are presented as an interesting curiosity that fails to give a student the business edge needed in this age.

Tough career choices await graduates. Everyone offers advice. The first step may "make or break you," warn those who hurry young minds. Decisions seem so irreversible. "Be serious about the future. Break from the starting blocks quickly," the advice continues.

Being human makes a person lonely. Not even a fast pace alters the need for companionship. "That's unfortunate. But timing is everything," advise the champions of speed. "When you are directed and settled, marry someone who shares your enthusiasm for The Rush. At the least, marry someone who will not interfere. Once married, don't rent." Early in life, new couples promise the bank that they will be subjects of The Rush for the next 25 to 30 years.

After consulting the trends and the appropriate movements for or against such things, couples decide to introduce a child into their lives. People warn them, of course. "What a commitment! It costs almost $200,000 to raise a child from birth through high school. Think of your careers, of your plans." Most adults bear children anyway; it is a human weakness, critics suggest.

Fortunate travelers simply worry about the usual debts that the fast lane brings. Those who have lost or traded companions rush harder to handle child support, visitation, and unwanted emotions. When can it stop? Well, retirement comes before you know it, but with inflation and the problems of social security, one **should**. . . .

The ghost of the present leaves us to reflect on our vision. What havoc can this two-headed beast reap? Unhappiness is created by an escalating divorce rate. Worse, couples live together without spirit, passion, or courage—couples who forfeit their relationships for the prizes of this world. Career burnout, depression, and appalling rates of suicide and alcoholism are seen. People are sustained by prescription drugs, weight loss centers, and cosmetic surgery. People run from death, but not quickly enough.

Like Scrooge, we fear most the visit from the ghost of the future. He comes to show us our children; they follow where we lead, down the highway behind us. Like each new generation, they want everything to be bigger, better, and faster. Yet, we notice in the vision that many are lonelier; their world is more dangerous. They own everything and possess nothing they love.

Yes, The Rush is both a friend and an enemy. It is where the wise who hear the call to adventure and take control of the wheel live vibrantly. Or it is the treadmill that forces us to run at its pace, to sacrifice today for a better tomorrow. Yes, the hero lives in The Rush. It is not The Rush that is evil, but our unintentional submission and devotion to it.

By knowing their mission in life and by following the passion for their inner spirit, those who make an adventure of life sidestep the dangers of The Rush. They say "No" when the world says "Faster." By turning their backs on many of the destructive treasures promised by society, wise men and women give birth to the longings of the heart. Mature adults retain the power to choose what is best for them and their families. Who is in charge, The Rush or us?

Sheriffs of the Rush

There are wise men and women who can help their fellow travelers respond to many of the challenging knocks upon the door. Sometimes they are professionals. But friends and loved ones also can free us to live with more vitality. Usually, such helpers are sojourners themselves enjoying the excitement of the excursion and the liberation that comes from self-exploration. Such people provide encouragement as well as guidance for our journey. They honor the human spirit and support the quest to live vibrantly within and beyond The Rush.

Some experts and friends, however, have never truly embraced life's greatest adventures. Their dedication remains to The Rush that trained them and now employs them, be they therapists, principals, public employees, or other professionals. Beware of those who have never smelled the salt air of the great seas. They cannot possess a vision that stretches beyond the shallow waters.

Belonging to The Rush, a few experts cross the line from advisor to police. They mold their clients to fit quietly into the system that pays the bills. Like those misguided football coaches who drug the broken bodies of their players and return them to the trenches to play ball, the Sheriffs of The Rush use any means necessary to return clients to the clutches of The Rush.

Not having journeyed far from safety, the Sheriffs misinterpret others' calls to adventure. All forms of depression, hyperactivity, suicidal thoughts, and other challenges appear to the Sheriffs to be symptoms of a sickness that must be fought as an enemy. Not knowing the thrill of adventurous living, such experts' immediate reflex is to eradicate the symptoms and return their clients to society's institutions.

Seeing symptoms as an adversary rather than a miraculous call, the Sheriffs battle against them tenaciously and predictably. Drugs are infused to make an uninspiring life more bearable. Behaviors are modified so that clients slide back into society more fluidly.

In the end, there is no difference between the Sheriffs and their clients. Neither escapes their own limitations. Neither responds to the voice of the inner spirit. Neither will experience the full excitement of human development's greatest adventures.

To find proper help, those who hear the most challenging calls of life must seek out the guides who know both worlds. Only those whose love for life's adventures is intense can help their spirit unfold. Yes, they will teach them what they must know about *living* within the system. But more important, they will nourish them in ways that allow them and their family members to experience the unique possibilities that their inner spirit longs to bring forth. The gifted helper or friend will enable them to open their sails, so that they can be filled with nourishing breezes from the sea.

POVERTY, HUNGER, AND IGNORANCE

Through no fault of their own, many people battle so fiercely for their survival that they rarely rise above the daily challenges that confront them. Numerous psychologists, including Abraham Maslow, have documented the inability of people to concentrate on love, self-esteem, and inner growth when their personal pursuit for safety, housing, and food empties their lives of energy.

The vicious cycle of poverty in Western nations is well known. Poverty generally leads to poor education, which closes job possibilities, which leads to another generation of poverty. The poor particularly fall victim to the Sheriffs of the Rush, not by choice but by fate. Sufficient money rarely finds its way from the rich coffers of The Rush to the hands of the poor.

Programs to tackle poverty frequently fail to carry either the vision or financial support necessary to alter the cycle. Those who envision, as well as those who deliver direct social or educational services, fight against difficult odds. Among those who control money and policy, there is too frequently no sincere expectation that the poor can ever escape their limiting conditions.

Poverty carries with it a haunting specter of the greatest fears of those dedicated to society's extrinsic rewards. To them nothingness is not the absence of spirited living, but the absence of comfort and material well-being. Therefore, the tendency to believe literally that "the poor are with us always" (Luke 12:8) becomes an excuse that allows the horrifying conditions of poverty to be overlooked.

In the Third World, poverty, hunger, and disease rage beyond belief. The same is true of America's inner cities and innumerable rural communities. Many people cannot see beyond their own lives and will not accept their fellow humans as neighbors. To them the poor are inhabitants of a distant world. Therefore, their plight seems irrelevant.

The wise know that we all live in one community. One child's hunger is our child's hunger. The early death from disease or malnutrition of any of this planet's travelers is the death of a brother or sister. In this short lifetime, we are all family members. It is not so much that "there but for the grace of God, go I," as it is "we are one."

The challenge to bring freedom from poverty to all people weighs heavily on all who accept life's challenges. To solve such enormous problems brings everyone one of the missions worthy of a lifetime.

The next chapters will discuss life's greatest challenges. On these great seas the reader will discover or continue to enjoy wonderful adventures. There will be ecstasy and tragedy, ends and beginnings. But for those of you with courage and vision, no matter how your story proceeds, you can be the hero of your own life adventure.

Chapter 2

THE MIRACLE OF CRISIS: A CASE EXAMPLE

Scrooge (to the ghost of Christmas future): "Where's Tiny Tim? I don't see him.
Mrs. Cratchet: "Tim, my little Tim."
Daughter: "Don't cry Mother. Don't."
Mrs. Cratchet: "I'm not crying, dear. It's the light. It hurts my eyes. Well, where's your father? He's past his time."
Daughter: "I think he walks a little slower these last few evenings, Mother."
Mrs. Cratchet: "I've known him to walk with Tiny Tim on his shoulder. Very fast indeed."
Daughter: "So have I mother."
Mrs. Cratchet: "But he was so light to carry. It was no trouble. No trouble at all."

Charles Dickens, *A Christmas Carol*

Ponderings. *Is the concept of human freedom and responsibility changing? By the mid-1990s, advancements in genetic research seemed to offer an explanation for almost every human frailty. In response, could it be that individuals and families shifted the responsibility for solving their challenges to the hands of experts—people who live outside of their families?*

Many argue that it is not the gifts people inherit, but how they use them that counts. If so, how can people work more effectively with science and professionals? For example, what is our responsibility for helping family members overcome their challenges and develop their potential to the fullest? Do we have the responsibility to ask ourselves tough questions: How does my behavior harm or liberate those around me? Could something in my marriage or in our family complicate or harm the life of someone I love? In this new era, what responsibility do we have to ourselves, our families, and others? What power do we possess to respond to the crises that may confront us or those whom we love?

Life does not always flow as smoothly as textbooks suggest. This chapter begins with the challenges of the Crompton family—four wonderful people whom I first met in family counseling. A crisis struck one of the Crompton children. Although the parents looked at the emergency as an unwanted intruder, I believe it now offers them a marvelous opportunity. Instead of an interruption to life, their crisis can be a call to awareness, which can lead to individual and family growth and development.

The call to adventure and change comes to each of us. The summons comes both to individuals and to families. Sometimes the summons gently appears as an opportunity, a door opening when we least expect it. At other times, the call assumes the cloak of a crisis or tragedy. Calls, if tragic, are often not overcome. Yet we all have read about those individuals who triumphed over tragedy— victories that led them toward more challenging experiences or greater contributions.

The vast majority of these heroes' stories never become public knowledge. Most appear to live ordinary lives. Many are men and women who accepted the crisis of a loved one as the invitation to lead their family on an exodus from stagnation to growth and adventure. To succeed, they followed a dream created by their inner vision and marched, at great risk, away from familiar, shallow waters. To do otherwise, to ignore or avoid the calls of family members, would have been easier but not heroic.

Calls involving family crisis are almost always unwanted and inconvenient. Conflict, however, shakes us from our contentment and urges us to regain contact with our directing innermost feelings. Such was the case with the Crompton family, when the psychological and educational challenges confronting their young son placed the family at a crossroads.

THE MIRACLE OF FAMILY CRISIS: THE CROMPTON FAMILY

When I asked, Emily Crompton responded that she had arranged the family's appointment because of Samuel, their 8 year old son, and his hyperactivity.

Samuel sat quietly beside his sister Sarah, age 10. Sarah looked like a treasured doll, perfectly dressed and groomed. Charles and Emily Crompton sat with the children placed carefully in between them, but more than two chair widths seemed to separate the parents' lives.

Quickly, Emily outlined the surface problem, the call to adventure. Samuel is disrupting his class. His teacher said he seemed hyper, and she just couldn't deal with him any more. So she sent him to the principal. The principal suggested that we put him on a drug called Ritalin to calm him down. All of the school personnel agree that Samuel suffers from an attention deficit hyperactivity disorder (ADHD). Last week I saw Samuel's pediatrician. He assured me that Ritalin would calm Samuel and that the medication could begin next week. But the doctor suggested that I see you as well. I would have only brought in Samuel, but your secretary said that you would want to see the whole family.

I looked at the "villain," Samuel. He sat quietly, almost motionless, staring at the floor. He was not sure how to behave in the presence of a stranger.

I observed, "Samuel, you seem calmer than my children."

"They say he suffers from situational hyperactivity," interrupted Mrs. Crompton. "He only loses control in school and in some social situations."

Samuel continued to gaze at the floor, his eyes unfocused.

Soon, I shifted the attention of the session to Charles Crompton to discover his role in the family. Charles slumped stoically in his seat. Obviously, only his body had been present until this moment: "Mr. Crompton, tell me a little about life in the Crompton home."

"Well," he struggled, "You probably should ask my wife. I'm a salesman for a major appliance dealer, and I travel much of the week. When I return home, I'm usually greeted by my wife's endless listing of Samuel's school offenses. Quite frankly, I think the schools just don't know how to discipline any more. I rarely have trouble with Samuel; he knows what he'll get if he misbehaves around me. Don't you, boy? Now Sarah, she's an angel. She doesn't give anyone any trouble—makes straight A's too."

At the mention of Sarah, Samuel slumped further into his seat. Obviously, he was frequently the victim of discouraging comparisons.

I talked with each child for a few minutes. Sarah was guarded, cautiously smiling at me after every response. Carefully, she gauged my reaction to each of her statements. It became apparent in our discussion that Sarah enjoyed few friends but basked in the praise and admiration of adults. Charles' description of her as an "angel" seemed accurate; what a tough role for a human to assume. What a difficult sibling for a young brother to follow.

Talking to Samuel proved to be difficult because Emily frequently attempted to speak for him. Obviously, Emily was immersed in his life. Samuel presented himself as an active young boy who hated school, a combination I remembered well from childhood. He enjoyed playing with a group of boys in the neighborhood. And, yes, he was often sent to the principal's office. Understandably, he disliked his teacher and the principal.

The conversation eventually worked its way to the Cromptons' marriage. "Tell me a little about your relationship," I requested of both spouses.

Neither spoke at first. Finally, Emily offered: Well, I guess we're very normal. As Charles said, he's usually out of town several days a week. I work full time as a legal secretary, so I'm always exhausted. I never seem to catch up on everything I need to do. We rarely go out alone because there's always so much work to do at home. And my husband is an avid golfer . . .

Angrily, Charles interrupted: Don't start that golf thing again. Doctor, I used to be a tournament golfer. Golf is really my only means of entertainment. I play twice a week, on the weekends. She knew when we married it was my one great love. I'm not going to give it up. Emily, I cannot believe you'd nag me about golf when we're here to handle Samuel.

Emily looked hopeless. She had thrown out the comment about golf hoping that a miracle would occur. Her husband's anger assured her that no such intervention would be forthcoming.

Often, when couples disagree on discipline issues, they are split on relationship issues as well. Couples frightened by the frailty of their connection often develop an unwritten contract to disagree only on comfortable battlefields. For Emily to mention golf violated their informal agreement.

Our discussions uncovered the history of Charles' and Emily's relationship. They attended the same college and began to date each other during their sophomore year. Charles was a history major destined for the business world. Emily majored in English, but was unsure of which careers might interest her. After graduation from college, Charles was offered a marvelous job. Emily accompanied him and the two married 6 months later. Fourteen months after their marriage Sarah was born. Mrs. Crompton shelved her career aspirations and began life as a full-time mother. Three years after the birth of Samuel, Emily took a job as a legal secretary to help pay the mounting bills.

By the end of the session, I realized that Charles was indeed a disciple of a rushed and frantic society. His business travels and his sports interests swallowed his days. As a father, he offered minimal involvement. Occasionally, he participated in family outings, but he rarely spent time with individual family members, including his wife.

In addition to working full-time, Emily tended to the children and took care of the housework. Apparently, her verbal exchanges with the children could be characterized as irritable and functional. Emily enjoyed no hobbies or diversions. Her present challenge in life, she believed, was to contain, not to liberate, the emotions and behaviors of her family. Emily Crompton's body posture testified to her lack of excitement in life.

As the initial interview ended, I tested the possibilities for extended family counseling. Charles explained that he did not see a reason for him to be there. After all, it was Samuel's problem. However, he agreed to attend if he must. Emily was anxious to return. Obviously, her unspoken hopes extended far beyond a quick cure for Samuel. Sarah did not express an opinion. She was willing to do whatever her parents decided. Samuel, who responded immediately to the bits of encouragement I offered during the session, quickly volunteered to return.

Thus the Crompton family reached the familiar crossroads, one where the call beckons. Their most important journey together would soon begin.

The Call: A Small Voice amidst the Roar

> The Emperor bowed graciously to the left and right, as the people cried, "How splendid are the Emperor's new clothes! How beautifully they fit! Such color, such rare and costly cloth!"
>
> Then all at once a little child cried, "But he hasn't got anything on!" And though his mother hushed him quickly, the Emperor had heard. Perhaps the child was right! The thought made his flesh creep but he knew that being the Emperor, he must lead the Procession through to the end. So he squared his shoulders and held his head high while the lords in waiting followed, bearing the train that wasn't there at all.
>
> *The Emperor's New Clothes*

The Cromptons drove swiftly into the night. Calls probably had come to the adults in the family many times before. The burning passion of humans demands an outlet. The Cromptons' marriage burned off too little of their emotion and desire. Therefore, their unspent energy, as in other fragile marriages, may have manifested itself in migraines, affairs, exhaustion, excessive drinking, avoidance of each other, or in countless nonproductive brushfires. But because Charles and Emily apparently ignored early alarms, the severity of the call increased.

More difficult calls always come later for those who lack the courage to respond in the present. But sometimes, when calls are neglected for too long, trials are passed on to another generation. The calls that children hear are rarely a result of their own creation.

As so often happens in the uproar of life, the voice of a small child can be clearly heard. Samuel's alarm invades the quiet of the night, announcing that the Crompton's car strayed dangerously from the center of the road. Samuel's life carries with it his own passion, but also the pressures inherited from his parents' neglect. Like a teakettle, he whistles for relief. What remains uncertain is his parents' response to the call, hidden within Samuel's crisis. Will they take control of the wheel?

For Charles the call initially appears to be a threat, not a miracle. He senses that he can lose what little he does possess. Therefore, his first reaction will be to horde his meager riches from external threats. As a dog hides his bones, Charles will try to bury his treasures. At this moment, Charles is blind to the possibilities for growth that await him and his family. Like his wife, he thinks only of containment, not of liberation. If only someone would take this crisis out of our hands, then we could escape without loss, reflects Charles.

Emily Crompton senses that Samuel's call symbolizes the family's unmet challenges. But she fears opening the floodgates by examining her own inner feelings. What would happen if she looked inside and discovered what she really desired in life? What would happen if she challenged the family to stop drifting in shallow waters? She receives Samuel's call with anxiety, with that haunting apprehension that this may be an opportunity to venture into desired but dangerous waters. Because no guarantee exists to insure the outcome of a bold adventure, Emily is reluctant to venture far from the stagnant, yet safe waters.

Calls come in so many ways. They come gently or with terrible force, but they come. For the Cromptons, the call came through a small voice. They hear, but will they respond heroically, or, like the Emperor, will they continue their parade, bothered but without change?

Spirits on Hold

Inward spirits are quiet but persistent. In The Rush of marriage, career making, and raising children, an individual's own swift motion and the roar of personal challenges may drown out the spirit's gentle, guiding voice. Nevertheless, the call—for a moment—gives the possibility of hearing the inner spirit's message. The Cromptons now are called upon to awaken from their hurried slumber.

That Emily and Charles Crompton have grown insensitive, and perhaps deaf, to the guiding voice of their spirits can be seen in their lack of personal excitement, the dreary state of their lives together, their inability to nourish each family member, and their fear to look within.

The Crompton's loss of connection with their inward feelings robs them of the true enjoyment of life's greatest challenges. But also their children will be poorly prepared to journey on their personal adventures. Their lack of inwardness prevents Emily and Charles from asking questions of ultimate importance: Where are we going? What are our dreams? What do we love? What is the purpose of our lives together? What gifts can we share with others?

Each family member keeps the spirit at a distance, but some occasionally feel its push. Samuel feels the force of his spirit the most, but his inward drive lacks the nourishing environment needed to find healthy outlets. Still it pushes. And the force creates frustrations that he is unable to understand. As a result, he plunges into symptomatic behavior—a plea for more nurturing guidance.

Charles' spirit is frozen by his fear of the future. Feeling excitement in life only outside of the family, Charles fears that changes within the family could rob him of the scant intensity he now experiences. Ironically, he sees the family as a predator capable of ripping to shreds the remains of his life. After all, what would happen if future, unknown demands made his golf scores soar or his sales drop? Charles Crompton's inward dragons roar.

Emily Crompton perceives that powerful forces within her beg to be unleashed. Because of this relentless urging from within, she harbors the hope that her life and her family's could be so much more than it is. But she too imagines disaster: the loss of her husband or the destruction of the comfort that the predictability of her life offers. Also, she feels hurt, neglected, and unappreciated. What would happen if her emotions erupted? Emily Crompton is unlikely to unleash the powerful forces within her on her own behalf, but to liberate her son, Emily Crompton might respond to the knock on the door. With a little courage and encouragement, she could engage the dragons in furious battle.

The person most vulnerable to losing contact with her inner self is Sarah. Quiet, conforming people often slide by in life unnoticed. Living to please others, they create little conflict. But often the price they pay is found in the distance that separates them from their inner selves. Sarah dances to the applause of others. Soon she will be unable to separate her own dreams from those of her parents, teachers, and society. Because conformists fill their days enjoying the songs of others, their only taste of adventure often comes as passengers on another's voyage.

The spirit in each member of the Crompton family is on hold. If only a liberator from within the family would arise to free them.

THE DRAGONS THAT ROAR

What prevents you from hearing the voice of your inner spirit? What stops you from experiencing its loving shove? Or what prevents you from striving to make the dreams of your inner self come true? Whatever forces stand in your way are your dragons.

The Cromptons' Inner Dragons

Fear of dying to the security and the prizes of their present lives imprison both Emily and Charles Crompton. Both cling to their meager treasures. If the clock could be turned back, I suspect it would be discovered that Charles was never a man who could let go of one stage of life to enter freely into another. Probably he never died to the ambitions and joys of the single life enough to become truly married. After all, didn't he report that golf was his "one great love?" By fiercely holding onto his passions for his career and athletic acclaim, Charles was not free to embark on a marital voyage with Emily. Never married in their goals, communications, or dreams, the two shared a marriage that lacked passion and a sense of togetherness. In truth, they owned a home and produced children, yet both remained single—one by choice.

Ignoring warnings to tend to their marriage, the Cromptons unwittingly awaited an alarm that could not be disregarded. The voice of the new call demanded a response to the fundamental question: "Can you die to your self-centeredness enough to give birth to mutual possibilities?"

Because Emily Crompton has less to lose, she may be more willing to accept risks. Her career brings her only scraps of happiness and her marriage offers little more than predictability. Nevertheless, her marriage is Emily's only experiment with "love." So now Emily Crompton is besieged by two internal dragons: "What if?" and "Yes, but."

Through Emily, "What if" demands: "What if you stir the waters and your husband leaves you?" "What if your children lose their father?" "What if you are left alone to face the world with your children?" Without the confidence and encouragement that her inner spirit can give, Emily Crompton feels power-less in the face of the dragon's threats.

After "What if" convinces its victim that catastrophe looms ahead of every risk, "Yes, but" begins its fiendish work. To every practical suggestion from friends or professionals, the dragon, through its victim, argues: "Yes, you're right; I should do this or that. But let me tell you why it won't work." Common sense and practical ideas are repeatedly tossed overboard. In the end, if the dragons devour Emily's courage, she may remain afloat, but only in a rowboat not capable of navigating across life's great seas.

Other challenges await Emily Crompton. "If only" is a demon of our later years. Already its voice can be anticipated. If only the Cromptons had faced their immortality. If only they had heard the seconds swiftly ticking, they might have realized that they were killing their youthful opportunities to meet life's most significant challenges. Internal dragons feast upon our fear to act when the future cannot be controlled.

The Roar of the Rush

After mortals taste the alluring fruits of a rushed and frantic society, addic-tion follows. At its worst, The Rush then orchestrates the family's every move-ment rather than the family freely playing the music it creates. Even when their frenzied participation in society brings little happiness or a legion of demoraliz-ing problems, the addict's participation in The Rush remains an obsession.

Addicted to The Rush's fruits, the Cromptons speed onward. Soon they own the rewards tossed to them by society: a house, cars, clothes, vacations, and educational funds for their children. In exchange for these, the Cromptons slave day and night, becoming wealthier financially and increasingly impoverished spiritually. Charles and Emily believe that no alternatives exist, that they are puppets controlled from without. Freedom to choose their future course in life becomes for the Cromptons an abstraction rather than a reality. In the end, the possessions the Cromptons own or can own become the captors that confine them to life as it is or worse, rather than the liberator they once dreamed their wealth would become.

The Rush infects its addicts with a fear of impending catastrophe. This terror declares that no matter what one owns, it is not enough. It hints that if an addict should rebel or wish to change the terms of his or her participation in The Rush, *everything* could be lost. An all-or-nothing, catastrophic world view aborts any attempt to create the sane adjustments that might place The Rush back under the control of its subjects.

Ironically, the Cromptons own more resources than they will ever need in order to be happy, more than the vast majority who live in this world or that past generations ever imagined possible. But once one tastes the fruits of The Rush, one becomes subject to its delusions.

Fully possessed by and addicted to the rules and customs of The Rush, Charles Crompton becomes easy prey for his internal dragons: What if I made career changes? Think of all that I could lose! What if I spent more time with my children? Think of how far behind I could fall. What if I altered my weekend priorities? Think of all of the happiness and contacts I would forfeit. Soon the ogres attack Charles' personal life as well: What if I tried to grow closer to Emily? Think of what a failed attempt might mean.

Once the demon "What if" finishes his monstrous work, "Yes but" completes the spirit's destruction. Yes, I could make this or that change, but let me tell you why that risk would fail. Soon Charles Crompton may convince himself that his wife and children need a provider more than they need a husband and father. His addiction erodes the foundation that supports his family's relationships.

Emily Crompton suffers from a secondary addiction to The Rush. Like the victim who develops cancer from the smoke of a loved one's cigarettes, Emily Crompton becomes yet another statistic in The Rush's files. She suffers, but without protest. Emily enables Charles to continue in his addiction by becoming a less willing, but nevertheless compliant, slave of The Rush.

If the Cromptons' dragons roam unobstructed, the family will remain imprisoned. They will be convinced that no alternative exists except to speed ahead as planned. "After all," they will recite to themselves, "everyone rushes ahead, don't they? When a crisis arrives, we'll tough it out."

If The Rush prevails, the call to Samuel will be viewed as a threat, as an external enemy. What will happen to Samuel? At the worst, he will be placed in the hands of the Sheriffs of The Rush. The Sheriffs are those who force others to fit into narrow roles in life. They are interested more in conformity and obedience than in expansion and liberation. The Sheriffs will muffle Samuel's spirit, modify his behavior, calm him with drugs, and allow Emily and Charles to ignore the call and continue their flight to nowhere. The dragons want nothing less than the Cromptons' souls.

The Sheriffs That Await

For every Sheriff dedicated to forcing people to conform at all costs, there are a host of committed professionals intent upon helping individuals develop their potential and abilities. Teachers, principals, doctors, and psychologists work daily with children and their families to help them develop positively. These professionals believe in their students' and patients' ability to transform crisis into growth. But in every school system and community there are Sheriffs. Usually, they are well known by those functioning on higher levels. But for those who are powerless or unaware of the potential for individual and family growth, the Sheriffs can destroy their attempts to grow and develop.

To surrender our personal crises to the Sheriffs of The Rush is a tragedy of our day. To turn their backs on the call to adventure and to hand over their symptoms to the Sheriffs robs a family of the opportunity to use their own minds, eyes, hearts, and souls to liberate themselves. How is it that many modern families have become so dependent, so blind, so unimaginative? Unless by accident or design we discover professionals who know the tremendous possibility for individual and family growth, we are doomed to allow physicians to tell us when to live and when to die, principals and teachers to tell us when our children need drugs, and therapists to bandage our wounds and return us to the whirlwind of The Rush.

Sheriffs know little about the inner spirit; they value order and speed. They are cogs in a fast-paced society that has no tolerance for those who fit imperfectly into the system and no time to allow people to discover their own paths.

Who can blame Samuel Crompton's teachers and principal? They already live under intense scrutiny and suffer harsh public criticism for not moving children along fast enough. His teachers demand manageable classrooms. They deserve them. Principals want orderly schools. Everyone agrees. But too often families do not want to be inconvenienced and troubled by their children's problems. So professionals try to relieve these families of their painful crises, the calls that if faced could lead to their liberation.

Many years ago Philip Slater (1976) coined the term Toilet Theory to describe how the Sheriffs of The Rush handle those who fit imperfectly into society. They are flushed from the main stream to orphanages, special classes, nursing homes, and, more recently with the homeless, they overflow into the streets.

Samuel does not fit snugly into The Rush. The Sheriffs stand ready to flush him. Because the Cromptons are disciples of the system, they will be tempted to surrender the custody of Samuel and their family's call to the Sheriffs. Then everyone—the schools, the doctors, and the Cromptons—can resume full speed ahead. Samuel certainly will not protest his own sacrifice; after all, he is only 8 years old and is dependent on the wisdom of adults.

After people become enslaved to the rewards of The Rush, they display the symptoms of their addiction. Their vision blurs, their hearts grow small, and their courage to stand up to the Sheriffs weakens. Is it any wonder that the Cromptons will require heroism to understand the miracle hidden within their family's crisis? It is so difficult to listen to the inner spirit whisper: "Samuel's life can be more than the Sheriffs envision. So can ours."

Family Change and Family Transformation

On making difficult choices, I defer to Hawkeye Pierce, the drive-em-crazy doctor in MASH, who said,

> Sometimes you have to leave the city of your comfort and go into the wilderness of your intuition. You can't get there by bus, only by hard work and risk and by not quite knowing what you're doing. But what you'll discover will be wonderful. What you'll discover will be yourself.
>
> *MASH*

Some families change and a few transform. Family change involves one or more family members making adjustments in living that decrease the symptoms of its members and increase the ease of living together. The changes usually are external and do not require a vision created by the inner spirit.

Family change occurs from without, coming largely because of the techniques used by professionals to alter family dynamics. Such changes are positive and might include an increase in communications skills, the acquisition of new parenting techniques, the gaining of benefits from assertiveness training, and a host of other techniques and skills that bring relief to clients. Families do not necessarily change within to make these external changes. Inner change is least likely when therapists rush to create goals and therapeutic plans before their clients come into contact with their inner spirits.

Family transformation involves a vision, a dream that the family creates and pursues. Transformation occurs when individuals, usually adults, become connected with their inner spirit. They no longer wish to be captives, but want to experience love, relationships, religion, or careers with more intensity. Their goal is to be liberated from a way of life that brought about the symptoms, not to eradicate the symptoms. While family growth originates from the outside and may or may not leak inside, transformation originates from the inside and bounds outward.

Transformed people question the purpose of life, seeking vitality in the limited days of their existence. Transformation does not take people away from society, but allows them to experience life and relationships intensely while harvesting only the healthy rewards of The Rush. Although transforming families may benefit from techniques and skills professionals teach, they use them to pursue their vision, not to eliminate their symptoms. Individuals can transform without their families. However, their metamorphosis does not insure that their families will also transform. In fact, when an individual grows from within in isolation from the family, additional problems may develop. For example, uneven growth patterns in marital partners may endanger their relationship.

Transformation requires that people see, accept and strive toward the vision their inner-spirit dreams. Professionals or friends who believe that living well requires vision and courage can help sojourners contact their inner-spirits. Also, they may encourage them to respond to their dreams. But, at best the Sheriffs of The Rush can only help the family survive its present crisis, for only the transformed can be midwives to transformation.

RESPONSES TO THE CALL

We left the Cromptons at a crossroads. To imagine where they might venture limits artificially the endless variety of journeys they may undertake. I share below three possibilities, representative of the types of choices frequently made. The first scenario tells of a common response: a retreat into the safety of an unexamined life. Two scenarios describe courageous journeys: one adventure that ends in the midst of struggles and therefore, in possibility, and one that ends on the high seas. In imagining these scenarios, I offer my apologies to the Cromptons and to all whose lives are guided by their inner spirits, for heroes enjoy unlimited possibilities in navigating the great seas.

Scenario One: Return to the Small Pond

Charles Crompton soon found family therapy to be a major hindrance to his career responsibilities. Much to his wife's disappointment, Charles dropped out of the sessions, although he urged Emily to continue. Emily, overcome by her responsibilities and disappointments in life, found it easier to allow Samuel to bear the burden of individual counseling and daily medication. Before she terminated therapy, Emily Crompton learned a handful of behavioral techniques to help her handle Samuel's misbehavior problems. Also, Emily accepted the challenge to follow her son's progress in school more closely. The Sheriffs were pleased with Samuel's progress. Soon, with a haunted feeling, Emily terminated all counseling.

Mr. Crompton won several sales awards in the coming years. On one occasion he won the club's open golf championship, defeating a host of competitors half his age. Pleased with his affair with his career and sports, Charles Crompton continued his passage down the highway of The Rush.

Although Emily Crompton occasionally thought of going back to college, she never seemed to make plans to do so. Her relationship with Charles never improved, but her children needed her. She had pills to monitor, time-consuming interactions with Samuel's teachers, and housework to face when her secretarial day ended. Once in a while she felt a gnawing inside, a dissatisfaction deep within. But through the years she attended to it less and less.

Samuel's behavior improved. His teachers were pleased with his new responsiveness to their directions. Certainly the medication seemed to help his performance, although Samuel never became an honors student like Sarah. From time to time, Samuel regressed and everyone worried as he fluctuated between conformity and rebellion. But the doctor always adjusted Samuel's medication, until whatever stirred inside of him released him. In some ways, Samuel may have even sensed that by keeping the center of attention focused on him, he not only found a prominent position in the family, but also he gave his parents something important to discuss. Meanwhile, Sarah became quite a young perfectionist.

Scenario Two: The Lonely Voyage

Charles Crompton soon found family therapy to be a major hindrance to his career responsibilities. Much to his wife's disappointment, Charles dropped out of the sessions, although he urged Emily to continue.

As Mrs. Crompton continued seeing the counselor to learn how to help Samuel, she began to mention her concerns about her marriage. First, it was a slight reference to Charles' lack of involvement with their children. Soon she confessed the hurt and anger she felt over their lifeless relationship. After she presented her concerns, she and the counselor attempted to bring Charles Crompton into the sessions. Their attempts proved to be fruitless; Charles was simply too busy. Consequently, the counselor worked with Emily to devise strategies that might encourage Charles to show a more active interest in their children. Again, all attempts to influence Charles' behavior failed. After several months, Emily abandoned her goal to alter Charles' role in the family and began to work on herself. Her first goal was met when she created more time to read and to exercise. As the weeks passed, Emily grew more in touch with her long, ignored dreams. She shared with the counselor her secret ambition to teach elementary school children. With his encouragement, Emily discovered which courses she needed to take in order to gain certification.

When her plans to pursue certification were ready, she presented her ideas to Charles. He reacted violently to her plan: Of course she shouldn't spend the time or the money on such craziness. Was she mad?

Emily Crompton stumbled into depression for a period of weeks. Her counselor, understanding the healing power of most depressions, supported Emily while she struggled inwardly. He offered her no drugs or quick escapes. To hear the voice of the spirit, Emily needed time to listen and to respond. Like a protective blister, the depression sheltered and nourished Emily until she was strong enough to emerge with her dream in hand. Now that she knew what she must do, nothing would stop her.

Emily Crompton stood up to Charles. Yes, she would take the courses necessary to become a teacher. Shocked at her first serious challenge to his authority, Charles gave in, but not without issuing a few bitter comments about how silly she was being at her age and how her counseling seemed to be creating problems for both of them.

Within the college environment, Emily Crompton felt the excitement of learning and the thrill of possibility for her future career. Unlike her college courses years ago, Emily's present work proved to be stimulating and purposeful. For the first time in almost 18 years, Emily felt good about herself.

Being with her husband, however, became less bearable. With excitement filling one part of her life, she knew she could no longer settle for the dullness of an unemotional relationship. On numerous occasions she pleaded with Charles to choose a counselor for the two of them to see together. He refused.

After pushing and pushing, Emily Crompton gave up. She issued an ultimatum: "Either we go to counseling or we must separate." Shocked and hurt, Charles packed his things and left the same evening that her challenge was made. However, Charles Crompton assumed that it would be only a matter of time before Emily asked him to return.

Life without Charles was little different than life with him. Her work load remained the same or was reduced if anything. Only now she did not face the terrible emptiness of their relationship every time she saw him. Only because of their children did Emily have second thoughts about asking Charles for a divorce.

Lonely and confused, Charles Crompton called Emily to ask her to pick a counselor for the two to see. She now felt reluctant to pursue counseling, but because of her children she assented.

In counseling, the therapist suggested that Emily and Charles date again to discover each other. On one occasion they even left their children with friends and took their first weekend trip in years. Charles Crompton worked very hard to court his wife again, but for Emily something basic was missing. Emily recognized that the two of them had never been married; they were separate spirits. Her feelings no longer poured out hurt and anger. Instead, she felt detachment. Worse, she felt herself torn between one voice that said, "Journey alone," and another voice that urged, "Don't give up hope." For now, she chose not to end either the separation or the marriage.

This couple is left in the midst of their struggle. Emily Crompton feels the excitement of growth and vision. She is in touch with her inner voice; Charles is not. He still fears losing what he has. As of yet, he has not smelled the salt air. His wife, once afraid of sea breezes, now can no longer live without them. In time, Charles may become a true sojourner. But for now, he remains a panicky creature. He sees Emily's movement, not as his personal call, but as an enemy that threatens his controlled world. These days, Emily Crompton knows that Charles is not, as of yet, a kindred spirit.

Scenario Three: When Life Becomes the Teacher

Charles Crompton soon found family therapy to be a major hindrance to his career responsibilities. Much to his wife's disappointment, Charles dropped out of the sessions, although he urged Emily to continue. Emily Crompton, overcome by her responsibilities and disappointments in life, found it easier to allow Samuel to bear the burden of individual counseling and daily medication. Before she terminated therapy, Emily Crompton learned a handful of behavioral techniques to help her handle Samuel's misbehavior problems. Also, Emily accepted the challenge to follow her son's progress in school even more closely.

As a result, the Crompton family changed but did not transform. Everyone seemed pleased. Samuel caused less disruption while on his medication and Emily Crompton more ably responded to Samuel's misbehavior at home when he was not taking his medicine. Sarah continued to be the ideal student and child. Charles continued to be known as a talented salesman and an exceptional golfer. Only Emily carried an aching in her heart that is caused by sensing, yet avoiding the knowledge that something was missing in their lives.

Then, on a stormy Sunday afternoon 6 months later, Charles Crompton's foursome rushed to finish the back nine as a storm approached. Caught on the course when the fury of the storm broke, the men began to hustle back to the clubhouse. Along the way, Charles felt severe chest pains and collapsed.

That was Charles Crompton's last memory before awaking in the hospital with tubes running into and out of his body. The nurses summoned the doctors as Mr. Crompton regained consciousness. Charles felt dazed and shocked. He quickly understood what had happened, but was startled to hear that if it were not for a doctor's presence on the golf course, his life would have surely ended.

Lonely days awaited him. Charles' days in the hospital dragged by. As the hours passed, he stared at the ceiling and reviewed his life over and over again. Then, to pass the time he created a game, trying to remember what he was doing in each year of his life. The days of his youth blurred together. All he could remember were the relationships he treasured: his parents, his siblings, his friends. Although he remembered the first golf tournament he won at the age of 12, his remaining victories seemed unimportant. As he began to review the years since his marriage, tears flowed. Once again, he remembered only the people he loved.

Where were the recollections of the great sales he had pulled off? Where was his memory of the burst of energy he felt after he rolled those long birdie putts into the hole? They seemed unimportant now.

With his reflections came grief and regret. What were Samuel and Sarah really like? How had Emily put up with him for so many years? For the first time since childhood, Charles felt his inward spirit arise. He cherished its song, its urging for him to feel emotions long avoided. Yes, he had ignored the spirit's calls before. But this one—this one literally struck with thunder. In these days of recovery, Charles became a man, no longer a god with endless years of life ahead.

Now, transformed from within, Charles greeted his family as the strangers who would mean everything to him. Knowing that he must adjust his life's pace to ease the tension on his heart was less the reason he wanted to change his lifestyle than his desire to discover his family.

Charles had spent time with his family before, but now he lived for those moments. Sure, there were the usual conflicts and discipline problems with his children. But they were not just annoying "kids" anymore;, they were his children, people he loved. When adults recognize their mortality, children no longer are inconveniences to be tolerated. Charles Crompton's children filled his fleeting days with energy and excitement.

Emily Crompton was not ready for Charles' increased attention. At times, she found his new attachment suffocating. Charles slowly learned to respect Emily's need for privacy and aloneness. As a couple, they confronted the usual challenges that occur when transformation in life begins with one person.

Charles Crompton discovered his wife was a dynamic woman, a person who for years had carried the entire family on her shoulders. He found her to be a dreamer, her dreams hidden from him because of the muffling of their inner spirits. So many of Emily's dreams were like his own. Together they explored their emerging interests and treasured their time with one another. At last, they became truly married.

Understanding the loneliness that his children had felt in their years without his active presence, Charles became interested in working with other young people. At first he became a volunteer in organizations that interested his children. Soon he was volunteering his time whenever he could make a difference. His golf handicap skyrocketed, although he occasionally played golf with his friends. Now it was the companionship of his friends and not the birdies that he loved.

Emily Crompton continued her work as a legal secretary and began to take evening courses to prepare for a possible career in teaching. Sarah Crompton became comfortable enough with her parents to complain about life, and even to be rebellious from time to time. Eventually, Samuel just grew out of his early problems. Although he did not reach the level of his sister's school achievements, he did well enough. Nevertheless, Samuel's achievements were less important to Charles than their relationship. So few years remained before Samuel and Sarah would reach the age when they would leave home.

To many cynics, frightened by their inner spirits, this scenario may seem like a fairy tale. That is a shame; fairy tales do come true when the inner spirit's dreams are pursued. Unfortunately, many fail to respond to the calls in their lives. They may spend all of their years doing what seems easiest only to discover years later that there was nothing there of lasting value. For heroes like Charles Crompton in this scenario, adventure does not remove them from the known world but allows them to live intensely within it. Charles does not know how long he will live, but he knows what living really is.

Chapter 3

LOVE:
THE GREATEST ADVENTURE

Love is the only sane and satisfactory answer to the problem of human existence.

Erich Fromm

Love is space and time measured by the heart.

Proust

Ponderings. *What are the ingredients of "perfect love?" Are there positive relationships that may be less than ideal? Why do many psychologists believe that a sound identity must be created before true intimacy is possible? How do men and women differ in creating their identities? How can this question "Who are you?" be answered? What factors can lead a person to marry the "wrong person?" What should marriage vows include and symbolize? Why do one-half of marriages end in divorce and many others seem to lack vitality? What qualities can be seen in couples who maintain exceptional marriages? Is marriage easier the second time around?*

IN SEARCH OF LOVE

Romantic Love

Although love may be one of the oldest human emotions, we are born without a single day of experience. Along the way, most of us observed some of the ways our parents loved. For many, this model becomes one to emulate; for others, it is one to avoid.

In the Western world we are captivated by the promise of romantic love that dominates the themes in movies, television series, books and magazines. The "right person" awaits us somewhere in the world, we are assured. This partner will become the love of our lives, the perfect mate.

Gone, at least in the Western world, are the centuries of arranged marriages that were created by parents and blessed by religious leaders. Passionate, romantic love once called by troubadours, "the sickness doctors cannot cure," becomes our steadfast goal.

Joseph Campbell, gifted writer and teacher, talked frequently about the advent of romantic love in the Middle Ages. In an intriguing discussion of how Western marriage has changed from being an impersonal, social arrangement (made by parents and blessed by the church) to a passionate union of two spirits who select each other, Campbell tells the bittersweet love story of Tristan and Isolde.

> . . . in the Tristan romance, Isolde is engaged to marry King Mark. They have never seen each other. Tristan is sent to fetch Isolde to Mark. Isolde's mother prepares a love potion, so that the two who are to be married will have real love for each other. And this love potion is put in the charge of the nurse, who is to go with Isolde. The love potion is left unguarded, and Tristan and Isolde think it's wine, and they drink it. They're overtaken with love. . . .
>
> (When) Isolde's nurse realizes what has happened, she goes to Tristan and says, "You have drunk your death." And Tristan says, "By my death, do you mean this pain of love? . . . If by my death you mean the agony of love, that is my life. If by my death, you mean the punishment that we are to suffer if discovered, I accept that. And if by my death, you mean eternal punishment in the fires of hell, I accept that too." . . . What he is saying is that his love is bigger even than death and pain, than anything. (Campbell & Moyers, 1988, pp. 190–191)

The power of love in human life is undeniable. My fascination with the romantic tradition began as a student in my early 20s. As a senior at Princeton Seminary, my world collapsed around me. I discovered that my personality and religious questioning were a poor match for the needs of the institutional church. And my secondary hope to become a poet crashed when I realized others did not share a passion for my poems! Soon pneumonia followed and I missed two weeks of class. Depressed, behind in my work, and without direction, I sought the counsel of my major professor in philosophy, Diogenes Allen.

Certainly, this former Rhodes Scholar and master-teacher would fill me with wisdom. Surely, he would advise me how to solve my conflicts quickly. I walked to our meeting filled with the anxious anticipation of knowing that my life was about to change inalterably. As I entered his office, Professor Allen sat amidst stacks of books and manuscripts. He peered at me between two mountains of written material and signaled for me to begin.

Confident that he could not only sustain the weight of my confession but also that he would free me of my purgatory, I bared my soul. My confusion, dissatisfaction, and frustration filled his sanctuary.

After my outpouring, the learned adventurer made but one observation: "You are not in love, are you, Ken?" Startled, I responded, "No sir, I am not." To this admission, he replied: "When you are in love, none of these things will matter. Good day."

That's it? I thought. This is the advice of the man whom I so admired? I left in more confusion and with more rage than when I had entered.

Time passed. I developed "the sickness doctors cannot cure." Then I understood: Diogenes Allen indeed was a man of wisdom, a traveler upon the great seas. But his advice bore a timeless truth that could not be packaged in a pill or be readily consumed by me or others of my impatient age. Only the engaging of life's greatest adventures could bring relief to the aches and pains of the empty heart.

How Has Romantic Love Fared?

> Whether or not you marry: you will be sorry.
>
> Socrates

> Love is the state in which a man sees things most decidedly as they are not.
>
> Friedreich Nietzsche

How has romantic love fared in our country? Not well. Nearly 50% of marriages end in divorce. Almost 60% of remarriages fail to endure. Many of the marriages that remain legally intact seem to be either battle-torn or lacking in vitality. Could it be that the vision of romantic love that brings couples together can become an albatross as love changes over time?

Love alters its appearance throughout our lives. When teenagers and their parents talk about love, they know they are discussing two different feelings and relationships. How insulted a youth feels when a parent maintains, "I understand your love." And how amused is the adult who hears from his teenager, "I, too, understand yours." Perhaps both know and discuss different types of love.

The Inuit people of Alaska have as many as 10 different words for snow. Could love be any less complex?

Robert Sternberg (1986, 1987; Figure 3.1) of Yale University stated that many types of relationships exist. A couple's love may change in nature frequently as they travel through the calms and storms of life. Careers, children, financial challenges, growing responsibilities, inner struggles, and personal growth join other powerful forces to influence the way in which couples love.

Sternberg's triangular model is based on his observations that relationships can include as many as three important components. These elements—the emotional, motivational and cognitive—may or may not be present in each relationship (Figure 3.2).

The emotional component or intimacy is a feeling of we-ness that couples develop. Intimacy is a feeling of bondedness that allows two people to feel like a couple or a unit. Symbols that the emotional component is present or growing include the couple's desire not only to be understood, but also to know everything about each other. Intimacy allows couples to be supportive, enjoy their time together, and share possessions.

The motivational component of love represents passion and a physical attraction to another person. Although the media may suggest that sexual intercourse is the ultimate expression of passion, the desire to touch, kiss, and hug represent the motivational component equally well.

The cognitive component involves various degrees of commitment. In the short term, this may include the willingness to share the decision, "I love you." In the long term, it extends into a commitment to remain in marriage no matter what hardships are faced. Engagement and marriage usually symbolize a growing commitment.

Sternberg describes eight types of relationships, which vary from having none, one, two, or all of the components described above. As time passes, a

Figure 3.1.   Robert Sternberg. Courtesy of Yale University.

Balanced Triangle

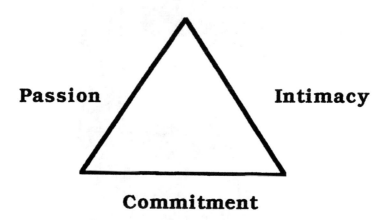

Figure 3.2.   Sternberg's triangular model.

couple's love can change from one type of relationship to another. Also, the triangle is not always equilateral. One component of love may be expressed most strongly, although each component may exist to some degree (Figure 3.3).

In *non-love,* the first type of relationship, none of the three components exists. This type of relationship might include a person's casual acquaintances in classes, in the workplace, or in a neighborhood. Each individual knows many people at a distance, but until they are known better, the relationship lacks any of the three components Sternberg describes.

Liking describes a relationship that is high in the emotional component but lacks both the cognitive and motivational. Good friendships are an example. Roommates may genuinely like each other and enjoy spending time together. However, they may not share a sexual attraction nor be ready to promise to be roommates for the rest of their lives.

Infatuation includes the familiar phenomenon called love at first sight. Someone may feel a strong motivational attraction to an absolute stranger. However, such a relationship does not extend beyond the physical. If physically based relationships do not mature, they may be characterized by periods of jealousy and misunderstanding. Without intimacy or commitment present, little mutual understanding exists and little trust for the future develops.

Romantic love characterizes passionate relationships that are high in the emotional and motivational components. Many high school and college loves are examples. Of course, romantic love can be found at any age. In romantic love, couples spend much of their time together and, at times, seem inseparable. These partners are not able to get enough of each other. They want to know everything about the other person, and they enjoy a physical attraction. However, commitment is missing. That is why many romantic relationships that blossom during college wilt after graduation. Eventually, partners travel their separate ways to create new lives for themselves.

Examples of Unbalanced Triangles

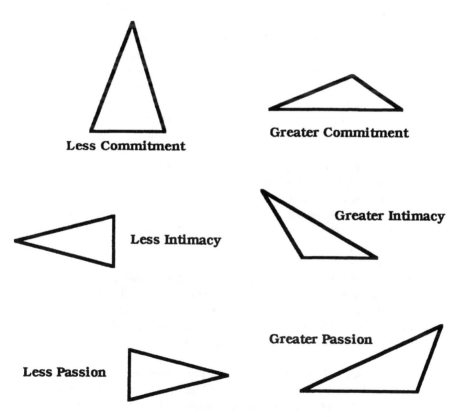

Figure 3.3.   Nonequilateral triangles.

Companionate love describes unions that are high in the emotional and cognitive components but are not highly passionate. For example, when people marry after long engagements, they may be like best friends who enjoy each others' company but lack a strong sexual attraction. Also, couples married for many years may enjoy the companionship of a partner but may not be physically attracted. Eventually these couples may prefer to sleep in separate beds or maintain private bedrooms. Companionate love can bring much happiness to people's lives.

Empty love seems to frighten more young people than any other relationship. In empty love, couples commit to stay together for a lifetime, despite the fact they do not feel a sense of we-ness and are not physically attracted to one another. In a sense, couples in these marriages agree to coexist. It is possible and not unusual for empty love to change into a more vital and enjoyable love.

Fatuous love characterizes those whirlwind relationships when couples meet, fall madly in love, and marry—all within a very brief time. These romances, which are high on motivation and cognition, are not uncommon among armed forces personnel or in Hollywood's fast lane. Fatuous love lacks the emotional component that allows a couple to feel like a unit. Couples need time to work out mutually satisfying patterns of working and living together. It requires time to, in a sense, build a wall around a marriage that protects it from unwanted intrusions. Without a firm sense of we-ness, relationships are more susceptible to outside interference. Because the emotional component requires time to build and solidify, relationships frequently blossom, then wilt in a short time.

Consummate love contains all three components. Consummate lovers feel united, are attracted to one another physically, and are committed to the relationship. Couples may drift in and out of consummate love. Others may enjoy consummate love throughout their lives. How rare is consummate love? It is hard to measure. Some estimates are as low as 10%. Optimists claim that 10% is too low; pessimists, of course, believe it is too high.

Unmoved by statistics that emphasize the alarming failure rates of lovers, an overwhelming number of young adults believe they will create a consummate love that will last for a lifetime. But a true marriage of souls is not easily forged and maintained. Treacherous is the journey that stretches from birth to the altar and from vows to an enduring relationship.

As in Ulysses' adventure, every seeker must overcome obstacles that test the inner spirit and insure the lover's worthiness. Any attempt to avoid the rigors of these trials promises almost certain doom. The first test comes not to the couple, but to each individual.

The Isle of Self

> Only he who knows himself will love with wisdom, and according
> to his powers, perform love's work in full.
>
> Ovid

Psychologists and philosophers have long maintained that one must complete one's identity in order to pass safely to marriage. If a map were formed to show travelers the safest route to marriage, it would show a long island separating childhood from marriage. Across this Isle of Self (Figure 3.4) one must journey to safely reach the marital waters on the other side.

There are those who look for shortcuts. Instead of taking the recommended route, they dive into the wild torrents of premature marriage that encircle the island. There a few survive to warn others to take a more cautious route. Many, but not all, who marry too young are crushed by the weight of a marriage too flimsy to survive the rapids.

A haunting, personal warning comes from those who survived and the many who shipwrecked in the waters of premature marriage: First, know thyself. Know who you are, what you want in life, where you are going, what you believe. To bypass the island is to lose yourself.

Erik Erikson (1964a), the renowned stage theorist, believed that people travel through eight stages in life. In each, a crisis is faced that requires resolution, although the struggle may reappear many times during life. Teenagers and young adults struggle to create an identity: to become relatively consistent in their beliefs, emotions, and behaviors. Failure to reach an identity may leave a person with identity diffusion, maintained Erikson, or an inability to know who one is, what one believes in, or where one is headed in life.

To achieve identity, James Marcia (1966, 1980) believed that adolescents need both crisis and commitment. The crisis need not be the tumultuous, stormy adolescence that early researchers equated with identity creation. Crisis does mean, however, that individuals begin a process of questioning that helps them decide what is true for themselves.

In this period young people examine their own beliefs and experiences. Sometimes their personal views will conflict with those maintained by their parents, church leaders, or the schools. However, despite their elders' fears, the basic values of most teenagers and college students remain very similar to their parents' values during and after identity formation. Some differences will occur, but for most families they are rarely earth shaking.

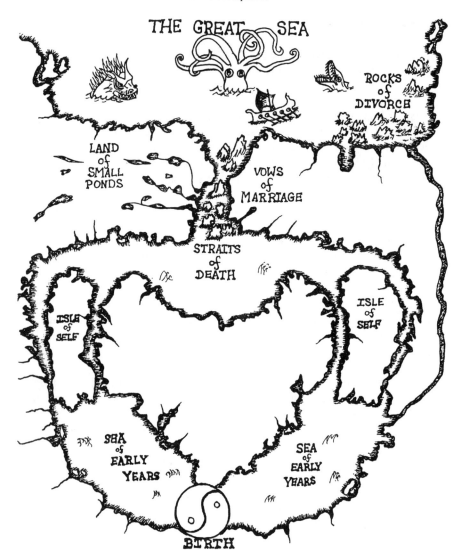

Figure 3.4.   Map of Isle of Self.

Questioning and crisis can only begin the process of identity formation; young people must eventually commit or decide what they really believe. When commitment successfully follows crisis, young people reach *identity achieved,* one of the four identity statuses described by Marcia.

When identity is achieved, individuals become more tolerant of themselves and others. Rather than being driven by emotions, they make careful decisions on the basis of their beliefs. Although valuing friendships, those with strong identities do not fear standing apart from their friends on important issues, nor do they shy away from gaining new insights.

Young people with identity achieved enjoy positive self-concepts; their beliefs and actions work in concert. In other words, there is little difference between who they believe they should be and who they are. Because of their stability and ability to accept others' differences, those with strong identities enjoy good interpersonal relationships. Is it any wonder that Erikson believed that intimacy with another person is not possible until identity is settled?

In *identity foreclosure* a young person displays commitment, but has not gone through the rigors brought about by questioning and crisis. Usually, this status suggests that young people swallowed their parents' values entirely and without examination. Sometimes, however, a young person might adopt the values of an organization or movement. The key is that those who foreclose live a life unexamined.

When identity forecloses early, people tend to resist inner conflict by becoming rigid. Although they may succeed in the academic world by following rules, they frequently spend much of their time and effort defending their beliefs. Usually, they have an external locus of control or a desire to please others, particularly those in authority. This need to please others frequently leads to successful degree seeking in the academic world. But self-growth is limited.

Although parents usually claim they want their children to develop their own beliefs, it has been my experience that many adults prefer their children be obedient and accept their family's beliefs and the values of people "like them." Adult development specialists, such as Daniel Levinson (1978, 1980, 1986) of Yale, believe that those who foreclose on identity early may experience crisis later during transitional periods in life. "Pay me now or pay me later" seems to be the motto of human development. At some time in life, most people question who they are, what they believe, and what is important. It is easier to ask these questions during adolescence and young adulthood than it is later in life when initial decisions about marriage, children, and a career have been made.

Another group of young people become stuck; they engage in the questioning necessary for crisis, but they are not able to commit to specific beliefs. *Identity moratorium* means that answers to questions and solutions to crises have not yet come. Although people in moratorium may feel positive about asking the right questions, they may also feel phony for not having answers. Not surprisingly, they frequently display high anxiety. Their behavior, understandably, becomes unpredictable. As college students they may change majors frequently or transfer to a number of colleges. As you might expect, these individuals are most critical of society and its institutions.

Although people in moratorium may be capable of very close relationships, they do not offer a solid foundation for long-term relationships. If married prematurely, the youth in moratorium may foreclose on an identity or achieve an identity that a marital partner finds unsatisfactory or even offensive. It is risky to marry a rolling stone.

Society might find the most challenging group of young people to be those who experience neither crisis nor commitment. *Identity diffusion* suggests that these young people, in a real sense, do not know who they are. Because they have not established a set of inner values and beliefs, they are most influenced by the peer groups surrounding them. Their philosophy seems to be, "when in Rome do as the Romans do."

This flightiness reaps havoc in relationships. Diffused personalities create shallow relationships that are frequently exploitative in nature. Because they are emotional and impulsive, an enormous number of personal and interpersonal problems seem to follow them. For example, they are more likely to be involved with drugs and to have a variety of personality difficulties. In college, they are drawn to the easiest majors and tend to work the least. "Let's party!" may be their most comfortable response to life.

Marcia (1991) does not believe young adults necessarily remain in one of these identity stances. Frequently, there is movement from one stance to another. Sometimes the movement seems positive and, at others, negative. One's parents and social situation can make the creation of an identity easier or more difficult. For example, how many positive choices does an inner-city adolescent have compared to an affluent teen from the suburbs? But in the end, Erikson believed that a strong identity leads to fidelity: the ability to be faithful to ideas, institutions, and people in whom one believes.

Identity does not come quickly or on a predictable schedule. The usual societal markers such as graduation from high school or college offer no assurance that identity is achieved. Of course, as many people unfortunately discover, a marriage ceremony may also fail to assure that an identity has been forged.

After Graduation

It requires longer than the average person realizes for most young adults' identities to stabilize. Although no formula guarantees success, many family therapists believe living and working on one's own for at least 2 years after the completion of one's education increases the prospects for a successful marriage.

Why? Through their work, young people will decide on the labors they love. From their struggles, they will discover which values they hold. In their searching, they determine the beliefs that liberate them. Because of their autonomy, they will learn to survive their disappointments, to heal their own wounds, and to have faith in their abilities.

Struggling to work and live independently will reveal characteristics of their inner selves to young people—some that are admirable and some regrettable—which are eventually acknowledged and, therefore, no longer frightening. Their emerging self-acceptance will prevent them from attacking the weaknesses discovered in others. But most important, in their tests and travels, young men and women may become confused and lost many times. Because they travel alone, however, they cannot be carried on the backs of others. Only by attending to and trusting in their directing inner spirits can they overcome their challenges. No lesson proves more helpful for the future.

When young people emerge from their personal travels, they are more self-confident, self-supporting, self-caring, self-loving, and self-directed. Only then are they "another self," one who transversed the Isle of Self successfully. When their identities grow strong, two spirits are prepared to join destinies and intertwine their adventures. The irony is that only when one knows that life can be faced alone can it be lived most successfully with another.

But Wait! Are Men's and Women's Identities Forged Alike?

> We need a world where affiliation is regarded as highly or higher than self enhancement.
>
> Carol Gilligan

Carol Gilligan (Figure 3.5) of Harvard University makes a compelling argument in her book, *In A Different Voice* (Gilligan, 1982) that men and women do not create identities in similar ways. Erik Erikson's theory, described above, depicts accurately the male struggle in identity formation.

Figure 3.5.   Carol Gilligan. Courtesy of Harvard University.

Boys and men tend to judge maturity by the ability to separate successfully from others. This search for autonomy begins with the early separation of toddlers from their parents. Then in adolescence, boys again seek autonomy from the family and institutions that nurture them. Even in marriage, a man who depends too much on his wife may be thought of as a wimp or Caspar Milquetoast. Male identity throughout the lifespan is tied to the ability to separate, to become autonomous or independent of intimate relationships that might interfere with achievement.

On the other hand, women discover a significant portion of their identity through relationships. While men point to their achievements in the world to describe who they are, women frequently emphasize their relationships as a daughter, sister, friend, or mother. For women, intimacy with others is prized over separation from others. The connectedness that men view as a weakness, women view as a virtue.

> Since masculinity is defined through separation while femininity is defined through attachment, male gender identity is threatened by intimacy while female gender identity is threatened by separation. Thus, males tend to have difficulty with relationships, while females tend to have problems with individuation. (Gilligan, 1982, p. 8)

What implications can be drawn from Gilligan's observations? First, it may take longer for women to form a clear identity. Part of their identity, in fact, will be determined after marriage by their relationship with their husband, their family of origin, their continuing friendships, their fellow workers and, eventually, their children. In many ways, identity formation may be more complex for women. And certainly, women's growth does not always fit into and should not be judged by the traditional male paradigms of "healthy" development.

Second, Gilligan calls into question the values associated with male development and achievement. A man's emphasis on separation may lead to advancement in a job. Figuratively, the successful male sits on the top rung of a ladder, having outclimbed his competitors. But for women, Gilligan maintains, the successful position is not sitting alone at the top, away from all others. Instead, the successful woman could be thought to be in the center of a web of connectedness (Figure 3.6). Because love, connection, and relationships are crucial to women, their identity formation may differ radically from that of males.

The Dragons That Roam

The Naked Seducer. "Love is two minds without a single thought" (Philip Barry). The first tempter of young adults comes dressed not at all. Sexuality

Figure 3.6. The Web. Courtesy of James Carico, Lynchburg College.

can bring with it unbridled excitement, instant closeness, unsurpassed euphoria, and a feeling of oneness with all of humanity. The lure of sexuality is not the danger, but the tempter's whisper, "sex is love," is what disorients the seeker. The words attempt to wedge themselves between the heart and mind of the youth. He or she wonders: "Could sex and love be the same?"

The heart responds positively: "I feel so close, so at one. Certainly, our relationship will last forever." The mind, an outsider in a relationship characterized by infatuation, offers a faint rebuttal: "But what do you share in common that will last? What do you both believe in? Where do you wish to journey? What hopes, dreams, and fears do you share?" At best, the heart and mind battle furiously.

However, should the heart spring forward and abandon the mind, young adults can be lured from the Isle of Self too soon. If prematurely married to the object of their physical desire alone, a couple who might not be able to share the same sandbox without squabbling will be cast adrift in a world that shows no mercy to the union of children. To fall for the external physical lure means to lose the internal struggle for self. As Kierkegaard noted:

> First love is strong, stronger than the whole world, but the instant doubt occurs to it, it is annihilated, it is like a sleepwalker who with infinite security can walk over the most perilous places, but when one calls his name he plunges down. (Kierkegaard, 1971, p. 96)

Unfortunately, poverty and ignorance also prove to be destructive demons in this first battle. Too often their destructive lies suggest that maturity is easily reached through the birth of a child or an early marriage. The opposite proves true. Without the development of self or strong relationships, young wives and mothers become frozen into perpetual dependence. Society offers the poor no greater disservice than to provide no accessible routes to individual identity. Without realistic career options, the poor must struggle to establish a meaningful identity.

Men and women must be wise in their early encounters with the naked tempter. To know the difference between sexual infatuation and a deep relationship tests the wisdom of young adults. To integrate sexual desire and delight with total loving proves to be a test of adult maturity.

Fear of Time's Passing. Love is a "temporary insanity curable by marriage" (Ambrose Bierce). For the next test, the tempter takes on not a visual image but a sound: the ticking of the social clock. The cadence is deafening as it beats louder and louder. This new assault attacks the mind not the heart. Throughout the island, the thundering clock announces—to all who will listen—when they should attend college or drop out of school, when they should marry, when they should have children, and even when they should die. In response, the anxious and obedient dance wildly to the pounding of the ticks rather than attending to the rhythm of their inner voices. The heart, of course, knows no time; only the mind marks the passing of the seconds.

Is it any wonder that psychologists believe the most compelling reason for most people's choice of a mate is timing? In other words, as long as minimal requirements are met, people marry whom they happen to be dating when they decide it is time to be married. It does not matter if the person is one of the least suitable people one has ever dated. What is most crucial is that he or she is there at the moment when the alarm sounds.

Each spring I share an almost identical conversation with successive graduating seniors. A student enters with this complaint: "Dr. West, I'm really depressed. All of my friends are engaged to be married. But I'm not engaged. There must be something terribly wrong with me."

I respond: "Are you in love?"

To which the student replies: "No, I'm not even dating anyone I particularly like. What should I do?"

My reply is always the same: "Celebrate. You're not dating anyone you love and you're not getting married. What a perfect combination. Think of all of those who are marrying simply because time demands it." After a pause, the young student looks at me in disbelief and leaves to seek more sympathetic counsel.

When society's clock seduces us away from our course in life, a relationship of convenience may be accepted prematurely. Possibly, a couple shares this or that common interest and may even enjoy the companionship of the other. But are they fueled by the depth of passion necessary to survive life's challenges, or with only enough energy to settle for what seems easiest?

In Chapter 2 the Cromptons never created strong identities or a sound relationship. Although Charles Crompton may have benefitted from his career, his wife never shared the dreams he created. As a result, she became the enemy rather than the encourager of his dreams. Emily Crompton married and had children too quickly to discover her own path or to develop a relationship that would sustain her needs for love. She followed the demands of the social clock and soon became enslaved by the results. Busy with children and a nonsupportive marriage, Emily lost sight of her inner spirit and, therefore, her ability to know what is best for herself. With the advent of Samuel's school crisis, Emily had the opportunity to concentrate on her own growth. However, development of the self at this point may endanger her relationships. Her growth may smash into the self-centered dreams of others. To develop the self after marriage or after the birth of children becomes a herculean and, sometimes, a frightening task.

A mature adult is aware of time but not driven by it. To be driven by time is to be controlled by outside forces rather than one's inner voice. It is crucial to allow time for identities and relationships to grow. As the young emerge at the northern end of the Isle of Self, they know they can live alone and cherish their own company. Also, the self-reliance and self-confidence built while traveling on the island prevent them from entering a dependent or unhealthy relationship. Self-contained at last, the hero is ready to set sail once more. But possibly the most difficult challenge looms ahead.

The Straits of Death.   "Each spouse has to give up part of his or her own ideas and preferences, losing individuality, but gaining belonging. In the process, a new system is formed" (Salvador Minuchin). The irony of marriage is that after appropriately centering one's attention for years on the development of the self, individuals must die to their self-centeredness in order to give birth to the union of two souls. Sacrificing for the relationship does not, of course, require people to surrender all of their personal goals. Far from it. But a relationship does require couples to work together in order that each person's and the couple's goals can be reached. If cooperation fails and one or both people live as a single person, then they become what I call unmarried-marrieds. Without being willing to sacrifice for the good of a relationship, there can be no bonding of two wills and spirits. As soon as adventurers emerge from the Isle of Self and join together as couples, they are drawn toward their fiercest trial: The Straits of Death.

The current quickly pulls couples toward the Straits where turbulent waters dash furiously against the cold, granite walls that surround the passage. Within the narrow pass, each partner's ability to move beyond total self-interest and toward nourishing the relationship is judged. If both lovers pass the test, then the fragile boat of first love transforms into a seaworthy ship with billowing sails, capable of surviving the rigors of the great sea.

However, if either or both members covet the self too much to abandon the personal altar, then the boat of first love leaves the straits without transformation. Having no sails and a paper-thin hull, their vessel soon will be dashed to pieces by the great sea, or they must forsake the greatest adventure for the safety of the harbor, where the unmarried-marrieds reside. Seeing the wreckage that litters the shoreline of the ocean, many blame marriage for the destruction. The truth is that the voyagers failed to sacrifice enough to create a vital relationship. Nature simply allowed time and the elements to destroy a relationship too flimsy to survive.

The Dragon of Self-idolatry.   Love is "a mutual misunderstanding" (Oscar Wilde). Self-sacrifice is an unnatural act. And many people are too worshipful of the self to nourish a union with another spirit. Rollo May (1981) once described the demonic as anything that consumes a person. During this stage of the voyage, the demonic can become a person's self-absorption.

When devotion to one's self-interest controls a voyager's life, then the self nourishes only itself. Such autoerotic travelers are touched by their own feelings rather than the feelings of a loved one and are inspired by their own dreams and not by those of their lover. The pain that moves the self, the hopes that lift it, and the hurt that humbles it are all self-induced. What results are solitary humans drowning in the waters that engulf them. Unfortunately, pulled under by their own weight, the self-lovers drag their relationships below the surface water as well.

What becomes sinful to the worshiped self is self-denial. One's own desires, ambitions, and experiences become the only goals worthy of pursuit. To deny the self pleasure or even the possibility of receiving stimulation becomes a cruel hardship to be avoided. If forced for any reason to sacrifice for the relationship, the self-possessed feels resentful and bitter. "Why must I make *all* of the sacrifices?" he or she angrily questions.

Those filled by their own self-concern become like giant sponges. If only one member of the couple is self-possessed, then that creature soaks up all of the energy that a partner can offer. Eventually the relationship becomes a one-sided atrocity. One member gives; the other member takes, and takes, and takes. Worse, the sacrificing member believes it to be his or her duty to give more and more to salvage the relationship. Ironically, no marriage ever existed; it is only the union of a host and its parasite. A mortal cannot survive a marriage to a god.

In some cases, two self-centered individuals ride the boat of first love. This soon becomes an angry ride of two children, each hating the other for not "playing by my rules." Acrimony fills the relationship, which is destined to crash and leave both partners bitter.

Worshipping only the self, the self-possessed become increasingly more isolated and alone. After all, gods find no companions on earth. Their goals ignore the needs of others, and their progress is hindered by anyone who might make demands or even requests. Because the unmarried-married attempt to create meaning through their own efforts, they fail to discover beauty in relationships with others. Not willing to search outside, they desperately look to their own creations and pleasures for life's meaning. Unsure that life has a purpose outside of their own creation, they can scarcely deny themselves anything.

Proper Balance: The Fruits of Self-denial. "Love is the reduction of the universe to a single being, the expansion of a single being" (Victor Hugo). Cooperation and occasionally sacrificing for another's good does not kill the self, but liberates it to create relationships with others. No longer totally self-absorbed, individuals recognize and support one another's hopes, dreams, pain, and despair. As a result, two individuals create a union of spirits, a relationship that becomes larger than the lives of either individual.

The Straits of Death require each traveler to reinvest personal gifts. Unlike money, human treasures multiply when given away. Part of each individual's investment still supports the pursuit of personal hopes and dreams, but now the account is balanced by concentrating love in the life of another and a relationship. This reinvestment process occurs frequently as life changes challenge the family.

In the life of the Cromptons, Samuel's crisis requires the family to reevaluate their commitments. Charles Crompton overinvests in himself and underinvests in the family. Emily Crompton, on the other hand, needs to reinvest much of her energy into her own self, which never properly emerged from the Isle of Self or grew within her marital relationship. After the adults balance their accounts, then Samuel and Sarah will be free to redirect their energies into positive, rather than negative pursuits.

The Straits of Death teach its travelers that love for another grows only when each can die to total self-interest. After two people pass through the Strait and successfully balance their giving and their retaining, then a miracle occurs. The young relationship stands ready for true marriage.

MARRIAGE: ON THE GREAT SEA AT LAST

What then, does the wedding ceremony accomplish? It provides a survey of the genesis of the human race, and therewith it grafts the

new marriage upon the great body of the race. Thereby, it presents
the universal.

Søren Kierkegaard

Marital vows separate the playful games of children from the unconditional commitment of adults. Children enjoy make-believe marriages. Everyone
knows that their ceremonies are pretend and will endure only as long as the
youngsters enjoy their conditional union. With the first signs of acrimony or
inconvenience, children quickly abandon their charade and their playful mates.

Modern society witnesses the childlike marriages entered into by countless
adults, some by design and some by coincidence. Many who fear life's challenges never intend to make their vows binding. Openly, they rewrite the language of their vows to declare "we shall be married as long as we both shall
love." By love they mean the experiencing of joy and exhilaration. They will
not be troubled by a relationship struck by perils or suffering. If theirs is a
choice well-considered, few will seriously contend with their right to choose
the safety and ease of a conditional relationship.

Others cannot make a successful transition from childhood to adulthood.
Although they intend to be married for life, many naive youth discover they are
unprepared to fulfill their vows. Unprepared for the challenges their marriages
will face, they may be overcome by the pain and turmoil that confronts them.

Many young couples believe they will remain married for a lifetime, but
many still harbor a storybook view of love. They picture love as a series of
celebrations, each more exciting than the last one. What falls in between pleasures seems only to be the time needed for careers and recuperation, much like
the week that precedes a college weekend.

After the vows are made, many are dismayed to discover that the Buddha's
warning that "All life is sorrowful" did not exclude them or their spouses. Also
overlooked are the serious commitments, such as those vows repeated by participants in a traditional Christian ceremony that foreshadow the potential difficulties in life: "in sickness and health, for richer or poorer, for better or worse,
till death do us part." Relationships face challenges from within and without
the marriage that require inner strength to endure and overcome. The sacrifices
a couple must make may be largely unknown until they are demanded.

At best, the marital ceremony measures the intention of the lovers. Will
their love be a childish one based on externals such as sexuality, children, companionship, conformity, or other conveniences that may soon become incon-

veniences? Or is their love based upon an inner commitment, vows that endure any tribulation that life may bring? How paramount will love be in the voyager's life? Will love simply be one of the most important parts of a person's life? Or will love be one's greatest priority? Only when love becomes a couple's supreme commitment will it truly be a marriage of the spirits, one that can "endure all things."

Wedding vows do something else; they place the couple on the universal seas of life. Couples are joined in their marriage to long lines of ancestors and to those couples who may follow them. No longer are they loners meandering through their limited days on earth. Now they experience the comfort of belonging to a present relationship and to time universal. The vows, however, only measure intentions.

On the Sea: Beware of Dragons

> [Ulysses,] square in your ship's path are Seirenes, crying beauty to bewitch men coasting by; woe to the innocent who hears that sound! He will not see his lady nor his children in joy, crowding about him, home from sea. . . .
>
> Steer wide; keep well to seaward; plug your oarsmen's ears with beeswax kneaded soft; none of the rest should hear that song. But if you wish to listen let the men tie you in the lugger, hand and foot, back to the mast, lashed to the mast, so you may hear those harpies' thrilling voices. . . .
>
> Homer, *The Odyssey*

Every seeker shares the struggles of Ulysses. Once marriage carries a couple onto the great sea, temptations and strife will assault and attempt to end love's union. Like Ulysses, modern heroes must reach inside to find weapons powerful enough to combat their external and internal foes. Clearly, not everyone survives the marital voyage. Like Ulysses' men, many wayfarers do not possess the wisdom to focus their eyes squarely upon the journey's goals or the inner qualities needed to ward off the seductive and crafty forces of our times.

Protecting the love that binds two spirits together is one of the greatest missions of the Odyssey. Love for people makes the journey through life rich and meaningful. And the love for one's partner is, at best, the crown of all loving. Archibald Macleish once observed that: "What love does is to arm. It arms the worth of life in spite of life" (1958). The voyage for most lovers will be long. Daily living, intriguing diversions, and tragedy threaten to sidetrack adults from completing their greatest adventure. However, those who keep an eye on the prize and listen to the voice of their inner spirit can survive.

In the end, those who reign victorious over the challenges of this world will have experienced the heights and depths of life. As a result, they will spend their last days free from the torment of the demons' voices: "What might have been . . ." and "If only I had . . ." Instead, they will celebrate a life loved well. As Arnold Toynbee wrote: "Love cannot save life from death, but it can fulfill life's purpose."

But beware! Dragons roam freely and the voyage is long.

The First Marital Storms.   The face of love transforms with time, as the appearance of a great mountain changes with the movement of the sun and clouds. All of the faces of love are beautiful to behold, but each differs in its excitement and pleasure. For those unprepared for change, each alteration appears to be a loss of love rather than a metamorphosis.

After the first months pass, marriage changes. For the unprepared, a reduction in playful love elicits shock and disappointment. No longer are love notes tucked away in hidden places. The kiss that joins and parts a new couple is, at first, occasionally forgotten, and then only occasionally remembered. With the loss of first love's frolic, young lovers feel hurt and angry. "Doesn't he or she love me anymore? What is wrong with us?" Their elders, if asked, respond: "Everything is fine." Youthful love matures into daily loving. Romance must find new expression, but the energy fueling love now comes from within and not from the frills and symbols associated with first love's push.

As first love begins to settle, unexpected problems perturb couples trying to adjust to the labor of daily living. More work and more responsibility are required to sustain a home than anyone anticipates. Most couples usually come to marriage unprepared to work at menial tasks. Almost no couple sat upon the banks of a river on a moonlit night and asked the truly important questions: Who will clean out the toilet? Who will prepare taxes? Who will take out the trash, wash the dishes, or sort the clothes?

So many thousands of tasks await young lovers. Somehow, one's partner's family never distributed the work load the way the other's family did. Feelings can be hurt easily as couples struggle to divide the never-ending cycle of work in an acceptable way. Often, the adjustment to the daily work of sharing a home momentarily diverts young lovers' attention from the great prize their union brings. Couples soon learn that neither partner's family of origin owned a sacred formula for the "right way" to do things, nor do counselors or advisors who live outside the home. Each couple accepts the terrible freedom and responsibility to manage their own daily living in a unique way.

Couples must adjust again and again to love's changing appearance. Each time the family adds or loses members, love transforms its appearance. Unforeseen events such as illness, death, or career changes revise the countenance of love. Natural events such as aging, midlife, retirement, and the advent of grandchildren also transfigure the image of love. Experiencing the process of change can frighten two spirits or it can allow them to celebrate together the changing image of love. Love is never static. Time proves to be a terrible adversary or an intriguing companion.

The Rush.   No dragon of our day threatens to scuttle the greatest adventure more than The Rush. Even couples with the best of intentions become easy prey for The Rush when facing the frenzy of raising children, enriching careers, meeting schedules, and earning money.

If uncontested, The Rush will absorb one's time, energy, and passion. Lovers can never do enough for their children, careers, communities, religious institutions, families of origin, social organizations, or personal enrichment. Each of these worthy commitments can possess an unquenchable thirst. For those who fail to battle and control The Rush, concentration on marriage may soon tumble from being one of life's primary commitments to an untended relationship. What begins as confidence that love can endure all things—without the vigilance of lovers—ends in the starvation of love through neglect.

Unless couples see The Rush as their potential enemy, they will soon become strangers to each other. No longer are they two spirits united, but two spirits who struggle alone for personal survival. Like the Cromptons, couples may discover that their days are filled with tasks but their lives together are empty.

The fiercest dragons always promise the world in exchange for the sacrifice of time. The Rush cannot be allowed to slowly, almost imperceptibly erode loving. Yes, The Rush will deliver its tangible goods and rewards as promised, but after years of heeding the call of The Rush, one may look inside one's heart and discover that nothing is there.

The Lure of Others.   As children, most adults believed in fairy tales that told them that a single, special person awaited them in this world. Only this one "match made in heaven" could attract them for a lifetime. Surely, others would pale in comparison to the brilliance of this single lover, or so it seemed. As the years pass, this fairy-tale view rarely survives. As children age, they become aware of numerous others who perhaps might bring them joy and happiness. What remains special about one's spouse is the *choice* of her/him and the vow to die to the lure of others. A break in the exclusive bond frequently springs a slow leak in the marital ship that if not patched perfectly can sink the great vessel to the ocean's floor.

Ulysses knew temptation. He was forewarned of the Seirenes whose haunting song could "sing his mind away." The lure of their song was so seductive that Ulysses, upon hearing it, begged his men to untie the lines that bound him. His men, with beeswax in their ears, dared not listen to the seduction of the songs. Out of allegiance to their leader, Ulysses's men bound him tighter as he struggled to free himself to follow the Seirenes' call.

No tune is as sweet as the love songs of new love. To resist them, they may symbolically need to be tied to the mast of their ship (commitments) or have their ears filled with wax. When experiencing their first love that leads to marriage, they allow themselves to be consumed. Then time passes and the love songs, once so alluring, become familiar. While familiarity brings with it contentment and joy, like Ulysses, each husband and wife faces the Seirenes' test—their voices so new, so beautiful, so irresistible. As with first love, the melody promises to "sing their minds away." And into the arms of the Seirenes, they may fall.

The allure of a new song can be seen in the statistics that suggest that as many as half of all married sojourners remove their bonds or unplug their ears to the voices of the Seirenes. Some couples agree to go through the seas unbound and may survive extramarital diversions. But for most, surrendering to the Seirene's song violates the trust that fastens together the hull of their marital ship. More, unfaithful detours signal that the couple failed to create enough marital heat to survive without the need to seek fuel from an outside source. Secret extramarital affairs usually symbolize a fundamental flaw in the structure of the relationship. The defect requires individuals to seek from without that which cannot be gotten within. Rarely is the defect the fault of one party but is the failure of the relationship itself.

Although couples may survive the tumult caused by a seducer's success, once possessed by the Seirenes, escape proves to be difficult. The heart that once trusted now feels the cold spray of the sea. As Mark Twain noted, in these situations "it is easier to stay out than to get out."

Seirenes also can prey on our inability to face death. To hear their voices erases the reality of our aging and the predictability of a mature relationship. Nothing could be farther from death than the energy new love or lust inspires. Marriage cannot grow complacent. It demands that its champions repeatedly give birth to loving. And one gives birth only through the willingness to die to those temptations that could unravel entwined spirits.

Denying oneself the first temptation is easier than the challenge to erase the memory of a broken vow. Lovers must continue to rekindle the thrill found in first love throughout their marriage. When excitement remains a part of loving, then death and aging are feared less. Only then may we experience the satisfaction expressed by Shakespeare (1981): "To me fair friend, you never can be old, For as you were when first your eye I eyed, Such seems your beauty still" (Sonnet XIV).

The Seirenes await each individual. The story of Ulysses tells of three options heroes might take; only two promise their survival.

Personal Dragons. Personal dragons—created most often in early childhood—freely besiege unfortunate travelers. Youth are often certain that their past will never interfere with their present adventures. Often unnoticed during the single years, these beasts may awaken and roar when marriage shakes them from their slumber. At times, these personal conflicts become so overpowering that one cannot hear, much less be guided by, one's inner spirit. When one's inner wisdom is ignored, love will always flounder.

The dragons take on as many shapes as there are stories told by ancient mariners. Sometimes would-be heroes find themselves in addictions that consume the passion of their marriage. Battles with alcohol and drugs are well-known. Also, many relationships that begin well soon become disturbed by a variety of predators. From past abuse to problems with sexuality to addictive relationships, personal problems are whirlpools that suck the marital ship into the vertex and spin it around and around.

In these critical situations, people cannot easily escape on their own. They may need help from a wise professional who can free them from their conflicts and return them to the great adventures awaiting those with courage.

Wise adults can overcome life's most devastating personal tragedies. In fact, in doing so they often transform crisis and tragedy into an example that inspires countless others who also have lost contact with their inner spirits. Men and women need to believe that they can once again feel the breeze of the salt air. Therefore, heroes always dream. And those visions of returning to life's greatest adventure will one day lead them home.

The Hero's Weapons

The hero of life's greatest adventure is not armed with spears or guns but with internal weapons and powers. The successful lover transforms from a childish creature who is tossed about unpredictably by external events to an inner-directed creature who endures the onslaught of the dragons of this world. The greatest weapon of any adult, as always, is the inner spirit that guides and directs his or her quests. Inside each person is a wise guide who senses what is best in his or her relationships with loved ones. When heeded, one's inner voice creates wise lovers, heroes much like Ulysses and Penelope. When the inner voice is ignored, individuals become robots that wander about their relationships without direction or purpose. To hear the inner voice one must be quiet and patient. One must be surrounded with love and encouragement. Constantly, the spirit pushes, but only those who believe in their own power to do what is best are likely to be led by this rich spirit. When adults listen to the inner spirit, other inner powers soon develop.

Loving Overcomes Being in Love.   Religion, mythology, and classical literature have long championed the virtues of our inner powers. Unfortunately, inner strengths are not good for the economy. The Rush and today's forces of greed benefit most from those who can be externally manipulated. Inwardly driven people are not so easily swayed by advertising and the pursuit of society's trinkets, nor do they seek their rewards solely from their careers in the marketplace.

In fact, in every age people must balance two forces: living within society and fighting its destructive powers. Erich Fromm (Figure 3.7) helped direct lovers by comparing their quests to the lives of artists in his popular book, *The Art of Loving.* Indeed, the consummate lover is an artist.

That is why the phrase "I love you" is an unfortunate one. It implies a stagnant state. One can say I am in a room, or I am in a car, or I am in England. But one is never *in love.* The declaration of love should be *I am loving you.*

On the greatest adventure, loving well implies action. Spouses actively care for their lover. They communicate, listen, and share. Most important, they support one another when the dragons roar and attack. Lovers nourish one

Figure 3.7.   Erich Fromm. Courtesy of Michigan State University Archives and Historical Collections.

another's inner spirit. They become the advocate, doctor, and chaplain needed by their spouses for the journey. Certainly, others play important roles in our voyages. It is crucial not to demand too much from our spouses. But in American society one's major support, at best, usually comes from the one who "is loving us" above all others.

Resolution.   For years, my sons wanted to be Super Bowl stars. Spellbound, they watched the locker room celebrations that followed the victory of the winning team. Unknown to my children were the long years of practice required, the injuries, and the discouragement that preceded that single celebration. Also lost to them was the pressure the following year would bring to prove oneself again.

Lovers celebrate moments of victory, but also they share periods of doubt and discouragement. Maybe they doubt they will ever reach their personal goals in life. Or, maybe their marriages face discouraging challenges. During these low periods, many abandon their journey. As with children who play at marriage, love no longer seems fun. Some simply abandon the "game" and go home. In these dark days, conflicts and strife create their greatest destruction.

Only those armed with internal weapons usually survive. So unpopular in The Rush are the internal traits of resolution, duty, hope, and concentration that the very words seem foreign and humorous to the Sheriffs. Essentially believing in little beyond the current system and self-promotion, they find the writings and beliefs of past generations to be useless. Generations of wisdom are tossed aside by the Sheriffs, who in one generation believe they have become omniscient. It is no wonder that only seekers can understand and be inspired by the encouragement Søren Kierkegaard's pseudonymous character Judge William shared:

> Duty comes as an old friend . . . It would not have been enough if he had encouraged them by saying, "It can be done, love can be preserved," but when he says, "It shall be preserved," there is in that an authority which answers to the heartfelt desire of love. Love drives out fear; but yet when love is for a moment fearful for itself, fearful of its own salvation, duty is the divine nutriment love stands in need of; for it says, "Fear not, you shall conquer." (Kierkegaard, 1971, p. 149)

Duty means that lovers become resolved to attend to each other and to nourish their love, not only in times of celebration, but also in darker days. Resolution becomes a consummate lover's most essential weapon. Without resolution, Ulysses could never have returned home. Without resolution, current sojourners may never create a home.

Concentration.   After lovers resolve to make marriage survive, they must actively love one another. To do so requires another inner quality: concentration. Complacency destroys loving. To spend hours before the television, for example, does not enrich loving. To babble with others at an endless string of parties or to talk only about children also fails to sustain loving. Couples need time alone. In these moments they may share once again those things that brought them together such as hopes, dreams, hurt, and fears. People change. If a lover does not concentrate on his or her beloved, soon he or she becomes a stranger.

Concentration on a relationship requires will and self-discipline. Of all qualities, these seem to be ones that easily escape our grasp. Even couples who resolve to remain married and intend to concentrate on loving too easily allow time to slip away. What remains is not a union of souls, but an arrangement that carries with it neither passion nor merit.

Concentration requires a couple to take charge of time. They must say "No" to diversions and commitments that devour their moments to be present to one another. Giving to another and experiencing daily something larger than one's self encourages a couple's vigilance. They should enjoy the world, but not allow it to overrun their marriage like kudzu vines overtaking the southern countryside. Knowing and remembering that an eternity is not theirs to enjoy reminds them that passionate loving is the greatest adventure.

The Miracle of Love: Expansion.   Eventually, at its highest, love leads one to serve others in this world. Seeing before us conditions that prevent others from loving well, true lovers wish to liberate fellow travelers from the bonds of poverty, miseducation, psychological handicaps, or other obstacles that interfere with their loving. It is a psychological verity that the unhappier and more anxious a person is the less he or she is able to give to others. Also, the opposite proves true: The more one gives, the healthier one becomes and the more, in turn, one wishes to contribute to others.

SHIPWRECK: DIVORCE AND NEW BEGINNINGS

No disguise can long conceal love where it exists, nor long feign it where it is lacking.

Francois de La Rochefoucauld

When two people are under the influence of the most violent, most delusive, and most transient of passions, they are required to swear that they will remain in that excited, abnormal, and exhausting condition continuously until death do them part.

George Bernard Shaw

Long ago I held a mistaken belief that all couples should stay together, that with work they could become a loving couple once again. My misguided conviction died on the night a couple I had counseled for months announced: "We met for dinner before we came tonight. We like you so much and know how much you want our marriage to work, but we decided it's best for us to go our separate ways. We knew this several weeks ago, but did not want to disappoint you."

It is difficult to understand how any loving couple—sharing the joy of a true union of souls—could tell a chronically unhappy couple not to divorce and to begin anew their quest for the greatest adventure. It seems that the only people who routinely oppose all divorce are those who believe it is sinful, or those who, having endured years of misery in a marriage, mistakenly believe their miscarriage of love to be a virtuous model others should imitate.

Clearly, some individuals do not escape the complications that beset new relationships. Many fail to cross the Isle of Self before they marry or cannot create a healthy identity within the marital relationship. As time passes, each begins to develop a self that may take the couple worlds apart. Not kindred in their beliefs, interests, or values, the two individuals can hardly become joined spirits. As a result, divorce does not end their marriage. It simply admits that a marriage does not now and may never have existed.

Other couples may not have survived the Straits of Death. They could not die to their own self-absorption, and in time they may realize they do not wish to. In such cases the marriage is not between two equals but is one in which one party unsuccessfully attempts to domesticate a recalcitrant spirit.

When a couple decides to divorce, it may indicate that the inner spirit still longs to be free. This situation is far superior to the one in which a poorly married couple's spirits were buried long ago, along with their courage to dream that life could be better.

Sometimes couples divorce before looking closely at their marriage and the alternatives that might resuscitate it. For example, the Cromptons still have many possibilities for revitalizing their marriage. To abandon their relationship now would be regrettable. In time, it will become clearer whether or not Charles and Emily possess the resources needed for transformation to occur. At this time they have not examined themselves or their relationship enough to be wise in surrendering their quest.

It must be remembered that divorce only ends a fruitless relationship; divorce does not insure that a second marriage will be more successful. Before a second attempt to navigate the great sea can be made, the travelers must once again journey to the open waters. First, they must cross the Isle of Self and then survive the Straits of Death. Too often second marriages fail because couples hear the social clock ticking away. Only after taking the time to build their marital ship the old-fashioned way—slowly and carefully—will a couple be ready to enjoy the voyage and survive the dragons that confront two spirits sharing life's greatest adventure.

Chapter 4

THE PARENTAL ADVENTURE: THE VOYAGES OF FUTURE HEROES

Woe to the man whose heart has not learned while young to hope, to love, to put its trust in life.

Joseph Conrad

Children today are tyrants. They contradict their parents, gobble their food, and tyrannize their teachers.

Socrates

The work will wait while you show your child the rainbow, but the rainbow will not wait while you work.

Unknown

Ponderings. What was your childhood like? If you could, what would you change about the way you were raised? What would you keep the same? What are the greatest challenges in society to children's healthy development? Why do some children seem to be so out of control? How should parents properly encourage and discipline their children? What special problems do children who live in poverty face? How well do schools handle children who cannot keep up academically with their peers? Who were the important people in your life who helped you overcome difficult life challenges? What did they do for you that proved to be helpful?

While journeying on their own adventures, many adults will influence their children's quest to become the heroes of the next generation. Before leaving childhood, children will undergo a series of voyages. While doing so, many young people will face challenges too personal to prepare for in advance. However, all children will encounter well-known hurdles. Some are created by predictable growth from within; they are changes or stages common to children of relatively the same age around the world. In addition, children face well-known external challenges peculiar to the cultures in which they live. This chapter examines the stages and social hurdles people encounter in the modern world. By anticipating the trials and dragons that await their children, parents can protect and nourish young adventurers.

Although all parents hope their children will be happy, it is equally important for parents to prepare young people to tackle the challenges of life wisely and without timidity. After all, happiness is not a goal to be reached; rather, it is a familiar companion of those who engage life's challenges, wonders, and despair. As the old Indian expression advises, "Happiness is not a destination one reaches, but a way of travel."

"The child is father of the man" (Cook, p. 59) claimed the poet William Wordsworth in his poem "Ode on Intimations of Immortality." Not only have developmental psychologists like Erik Erikson confirmed Wordsworth's wisdom, but also they have assured parents that the good they do daily in their children's lives will not be lost in the years to come. The strengths forged in childhood will enrich their adult years. And then, the children will pass these precious gifts to their own children. William Faulkner certainly understood this when he wrote: "The past is never dead; it is not even past."

Although teaching children to flourish in the adventures of life has been and always will be among the most crucial work of adults, for the moment The Rush finds the needs of families to be an annoyance. Therefore, contemporary society frequently talks about significant changes, but does little to elevate parenting to the position of respect it deserves. The Rush's indifference toward parenting is seen daily in its reluctance to meet even the most basic family needs (the need for quality day care, family health insurance, and other family issues that will be discussed later) of parents who work full time to enrich society. Those who labor primarily in the home were abandoned long ago.

To make a decision to commit oneself to parenthood as a career or balanced with a career is more and more an act of heroism. In many cases, it is an act of rebellion. Contemporary values rush people away from their families and away from preparing new generations to inherit this planet. Adults must be guided by their inner convictions in order to navigate against the tide of current values. For parents to give selflessly to a new generation, they must journey toward the great seas where relationships, love, and courage reign. There it will not seem aberrant to sacrifice some of their own self-advancement and many of the rewards of The Rush to enrich the next generation.

Parents are the captains of ships that transport the future leaders of this world. These new voyagers possess a budding spirit that moves them toward growth and self-actualization. The survival and nourishment of each child is placed squarely in the parents' hands. Unquestionably, the responsibility for protecting and guiding young people today is enormous.

Occasionally, parents may stray off course; after all, they face problems and conflicts of their own. On occasional dismal days adults may dream of steering without the responsibility and challenge their young passengers present. But wise parents always seem to regain their vision, see the channel markers clearly, and return to the wheel to accept life's most significant challenge.

Not all parents succeed. Those who fail to develop their own identities or face tremendous obstacles in their personal lives may be overcome by their challenges. As a result, the needs of their children become obscured. Unsure of what is important in their lives or even that their own lives are important, disoriented captains run aground. Because they are unable to value themselves or others, they cannot communicate effectively or resist routes that may prove harmful to themselves or their passengers. As a result, they journey into waters where the spirits, and even survival, of their children will be jeopardized.

Many maps have been passed down that show the routes previous generations followed. All have merit. The well-known map created by Erik Erikson (Figure 4.1) is used below. Its familiar shorelines and channels remind parents of the opportunities they have to nourish their children's inner lives. Also, the map tells of dangers to be avoided. Dragons alter their appearance from generation to generation. However, the child's journey and the parents' responsibilities remain the same. Of course, the children's adventures will not proceed without enriching their parents' lives, for the parents also grow along the way. After all, without the dependence of children, parents might never discover their own maturity.

Erikson's Early Stages

Stage	Age
Trust vs. Mistrust	Birth to 18 months
Autonomy vs. Shame	18 months to 3 years
Initiative vs. Guilt	3 years to 5 years
Industry vs. Inferiority	5 years to puberty

Figure 4.1.   Erik Erikson. Courtesy of Harvard University.

THE FIRST VOYAGE (BIRTH TO 18 MONTHS): THE TRIAL OF TRUST

Paradise might be the best word to describe fetal life in the mother's womb, at least, according to early psychoanalytical thought. Then, as birth begins, each baby abruptly discovers life's most repetitive and demanding challenge: "No! You cannot have it this easy way forever!" With this declaration, life thrusts the baby from paradise and into the first trial of life. And how does a healthy baby respond after birth? With a cry from the spirit that vows: "Yes! But I shall overcome."

Of course, infants cannot survive on their own. Totally dependent, they figuratively and literally place their survival in their parents' hands. From their caretakers, babies will learn if loved ones can be trusted and if life is worthy of the continuous struggle required to conquer new challenges. In 18 months, babies discover answers to crucial life questions: Will my cries be heard? Will my hunger and thirst be satisfied? Will my pain be soothed? Will my life be valued? Will people support me when I need them?

The Trial of Trust examines the relationship that infants and their parents create. Can they work together, responding predictably to each other's needs? As their first trial ends, most children develop a mixture of trust and healthy mistrust. Their trust will allow them as future adults to believe that loved ones will hear their cries, nourish their inner lives, heal their aches, and stay close to them when they are needed. And of equal importance, they will trust themselves and will believe that they too will be able to nourish and to be faithful to those they love. As their trust emerges, a vein of mistrust also develops. This strand of mistrust will protect them from being easily misused by others.

Despite the fact that it is now known that life within the womb may not be paradise, the psychoanalytical paradigm remains a beautiful symbol of the human spirit's determination to overcome adversity. At the end of each stage in our lives, life declares: "No! You cannot have it this easy way forever!" And just as often the hero declares: "Yes! But I shall overcome."

The drive for self-actualization that survived the trauma of birth continues to spur children onward. Soon toddlers attempt to walk, although crawling is easier and faster. Unstable on their feet, children stumble, fall, and cry. With encouragement, they will arise to try once more. Words come slowly at first. No one understands and the frustrations mount. Yet each child pushes ahead, longing to communicate with loved ones. Curious, toddlers actively investigate a world filled with toys, boxes, mobiles, fireplaces, and electrical sockets. Their inner drive propels them forward as they actively engage their small worlds.

In the end, a parent's dedicated hours of rocking and feeding babies, changing countless diapers, responding to tears, and protecting their children from harm gives young people a gift of trust that will enrich them throughout their years. Although children and adults always must balance trust with a healthy dose of mistrust, trust needs to be more influential. On the firm foundation of trust, young people will build enduring relationships, secure in the belief that their lives are worthwhile. As a result of their trust, hope for the future develops.

Trials, however, sometimes lead to unfortunate results. Infants who do not receive the concern and love of their parents feel mistrust swell inside. Theirs is not a life championed by the captains of the ship. Not feeling the warmth and sunlight enjoyed by children raised on the main deck, they may withdraw from others and endure the darkness, danger, and uncertainty encountered deep within the hull of the vessel. Alone and unloved, they grow into adulthood unable to sustain relationships that require foundations of trust. Feeling awkward on the main deck, mistrusting adults will lack assurance that the ships they now captain have any worthy destination. These dark souls have fallen victim to the dragons of childhood (Figure 4.2).

Demonic Self-centeredness

Parents of infants and toddlers are known by a certain exhausted-yet-fulfilled look. No job tires the body and mind more than the 24-hour vigilance that babies and toddlers require. Mature parents sense when and how much they must die to self-centeredness to meet their children's needs. Most, as mentioned earlier, have already made this sacrifice once before when passing through the Straits of Death that precede marriage. In the place of self-absorption, a balance again must be struck between pursuing one's own desires and attending to the constant needs of children. The vast majority of parents in all social classes and careers successfully merge devotion to their children with the desire to meet personal and professional goals. A few, however, develop a "demonic" self-centeredness.

"Man's goodness is in direct proportion to his potentiality for evil," warned Carl Jung. Demonic self-centeredness means a parent's deliberate choice to follow personal ambitions and desires rather than to attend to the primary needs of their children. Self-possessed parents shove their children into the hull of the ship, where they must survive with minimal warmth and nourishment. Demonic parents feel no guilt and militantly justify their selfish decisions.

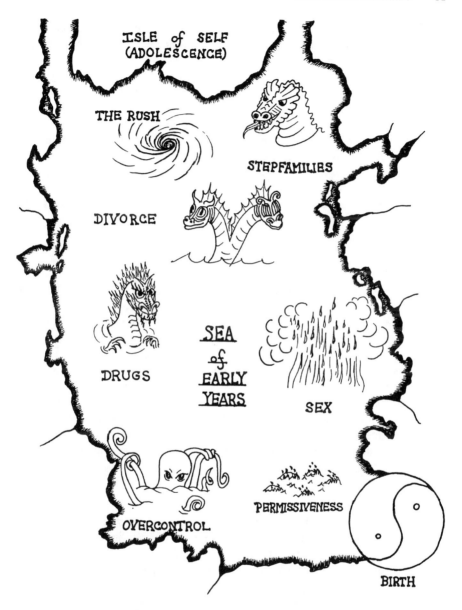

Figure 4.2.   Map of Early Childhood.

Some self-concerned parents manage only to feed and water their children, as a youngster might care for a gerbil or hamster. Warmth is never shared; their children are rarely rocked and held. Other adults fail to provide proper nutrition or medical care for their dependents. Still others neglect their young, forcing them to survive the dangers of their immediate environment alone.

However, most self-centered parents do not willfully mistreat their children. Instead, they pass on the sins of their parents and a too frequently unsupportive society to the next generation. Although they may sense that it is wrong to neglect or to physically harm a child, these unfortunate adults reproduce the damaging relationships that they themselves experienced in childhood. When nothing new is learned in society about caring for themselves and others, ignorance reigns. The child's spirit flickers.

Poverty

"A hopeless, helpless parent produces a hopeless, helpless child," observed Bernie Siegel (1986, p. 88). Nowhere can this tragedy be seen more clearly than in the lives of parents whose ships lack the provisions necessary to survive the voyage. For these families, food may be scarce and medical treatment often unavailable. The ship, through no fault of its captain, simply fails to be seaworthy. Everyone aboard risks immediate ruin. Poverty reaps its destruction most viciously in those Third World countries besieged by war and famine. Also, in the richest countries in the world, the visible homeless and the invisible poor struggle to meet their families' most basic survival needs. When life's adventure is reduced to day-to-day existence, nourishing a child's inner spirit with warmth and attention becomes a secondary priority. The child's spirit languishes.

Spiritually Impoverished Parents

Through their personal quests for truth, most parents validate life. Those who develop faith—in formal religion, in humankind's ability to solve its own problems, or in an active search for meaning in life—believe that life is positive and worthwhile. Parents with affirmative beliefs pass on their assurance to their children. Optimistic parents lovingly nourish their children's inner spirits with acceptance, support, and love. Feeling their parents' hope and constancy, most children will share their caretakers' belief that this world and life itself is worthwhile.

But adults who fail to believe in life's worth may be unable to nourish their children's inner spirit. Abandoned to the course of a rudderless ship and lacking any assurance about life's value, these unfortunate children are destined to share their parents' cynicism. Not wishing to navigate toward the great seas, the captains wander away from the deep channel and slam violently into the shores of mistrust. As adults, mistrustful people usually become part of the dark forces of this world. Because they cannot create meaning, the most disturbed feel powerful only when they destroy. Their targets for destruction are the lives and institutions of those whom they believe are worthless: themselves and all others.

But even if parents stray, a child's spirit proves to be resilient. As the founder of Client-Centered Therapy, Carl Rogers stated in a speech given shortly before his death: "In a cellar the potato's sprout grows toward the light." Thus, even children in the dark hull of a ship still strive for freedom and warmth. Theirs will be a more difficult voyage, but life itself often heals broken spirits.

Fortunately, most infants are raised by imperfect but determined parents. On the main deck, their children bask in the warmth and constancy needed for healthy growth. As a result, the trial of trust ends as children learn that they can depend upon the actions of loved ones and the value of life. Trust abounds.

THE SECOND VOYAGE (AGES 1 1/2 TO 3): THE TRIAL OF AUTONOMY

"*No!*" shouts the almost-two-year-old child to his parents—and to the world. With this proclamation the trial of autonomy begins. This first declaration of independence announces: "I am a person. I am not my Mom. I am not my Dad. I am *Me*."

The days of infancy and toddlerhood abruptly end when life once again announces: "*No!* You cannot have it this way forever." Now attention shifts to the interaction between parents and their children over control and discipline and the trials created by children's emerging wills. As in the days of adolescence when the second declaration of independence will occur, life for the captains is not easy. Their task is to support and nourish their children's desire for autonomy without allowing them to commandeer the ship. To maintain their course in life will require all of the captain's wisdom and patience. Also, there will be few times in life when support and encouragement from a mate will be needed and enjoyed more by those fortunate enough to share a cooperative marriage.

Most of the time parents are thrilled to watch their children grow in independence. Not only can youngsters walk without help, but also they gain control of their bladders, bowels and language. Only months before these young-sters required total care, but now they regularly announce: "I do it myself." The inner spirit's drive toward independence is clearly seen.

These positive autonomy requests become mixed with mutinous demands, and it is the mixture of the two that tests the mettle of the parents. Car seats and seat belts are resisted. Meal times become problematic, and the nightly summons to bathe and sleep become battle calls. While desiring to support their children's positive assertions, parents must also sidetrack demands that threaten to topple all authority.

No adult feels perfectly balanced in the midst of these storms, but parents who keep their eyes on the prize—autonomy—weather these trials best. When autonomy develops, children become self-confident and willful. They work more independently, without demanding constant assurance, prodding, and assistance from others. Eventually, as autonomous adults they will not suffocate their loved ones by demanding too much of them. Feeling confident, children also learn to stand up for themselves. In future year, an autonomous young person will be less subject to the temptations of peer groups and less likely to submit to the pressure to go along with the crowd. To say "NO!" to others means to say "*I*" to myself: I have rights. I have dreams. I have standards. I know what is best for me.

Most parents handle their children's autonomy demands well, at least most of the time. However, many adults take extreme stances, either forbidding their children to say "NO!" or allowing children to dominate the household. Not allowing feelings of autonomy to develop creates a lack of self-confidence in children. The "I" is troubled by feelings of self-consciousness and low self-worth. On the other hand, children allowed to dominate a home become despots. The overbearing "I" soon fails to recognize the rights and needs of others.

Parental Inner Dragons: Of Tyrants and Servants

Only one light can shine on a tyrant's ship. The autocrat's needs, desires, and dreams alone are recognized. Others' spirits must seek refuge below deck or submit to the tyrant's self-centeredness. The tyrannical parent sees the child's demands for autonomy as nothing more than the rebellion of an unruly under-ling. To the tyrant, the inner spirit that promotes this discord is an evil source that must be destroyed.

Not allowing the child to say "NO!", not having the patience to hear "I do it myself," and having no desire to sidestep temper tantrums or power struggles, the tyrant attacks the child's autonomous behavior and pollutes the inner spring from which the spirit flows. Instead, self-doubt and self-consciousness begin to cloud over the morning sun. Defeated spirits hide below the main deck or dance mechanically to the whims and wishes of the commander. If overwhelmed by the tyrant, a child surrenders the quest for self. Lost are the declarations of autonomy: "I am somebody. I am unique. I am worthwhile."

Lacking the confidence to burn brightly in the sky, children filled with self-doubt become like pale moons. Their lives reflect the light of others rather than generate their own brilliance. As adults, the least confident may even fall from the heavens, unable to discover their own orbit. Others may once again attach themselves to tyrants, where they will passively reflect the rays of their masters. Although some children survive a tyrant's hand, most carry the shadow of the oppressor within them in adulthood. For those who fail the initial trial of autonomy, no "I" or "Me" emerges to journey through life's greatest adventures.

The opposite of tyrants, some captains—with little autonomy of their own—surrender control of the wheel. Unable or unwilling to distinguish between the legitimate and illegitimate demands of children, they meet each ultimatum with acquiescence. Children swell in power until they take over the family ship. Whatever the child-captains wish, they receive. Eventually, they dominate mealtimes, bedtimes, family outings, and even the family's safety standards. But the fiery heat from these runaway suns threatens to consume the defrocked captains and the ship itself.

Wise parents control the wheel and nourish the autonomy of their young, a difficult balance. Fortunately, many books and parenting courses can instruct parents in the art of setting limits and creating consequences for misbehavior, but knowledge rarely transforms tyrants and servants. Before change is possible, parents must truly want their children to be shining suns. Also, they must appreciate the beauty of order in nature; every sun needs the security of its own orbit.

The Rush

At the end of the 20th century, The Rush retreated into history and revived the ancient practice of treating children as if they were miniature adults. No longer does The Rush have time for childhood. Gone are the backyard baseball fields worn dirt-bare by neighborhood games. Replacing them are official practices scheduled on official fields, played in official jerseys, and coached by official adults. Gone are the hours when children enjoyed solitary play such as tea parties, wars between the forces of good and evil, and tents constructed with sheets over tables.

Or, are those days gone? In the homes of insightful parents, childhood still thrives. Surely the framework of childhood has been changed, just as economic and social changes have created the need for dual-career couples and other family modifications. Nevertheless, wise parents understand that a child's inner spirit requires time and space for healthy growth. They, therefore, resist the spirit-crunching pace of The Rush. David Elkind, a gallant champion who fights against the challenges of The Rush, explained the consequences of abandoning children to the frenzied pace of this era:

> Hurried children seem to make up a large portion of the troubled children seen by clinicians today; they constitute many of the young people experiencing school failure, those involved in delinquency and drugs, and those who are committing suicide. They also include many of the children who have chronic psychosomatic complaints such as headaches and stomachaches, who are chronically unhappy, hyperactive, or lethargic and unmotivated. (Elkind, 1981, p. vii)

Disciples of The Rush run their children from sitter to sitter, from lesson to lesson, from achievement to achievement. At the end of the day, parents and children both seem frazzled from the pace. Nerves grow raw as dinner, clean up, baths, and bedtimes fill the few remaining moments of each day. On the weekends, more lessons and games are scheduled in between the massive work catch up that always awaits adults. Children, pushed beyond their years, mirror their parents lives: stressed and overcommitted.

Within the undertow of the modern world, courageous parents create a spiritual sanctuary free of powers of The Rush. A spiritual sanctuary is not the same as the elusive quality time, which people can neither describe nor grasp. Instead, it is the ongoing relationship of fellow voyagers who treasure and nourish the inner spirits of their loved ones. Parents who respect their children's inner spirits, notice and attend to the needs of their young. Sometimes children need to be alone, but often they need their parents' companionship. At times, children seem to handle the daily pace of their lives quite well. A spiritual sanctuary requires verbal and nonverbal communication among family members, as well as the parents' commitment to protect young people from the demands of The Rush.

Valiant parents know that in this era less is often more. Therefore, they say "No" to immoderate television watching or to an exorbitant number of lessons

and games. They battle against unhealthy academic pressures and the p\
children to mature too quickly. The spiritual sanctuary becomes a shie\
deflects the dragon's fiery breath.

In these days of science, parents often demand a formula. "Exactly how do we create this shield?" some ask. No simple formula exists. The sanctuary is an ongoing relationship between parents and their children. Following their inner feelings, parents sense what is necessary and what is not, what is helpful and what is harmful to their children's lives. To succeed, parental heroes, like the storybook Jedi knights, ignore the clamor of external shouts and listen to their own and their children's inner voices. Children's needs can be discovered in their voices, temperaments, misbehavior, and health. When children feel too much pressure, they begin to be dysfunctional. Their pain can be seen, like Samuel Crompton's, in their school work. Or, it can be seen in frequent health or behavior problems. The earlier that parents recognize that their children's spirits are protesting against the pace of the world, the easier it becomes to shield them from unhealthy pressures. Heroes live in this world but also apart from it. Within the circle of their parents' love, concern, and protection, children can retreat to a sanctuary in which they can rest, play, and grow before returning to the pace of The Rush.

To the Sheriffs, a spiritual sanctuary seems alien. Sheriffs usually solve problems by pushing the accelerator harder. How, they ask, can parents delay their children's entry into school? How can parents limit their children's participation in organized events? How can parents allow their children to "waste time" playing at home and in the neighborhood when others are achieving skills in music, sports, and academics? How can they? Because reflective adults know that character is built from the inside out, not from keeping up with external demands of The Rush. For young children, the quality of their adult lives usually depends upon the quality of their childhoods. And healthy children are, above all, children.

THE THIRD VOYAGE (AGES 3 TO 5): THE TRIAL OF COURAGE AND INITIATIVE

"Follow your bliss!" This advice of Joseph Campbell (1988, p. 190) could easily be the watchwords of heroes. Not only do they know what they love, but also they possess the initiative to pursue it. From where does this initiative come? Children's innate drive for growth propels them to investigate the world, test their physical abilities, and ponder why the world works the way it does.

No sooner do children become autonomous than they begin to explore the ship that carries them. Up the riggings they climb as their captains watch with wildly beating hearts. The preschool child tries almost everything once and repeats over and over their favorite mental and physical activities. Soon, the ship no longer can contain the curiosity of children, and for the first time they peer over the rails and wonder at the great seas ahead. Dreams begin. Spurred on by their growing imagination, children pretend to be explorers, doctors, teachers, actors, and athletes. All is possible in the minds of dreamers.

The stage of initiative vs. guilt begins when parents must repeatedly react to their children's wandering spirits and activities. Psychologists report that parents must intervene in their preschool children's lives on the average of 85 times each day. However, it is not the individual responses that matter, but the parents' attitude toward the child's growing initiative that stands trial. Will the parents' own fear of experimentation lead them to prohibit their children from taking the risk of climbing trees, exploring the woods, or walking along the rail of a fence? Or will parents applaud their children's love for adventure and limit only their high-risk investigations? Will parents take time to answer the probing questions of young children, or will they find their inquisitiveness bothersome?

Parents who achieve a balance between encouraging healthy experimentation and channeling wayward behavior into acceptable channels encourage their children to feel "I can do almost anything. I can be anyone I wish to be." These children have initiative and are not paralyzed by a fear of failure when they become adults. Their lives become purposeful. They strive toward their dreams and seek to live life fully and courageously.

As usual, extreme stances taken by parents create problems. Parents who overly restrict inquisitive spirits crush their children's initiative. Children begin to internalize their parents' fears. As adults, these children may feel too anxious and inhibited to take risks. The shallow but stagnant waters become a safe place that shelters its inmates from potential dangers in life, whether the imagined hazards might arise in interpersonal relationships, career experimentation, or truth seeking.

On the other hand, parents who fail to restrict or to redirect the misguided words and deeds of their youth may discover that their children charge out of control. At times, they appear to be ruthless. Knowing no limits, they may ram up against the authority of teachers and the law. Never being restricted, out-of-control children fail to respect the rights and needs of others. The trial of initiative measures the heart of future voyagers: Will they possess the initiative to undertake challenging adventures and the self-restraint to respect the voyages of others?

Encouragement: Fuel for the Spirit

Throughout their lives, people blessed by an encouraging nature spread their courage to others. No gift is more enabling and empowering than the encouragement that parents provide their children. Young people need to know that they are meeting not only their own expectations, but also that in the vast majority of situations they fulfill their parents' expectations as well.

Encouragement, as the word suggests, offers courage to another. If children fail the first time, encouragement does not waiver. It urges them to rise up and try again. Of course, encouraging parents must intervene when their children's interactions harm another or to prevent the truly dangerous escapades their children may plan. As encouragers they dwell upon the positive, always seeing their children's endeavors as half-successful, not half-failed. When in contact with an encouraging person, one finds little time wasted on negativity. Although encouraging parents can clearly see shortcomings and restrictions, they prefer to emphasize strengths and opportunities. Those who do well at encouraging listen to the dreams and hopes of their children. Then, they affirm their aspirations in a way that enables their children to believe that anything is possible.

Encouragement rarely comes easily or naturally for those living within The Rush. Today's parents and children live amidst astounding negativity. The media dwells upon catastrophes and human frailty. Following every speech of elected officials, newscasters and experts stress the imperfections of their ideas. Presidential elections have become little more than glitch hunts. With the precision of sharpshooters, sports announcers target the weaknesses of every athlete and athletic performance. And even teachers often report on only the poor work or misbehavior of school children. Is it any wonder that parents who live in this era criticize their children, hoping that such negativity will encourage an already discouraged child?

The opposite actually results. Criticism kills initiative. Dwelling on the negative creates cautious children who soon become discouraged. Losing courage, children learn to play it safe or never to play at all. As discouraged children move into adulthood, they may fail to follow their bliss or may even be unable to identify their bliss. Many people cannot imagine what actions might invigorate their lives, or cannot envisage making their dreams come true, even after receiving suggestions. As one psychologist observed, their watchword becomes "Nothing ventured, nothing lost."

Heroes love the action on the great seas. To them life is not a performance to be graded but the pursuit of experience, relationships, and truth. Parents' enchantment with their own quests allows them to encourage their children to engage life's greatest adventures without reluctance. To enable children to pass safely through the trials of initiative, parents should encourage them to follow their bliss.

Inner Dragons: Perfectionism

Few are anchored more hopelessly within stagnant waters than are perfectionists. Always trying to control their own lives, and too often the lives of their children, they avoid all risk taking. Because only God is perfect, perfectionists deceive themselves by living in a fictional world of their own creation. Perfectionists fear journeying into deeper waters where failure, disappointment, and death accompany the risk of living well. Perfectionists live a life of prohibition, not of openness.

Spotless houses, immaculate children, impeccable speech, faultless behavior, and excellent grades become the minimally acceptable standards of perfection pushers. Whatever their children do either is perfect (which to them means acceptable) or not good enough. When more than one child divides the sibling turf, the perfectionist compares the weaknesses of one with the excellence of another. Comparisons always lead discouraged children to feel more discouraged.

If children accept their parents' mythology that perfection is the minimal standard for acceptability, they soon begin to limit their own dreams and activities. Only what can be achieved perfectly is worthy of pursuit. Those who fail to meet their parents' expectations are doomed to feel they are not good enough. As adults, they will feel as if someone is always looking over their shoulder ready to criticize them. Too self-critical to venture from port, discouraged adults may fail to develop their talents or to take advantage of the opportunities that surround them. Or, they may discover their niche only by severely reducing the world to its most controllable parts. Perfectionism is a cancerous life stance, which, unfortunately, proves to be contagious. Its victim always is the inner spirit. Follow one's bliss? Not for a perfectionist. It is far too risky.

Dragons Ahead: Television, Home Video Games and Media

Television shares many beautiful messages. For example, children today grow up to understand that the world is small and we are all interdependent. Despite the criticism of parents, television will remain an influence in children's lives; however, like a drug, its benefits can become transformed into a nightmare of addiction.

Neil Postman effectively alerted parents to the perils of television many years ago. In *The Disappearance of Childhood*, Postman (1982) explained how the knowledge of sex, sin, and evil that once served as a wall dividing adulthood from childhood first came tumbling down when children learned to read. With the advent of television, adult secrets bombarded children much earlier and more explicitly than ever before. As a result, "having access to the previously hidden fruit of adult information, [children] are expelled from the garden of childhood" (Postman, 1982, p. 97). Television is a ravenous beast with an appetite that must be limited by parents. In addition to pushing children prematurely into the adult world, television and similar activities (such as home video games) may consume a child's initiative.

According to recent reports, average children watch television for 2 of their initial 18 years of life—more hours than they spend in school. What would they be doing if the television were turned off for much of that time? They would be creating their own adventures instead of watching those of television characters. They would be making the winning last shot in imaginary games rather than applauding the heroics of others. They would be interacting with friends and family members rather than observing the shallow relationships modeled on a multitude of mindless shows. Nothing is more crucial to the development of initiative than time. Children need time to dream and explore their own worlds, not the worlds presented to them through the media.

Along with its consumption of initiative, television dangerously habituates children to poverty, hunger, and violence. Viewers are overwhelmed by the evil and tragedy of this world. Believing that "the poor are with us always" seems to justify inaction. Heroes strive to liberate people from enslaving conditions, but if our future adults feel powerless to alleviate people from their life-destroying conditions, then poverty and violence will become the acceptable norm for the lives of our neighbors on this planet.

Articles and books abound with advice on how to use television wisely. In the end, all agree that parents need the courage to act, to turn off the television when shows not agreed on in advance are watched. Concerned adults cannot do otherwise. They value the inner spirit too much to see it put to sleep. Parents should liberate their children's time and give them the opportunity to explore the main deck and to dream of life beyond life's shallow waters. Too soon the days of freedom and joyful activity will end at the schoolhouse door.

THE FOURTH VOYAGE (AGES 5 TO PUBERTY): THE TRIAL OF INDUSTRY

School offers the first organized challenge to all young people that occurs outside of their home. Before school begins, parents can carefully choose the adults and the environments that will nourish their children. But when the school bell rings, most parents enjoy little choice in the care of their children. For the first time, the law orders parents to deliver their children to the Isle of Academia.

All is not well upon the island. Too much is expected from the schools and too little support is provided. As a result, the schools must receive and educate every child in the nation, many of whom are severely disabled by the conflicts and turbulence of childhood. Not surprisingly, the schools cannot handle every challenge. Quickly, within the first six grades, two rivers spring forth upon the Isle of Academia. One river carries children toward achievement and success; the other leads to discouragement and failure. In between these rivers, many children flounder while trying to find access to the waters of success.

American schools celebrate the lives of well-prepared, achievement-oriented children who come from healthy families. Most mainline children prosper in Academia, discovering their inner strengths and thriving amidst the praise and encouragement they receive. Quickly, they develop a sense of accomplishment and competence, feeling that they will continue to flourish when they reach their careers. Success breeds success. Those who possess unearned privilege— advantages enjoyed by the accident of birth—prosper. Early reading skills and positive attitudes speed the accomplished into higher level classes that will lead to college preparatory classes, a college or university education, and a career that will showcase their abilities.

Trials for the socially, psychologically, and academically fortunate exist, but their legs are long and the hurdles are low. However, The Rush, as always, pushes many too hard too fast. In the early grades, even the successful may suffer from symptoms of stress such as headaches, stomach ailments, or thunderous dispositions. In later grades, boredom becomes their worst obstacle, but by then they understand the system, may be challenged well by a few excellent teachers, and streak onward toward the lure of college admissions. Despite their grievances against the schools, most of the fortunate survive with a feeling of confidence. They know they are able and their abilities are appreciated. For them, the trials of school are passed successfully. Their inner spirits emerge slightly drowsy but ready to burst forth.

Woe to those, however, who fall away from the mainline! Children poorly prepared for the academic world face walls rather than hurdles. Slow starts and short legs will prevent most from clearing the obstructions that tower before them. Slamming into the walls of school failure, they quickly take the river that leads toward feelings of inferiority. Failure breeds failure, whether its roots are poor academic preparation, true learning disabilities, faulty motivation, or psychological upheavals. Most youngsters placed in slower classes quickly realize they are different from mainline children.

Discouragement whittles away at the inner spirits of failing children. If school success seems impossible, the force of their spirits whips children back and forth like fish caught in nets as they desperately attempt to survive. Those who internalize failure or cannot handle the pressure of The Rush seek acceptance in cliques, that demand lower entrance standards. Drugs prove to be an easy admission ticket, as does the wholesale defiance of the very schools which served as midwives to the birth of their inferiority feelings.

In the river of failure, countless youth scurry about like the humans thrown into the mythical labyrinth where they searched for a safe exit before the Minotaur devoured them. In order to escape, these children need an advocate to hand them a string that will lead to their liberation.

The Dragons: Poor Preparation

Parents who failed to harvest their own talents in school often struggle to survive in society. Beset by economic, personal, and health problems, many lack the energy and foundation to prepare their children for the rigors of school. Without the help of successful early intervention programs, these children are destined to swim in the river leading to school failure. After failing in school, most young people will not share in the fruits of our economic system. Struggling to survive—as their own parents did—they will be unable to prepare their children for a better life.

Only a revolution in society's thinking will break this cycle of failure and poverty. School reformers and special educators continue to suggest many creative ways to reform the system, but reform is slow. As a consequence, many spirits die, wasted by failure. Ignoring the need for massive reform, Sheriffs of The Rush prefer to provide a larger drug enforcement militia and to build bigger jails to arrest and confine defeated spirits. Some day the specter of this national failure will either scare the guardians of our contemporary system into making massive reforms, or the system—like the Berlin Wall—will tumble from the weight of its own incompetency.

Along with the poor, those who carry the psychological burdens of their families drift aimlessly. Children like Samuel Crompton are unable to feel treasured and secure. Many talented children work below their ability level. Experiencing turmoil in the home and failure in school, they cannot survive the currents of the fast, academic river. Soon they drown in the classroom. Their public failure leads to increased humiliation. Eventually, the Sheriffs of Academia come to their rescue, but too often their treatment accelerates a child's sense of failure. Publicly, the Sheriffs stamp and label struggling youth. The victims of social inequalities, family disharmony, and true learning disabilities are frequently treated like the junk of the academic world.

Dragons of the Isle of Academia: Early Labeling

Schools have become society's whipping boy. Falling behind other nations in academic achievement, our country pushes teachers and administrators to increase achievement. In turn, the Sheriffs of Academia push children harder. Those students who fail to travel at the institutional pace are flushed from the academic river. Most receive a label, which is as highly conspicuous as Hester Prynne's scarlet letter. Once labeled, children live up to the expectations made of them. As Elkind explained:

> The child who cannot keep up in this system, even if only temporarily, is often regarded as a defective vessel and is labeled learning disabled or minimally brain damaged or hyperactive. Yet these same children can easily demonstrate how much knowledge they acquire from television and how quickly they can acquire the skills needed to operate electronic games. The factory system . . . hurries children by ignoring individual differences and by prematurely labeling many children defective. (Elkind, 1984, p. 48)

In America humanistic theories are used to explain one's possibilities, and deterministic theories are used to explain one's limitations. In the first instance, Americans choose to think of themselves as free, and in the latter they wish to believe they are simply the product of genetics and past training. Unfortunately, biological theories prove to be neat, easy theories that solve the problems facing the Sheriffs of Academia. Sometimes the theories are correct and the resulting treatment is helpful, but for many children, it is a tragedy. By blaming all forms of learning disabilities and attention deficit hyperactivity disorders solely on organic difficulties, parents and schools are relieved of the responsibility of treating the complex origins of many children's conditions. Drug therapy combined with a shallow exposure to behavioral management techniques allow schools to process quickly the large number of children who cannot keep pace. Unfortunately, as in the Crompton family's situation, the call for transformation is ignored.

Richard Gardner is a Clinical Professor of Child Psychiatry at Columbia University. In his book, *Hyperactivity: The So-Called Attention-Deficit Disorders and the Group of MBD Syndromes*, he noted that:

> The biological approach is certainly an attractive one. Rather than spend long periods going into background history; rather than undergo the tedious process of trying to understand the multiplicity of factors that have produced the symptoms; all one has to do is supply the medicine that presumably will correct the biological abnormality that is theorized to be the cause of the disorder.
>
> . . . This biological approach is also more attractive to schools and institutions where large numbers of patients must be "processed" and provided services. There was a time when doctors treated patients. Now the lingo calls us "providers" and our treatment "delivery of services"...The result of all of this is that the "customer" is being ripped off. The "product" being provided is often of specious, if of any, value at all. And the ADD (Attention Deficit Disorder) diagnosis and its treatment is an excellent example of this phenomenon. (Gardner, 1987, p. 185)

The losers in these trials are hundreds of young people. Feeling inferior to others, humiliated by labels, and receiving inadequate treatment and services, these children's inner spirits begin to dry up. Children who struggle need advocates. Someone must believe the truth in the title of the children's song, "God Don't Make Junk."

Heroes as Advocates

So often a single person saves the spirit of the child who struggles to feel competent and able. Usually, it is a parent who encourages the child and transforms the family into a sanctuary that nourishes and liberates the child's spirit. Special teachers, coaches, youth workers, or counselors can also provide the critical care needed to overcome feelings of inferiority. A child's inner spirit thrives only when others recognize and nourish it.

The Sheriffs of Academia's main interest centers on the system's smooth functioning, not on individual children's welfare. Individuals' spirits are not expendable, however, even when they fit imperfectly into the contemporary system. Children with special school challenges need heroes in their lives, adults who shield them from the crunching academic system. How often adults who struggled in their childhoods recall: "She (he) believed in me when no one else did. And her faith and encouragement made all of the difference in my life." One adult *can* make all of the difference between success and failure in a child's life.

Passing through the trials of childhood, children grow in their trust, autonomy, initiative, and competence. Now they are ready to spread their wings. But before they become successful in the adult world, they must survive their flight through adolescence.

Chapter 5

ICARUS AND THE DRAGONS: TEENAGERS, THEIR PARENTS, AND BEYOND

When all was prepared for flight [Daedalus] said, "Icarus, my son, I charge you to keep a moderate height, for if you fly too low the damp will clog your wings, and if too high the heat will melt them. Keep near me and you will be safe." While he gave him these instructions and fitted the wings to his shoulders, the face of the father was wet with tears, and his hands trembled. He kissed the boy, not knowing that it was for the last time. . . .

Bulfinch's Mythology

Ponderings. *How do the lives of teenagers and their parents differ? Why do parents sometimes seem to be more cautious than their adolescent children? What issues generally generate the most disagreements between parents and their teens? What strengths do teenagers enjoy that contribute to their own lives and the lives of others? What changes and challenges do midlife parents encounter? What new strengths do midlife parents enjoy? What are the major tasks of young adults in their 20s? What childhood myths break down as people journey through the 20s? Are the 20s difficult or relatively easy years for most young adults?*

Mythology is intriguing. In fact, new myths should be created and passed down to future generations. With this hope in mind, a part of the well-known myth of Icarus will be revised below. In the place of Icarus' parents, the image of dragons will appear. In mythology, dragons are not always dangerous creatures like the ones discussed in other chapters of this book. To the contrary, dragons often are kindly animals filled with good will. In the following recreated myth, these well-intentioned dragons represent those in midlife who do the best they can to raise their adolescent children well.

ICARUS AND THE DRAGONS

Icarus, the teenager, lives with the dragons, his parents. On most days they make good, even if unnatural, company. They enrich one another. Yet, on occasion their differences irritate each other.

Icarus, it may be recalled, has beautiful wax wings. Untested by time and unbothered by his inexperience, Icarus wishes to fly. The higher and faster he flies, the better. He soars and glides to his own rhythms and to the songs of his time.

For Icarus, everything will be different and improved. His future marriage will reflect perfection; his love will remain heated and passionate for eternity. He will ascend some day into the heavens of career opportunity, will never compromise his values, and will never accept routine. Surely, the world will change for the better because Icarus understands its problems. His will and purity of heart will certainly transform society. How beautifully Icarus soars through the sky.

But at times Icarus drifts perilously close to the sun. His parents, the dragons, tremble. They fear the melting of his wings and a fall to earth that may prove fatal. Yet their warnings and their caring go unnoticed.

Early in life Icarus' parents, the dragons, soared. Though they still own wings, their wings seem smaller. They can fly, but the weight of reality and experience holds them close to the earth.

Dragons know the limitations imposed upon them by their talents, their personality, and this world. They understand the difference between young love and mature love. Their love has known as many winters as springs. Also, the dragons discovered the complexity of the marketplace. Even with success in careers, they know well the ferocity of competition and the costs of advancement.

Like Icarus, the dragons were once so certain that the world would change upon demand; now they accept the lessons learned over time. War, poverty, ignorance, and earthquakes face each generation. Wisdom, fidelity to religion, and one's will do not always transform what is. Change comes slowly, if at all.

Dragons feel firmly entrenched because of their responsibilities in this world. Their huge feet seem solidly mired in the logistics of savings accounts, taxes, checkbooks, house cleaning, yard maintenance, health concerns, and the demands of raising young Icarus.

The dragons plead with Icarus to stay closer to earth. Icarus retorts, "You've forgotten how to soar." Therein lies the irritation.

At a time when parents only dream of flight, Icarus parades their weaknesses before them. He reminds them of their bulkiness, of their lack of dexterity. Icarus sees as weakness what his elders know to be experience. The dragons growl.

In return, the elders warn Icarus of his lack of reality. He flies without direction, without realizing the consequences of uncharted flight. The dragons see as irresponsibility what Icarus knows to be the human spirit. Icarus soars higher.

And thus these unnatural companions share a home and different worlds for a few short years. Conflicts will naturally occur, but maybe the unnatural will also happen.

Instead of taking offense at Icarus' protestations, maybe the dragons should examine the criticism. Could it be that they have become too entrenched? Maybe Icarus, seemingly so innocent, offers needed wisdom. Have the dragons forgotten that they too have wings?

And maybe upon seeing the dragons begin to fly in their controlled way, Icarus will value more the ground that is his home. Maybe he will better understand the security of the earth.

Instead of fearing the differences between their ways of living, Icarus and the dragons should listen to one another's message. Can they not, at times, share the best of two worlds?

FROM THE CROW'S NEST OF MIDLIFE AND ADOLESCENT VOYAGES: PERSPECTIVES ON SEVEN DIFFERENT VISTAS

It is as challenging for an adolescent to live with midlife parents as it is for parents to live with a typical teenager. Both ages represent turning points in life. Adolescents leave childhood as they sail toward an adulthood that seems never to arrive quickly enough. Their parents pass through young adulthood and begin the last half of a voyage that now passes far too swiftly. On different legs in their journeys, teenagers and their parents look out from the crow's nest and see the same world differently. Their divergent views can make living together exciting or tumultuous. Most families probably experience a strong mixture of both.

For logistical ease, authors of developmental texts separate their chapters on adolescence from their studies of middle adulthood. If adolescents lived in segregation from their parents, this approach would work nicely. But the truth is that the worlds of adolescents and their parents always meet and, at times, collide. For parents to truly understand their teenagers, they must first be aware of themselves. Although adolescents' lives seem filled with motion and obvious changes, their parents often experience equally dramatic, although sometimes less visible, alterations.

Below are seven vistas that are seen quite differently from the perspectives of adolescents and their parents. Each vista represents a challenge to the voyager, one that elicits a variety of reactions. To some trials, sojourners, whether younger or older, respond in ways that bring equilibrium and even tranquility to family waters. To other challenges, their reactions create typhoons and whirlpools.

Because parents and teenagers react in such a variety of ways to each of life's challenges, this period of family life becomes one of life's most complicated and fascinating. Below are a few of the more frequently observed reactions to seven of life's challenges.

VISTA 1: THE PHYSICAL TIDE

Middle Adulthood

Carl Jung was right. When my first child, Patrick, reached his teenage years, his sun burst brilliantly into the morning sky. And, at the same time, mine passed noon and began its slow descent through the afternoon sky. For the first time, the years left in my life became less than the number lived.

For parents in midlife, life becomes emotional and, at times, difficult. Events in one's life become more poignant, meaningful, and dramatic. Sometimes these events are understood by everyone; at other times they are deeply personal.

At the age of 44 two events symbolized my transition from young adulthood to middle adulthood. The first would never be noticed by others because of its presumed insignificance. Each day since my three children learned to walk, I raced them to the front door as soon as our car stopped outside of the house. Sometimes I won the race; at other times, I allowed them to win. But early in my 44th year, my youngest son beat me to the door on his own. I was never to win another race; the physical torch was passed to another generation.

During that same year my mother suffered a long, cruel illness. As a member of the famed sandwich generation (sandwiched between the needs of the young and elderly), I never felt as if I could do enough for my mother, my children, students, wife, or friends. It was as if I tried to keep hundreds of balloons in the air at once. As soon as I pushed one balloon skyward, several others came perilously close to striking the floor. Emotions raged inside as I tried to do my best to help everyone, but my efforts always seemed to fall short.

After being ill a year my mother died, six years after the death of my father. Suddenly, I became the oldest member of my immediate family. Now, if life follows the course I hope it will, my wife and I will become the next generation to die. The realization of aging and one's certain death brings with it some discontent, restlessness, and desire for change. Also, the simple things in life arouse increased passion. Sunsets become more radiant because of the knowledge their number will not be endless. Friendships seem increasingly important because friends will enjoy a limited number of nights together. Marriages become more vital because partners know in time their lives together will be no more. Life changes for a midlife person. There is passion, dissatisfaction, anger, hope, and love. And if ever one tends to forget the lessons of midlife, the mirror will always reflect the reality of aging.

"*No!*" You cannot have it this easy way forever." Life declared that many times before, but in middle adulthood the body becomes time's constant messenger and reminder. Wrinkles appear. The legs no longer carry the frame as swiftly around the tennis courts. Aches and pains mount. Menopause approaches. Soon, worries about mental capacities will arise. Although probably unfounded, midlife adults worry: Am I slower to remember names or have I just met so many people? Can I keep up with the new technology and new discoveries in my field? These questions become the mental undertow that accompanies life's receding physical tide. For those who rejoiced in the appearance and strength of their youthful bodies, these midlife years may present unwelcome challenges.

For those who react positively to their physical changes, comfort is found in moving with time, not against it. For the first time, many personal limitations become obvious and can be accepted more readily. Because time now seems to pass more swiftly, the days become increasingly precious. No longer does one wish away the seasons of life. For instance, rarely would a midlife person say with conviction: "I cannot wait for winter to end." Because future winters are limited in number, the long shadows and cold mornings appear like lifelong friends who bring comfort and even companionship. Biologists capture the poignancy of the human situation well when they point out that humans alone among living creatures are able to observe: "I am growing older."

On the other hand, many adults fight against the rhythms of nature. Instead of moving forward, they throw themselves onto the hands of time, hoping to sabotage Mother Nature's clockworks. Hair transplants, tummy tucks, face lifts, and such ploys become desperate attempts to deny the passing of the years. Those who refuse to dance to the rhythm of time are dragged across earth's ballroom floor, kicking and screaming without grace. It is into this parental world of diminishing time that adolescents spring forward. Parents who already feel like a part of nature's rhythm will fare far better in this era than those who rebel against the passing of the years.

Adolescents

Not long ago sleeping children were carried in from the car and placed in their beds alongside their treasured animals. Suddenly, puberty strikes and childhood is no more. With their metamorphosis to adolescence, children become new, almost strange inhabitants of the home. Voices change, bodies leap in growth, and minds become keen and critical.

For most maturing adolescents, these changes bring with them excitement and anticipation. Unlike for many of their parents, the teenager's mirror becomes a constant friend and companion. Optimism abounds. And these years— treasured by their parents—cannot pass quickly enough for the young who long for adulthood.

In these years, most adolescents experience periods of gloom; in these moments, their tongues attack their most available prey: parents. Frequently the young's emerging mental powers focus on their parents' weaknesses, as if their parents were not keenly aware of their own shortcomings. Unfortunately, adolescent critics emerge at a most sensitive time in their parents' lives.

Not all adolescents find that physical growth is a blessing. Many worry about early or late development. Others' bodies do not seem to measure up to society's unreasonable standards. Teens who become unhappy with nature's rhythms will also increase the strain in their parents' lives. If by chance parents and their children both dislike nature's progression, then home life can become volcanic.

Possibly, all adolescents and parents feel some natural tension as their suns pass by each other in the sky: one is rising and the other declining. However, when parents and children feel comfortable with the physical changes they experience, their life together will be much calmer. On the other hand, it is difficult and challenging to share a home with a disappointed and angry person of any age.

VISTA 2: DEATH

Middle Adulthood

Time may heal all wounds, but it does not fill the emptiness left in death's wake. Anyone who has lost the presence of a loved one understands the permanent void their death leaves behind. Sometime during midlife, most adults are thrown out of the mythical garden of eternal, earthly life. Not only do travelers begin to lose older relatives, but they are also shaken by the natural deaths of a few of their peers. The reality of their own future deaths promises that their suns are in descent and the night will surely come.

This is a nightmare that will not leave when morning breaks. Instead, death becomes an ever-present part of reality. Positive sojourners eventually accept death, not as an unnatural evil but as a necessary beat in nature's rhythm. Instead of resenting their mortal status, most in middle adulthood give birth to something that will last beyond their years. Giving to the next generation, directly or indirectly, becomes the major focus of most travelers. A shift from feeling remorseful to giving to others also eases the tension often felt in the home.

However, a few parents continue to see death as the enemy, as an evil outsider. The Grim Reaper, they believe, must be ignored or avoided. The ones who are fearful run from death and enter frantically into activities that help them to deny death's existence. Parties, work, alcohol, sports, and sex can enhance life, but overindulgence allows fugitives to forget the promise of death. It is as if the fearful seek an eternal life on earth, but to no avail. Those preoccupied by their fear of death will feel doubly threatened by the feelings of immortality felt by their teenagers.

Adolescence

For adolescents death is a curiosity. Intellectually aware of the nature of mortal life, adolescents, nevertheless, are armed with powerful defenses. To most, death appears to be a distant visitor who rarely demands their attention. However, there are days when death intrudes. By accident, a friend may die, or older relatives may end their journeys. In these moments death becomes a teacher.

Discovering that death shows no mercy, sensitive young people become outraged at a world where starvation and war end the lives of innocent children. Teens valiantly cry out against any unnecessary destruction of life. To some extent the young understand that they too are vulnerable, but their defenses prevent them from dwelling on their own mortality. For most, possibilities far outshine any potential limitations.

However, the promise of death does overcome a few. Disillusioned, they shout: "Why should we do anything if it all must end?" For some adolescents, depression and inaction seem to be the only possibility of robbing death of its spoils. Others, intrigued by death, respond by challenging death with heavy drinking, fast driving, and dangerous risk taking. After all, they feel, perhaps death can be eluded forever.

When parents and children live positively in the face of death, their years together are more likely to be cherished. If either or both cannot adjust to the shocking truth that death will come, life can take destructive detours. At the least, parents who cannot resolve their own fear of death may become too anxious and fearful to allow family members to risk living courageously. As a result, young Icarus may become grounded in the mire with his fearful parents.

VISTA 3: LOVE

Middle Adulthood

Mature love no longer resembles a National Geographic exploration into virgin territory. Years of living together leaves few physical wildernesses unexplored. Yet familiarity need not breed contempt. Indeed, time can usher in new ways of loving. For those whose marriage has thrived over many years, joy in the relationship now comes from companionship, encouragement, faithfulness, and sexual contentment. More like marathon runners than sprinters, mature lovers learn to celebrate each mile passed, to replenish themselves regularly, and to look forward to the experiences and challenges ahead. Partners who stand together on a firm marital foundation are most likely to withstand successfully the vibrations created by growing adolescents.

Not every couple completes the course. Some cannot endure the highs and lows experienced over the long distance. Instead of feeling renewed, many experience only the bitternesses and resentments that have collected over the past miles. No longer able to encourage their partners or to receive nourishment from them, they abandon the marital route with the hope that new companionship will bring renewed vitality. Other couples, unfortunately, abandon the course to sit listlessly together along the side of the road. No longer participants, they accept their fatigue, exhaustion, and loneliness as the fate of a marriage that must be endured. Adults who experience marital stagnation, turmoil, or divorce while their children are teenagers may find the typhoons of adolescence to be frequent and severe.

Adolescence

Are any thrills so intense as those of new love? For the first time, a young person feels completely understood and cherished. Sexual excitement and exploration add to the unbearable anticipation that precedes the hours to be spent together. Swept up with the newness of love, adolescents seem possessed by the adventure. In school, their minds wander. Secret notes are left for one another, excitement builds, and fulfillment seems at hand. Certainly, they believe, no one ever experienced such love before, for this is perfect love, an eternal union.

Despite the thrill of new love, most teens recognize that love is a relationship, not a possession to be owned. Dating, going steady, breaking up, and beginning once again teach valuable lessons. None, however, is more instructive than the loving of their parents, that ironically may seem so imperfect to the young. It is the parents' model that teaches young people that relationships involve the cherishing and building up of another person as much as receiving what may be offered.

The mature teen flourishes in the passion of first love but also understands that love is a great adventure, not a short expedition. Despite their allegiance to love, most youth are able to balance their love with other dreams for the future. Although love may be their brightest creation, achievement in school, friendships, personal interests, and the promise of future careers also bring light to their days.

On the other hand, frantic teens lose their balance. For some, the need for love becomes desperate; for others, the fear of love leads them toward isolation. Sometimes parental models paint an ugly picture of love as a relationship filled with bickering, unhappiness, and desertion. As a result, young people become anxious and grasp at love as if it was gold dust slipping quickly through their fingers. In other cases adolescents may lack personal stability. Seeing love as salvation, which must be obtained at any cost, they abandon their dreams and interests in order to capture it. Possibly, they believe, early marriages or furious sexual involvement might help them entrap love. Their parents, who may have experienced such folly, are terrified by their children's desperate tempo, for the long course ahead cannot be conquered with the pace of a sprinter. Parental warnings, of course, may go unheeded. As a result, those relationships cemented before young people travel across the Isle of Self are destined to face serious challenges.

Fearful teens often run away from love. Feeling too unlovable or frightened to be attracted to others, they wait in isolation destined only to observe the relationships enjoyed by the "blessed." These teens fear love and/or the loss of love, but by avoiding commitment and intimacy entirely, they postpone the opportunity to practice building intimate relationships.

For love to go astray in the life of any family member brings storms to a household. If the adults' love shipwrecks, then the intensity of the typhoons double. If in addition to the adults' shipwreck, teens' relationships crash, then storms may rampage out of control.

VISTA 4: DREAMS

Middle Adulthood

George Bernard Shaw wrote, "There are two tragedies in life. One is not to get your heart's desire. The other is to get it" (1955, p. 155). By midlife, most adults understand the wisdom of this maxim. As a child I dreamed of reaching three goals: to become a great poet, to reach the finals of Wimbledon, and to share a life of loving with another. Like so many of the ground balls hit toward me in my youth, the first two dreams passed me by unhindered. And the third, while realized, still requires constant vigilance to maintain.

As life passes, adults realize that few of their wildest dreams will come true, and even when some do, their achievement does not bring with them the total happiness that was once anticipated. As a result, in middle adulthood people reevaluate old dreams and often create new ones. Most maturing adults begin to place an emphasis on goals that enrich relationships or contribute to the next generation's fulfillment. That is not to say personal goals are not created, for it is a dull person who strives toward no vision of the future.

But freedom to pursue personal dreams becomes more restricted in midlife. Through the years most adults collect numerous obligations and constraints. Many are financial, others involve caring not only for youthful family members, but also for aging relatives. On top of these commitments are piled career and social obligations. No longer are people free to drop everything to follow their bliss. But the everything usually becomes a significant part of life's bliss. Often, more personal dreams must be pursued in one's spare time or held on to for future attainment. Life seldom turns out the way one dreams it will. Yet for adults who adjust their dreams and reinvest their energy positively, family life becomes a mutually fulfilling adventure.

A number of adults, however, never adjust to life's disappointments. Some hold on to their unfulfilled fantasies, blaming their spouse, children, boss, or life itself for their failures. Bitter, they remain haunted by their unfulfilled ambitions. At the other extreme, many adults toss aside their goals and dreams. In their place they latch on to their children and push them to succeed. In these cases, the children's success or failure governs the parents' happiness. Unfortunately, few children thrive when given the responsibility for their parents' emotional stability.

Of course, there are always a few adults who create new goals, then abandon everything they have created to pursue them without restraint. In fleeing from old responsibilities, they usually prevent family members from fulfilling their needs. In any situation, unfulfilled parents rarely react appropriately to their children's aspirations.

Adolescence

"I can be anyone and do anything," publicly or privately boasts the healthy adolescent. Not bothered by years of reality testing, many teens believe their destiny will include glory and honor. Elkind (1984) wrote about the personal fables constructed by young people that lead them to believe they will someday be famous beyond anyone's expectations.

Dreams of future success can motivate teens to pursue positive goals. Understanding that their dreams will not be reached without hard work, most learn to defer their gratification and choose instead to study and prepare for future careers. Wishing to excel, sensible young people begin to develop their talents and broaden their abilities. By doing so, they create a sturdy foundation that will support their career and ambitions in future years.

But for teens who have experienced too much failure, realistic dreams do not sprout. Their sense of inferiority grows and their dreams become either prohibitively grandiose or far too limited. If their parents also feel unfulfilled, the home can become a whirlpool of negativity. Eventually, discouraged teens may drop out of school and begin their uphill struggle to succeed. Sadly, too many of these discouraged youth soon fall victim to unemployment or to the lure of crime.

Destined to live in a different type of prison, a number of adolescents adopt without question the dreams their parents push upon them. Later they may discover they obediently entered fields that offer little or no bliss. As disillusioned adults they begin late in life the struggle to create their own identities, a process that should have begun much earlier.

Parents who come to terms with their own life dreams will encourage their children to pursue theirs. However, discouraged parents rarely can encourage their children properly. Parents disappointed with their own lives tend to either push their children or to place unnecessary roadblocks in their way. The older generation's ability to dream well is deeply entwined with the younger generation's ability to create healthy goals.

VISTA 5: CONTROL

Middle Adulthood

By midlife most adventurers realize that life cannot be controlled. The aging process proceeds at its own pace, despite any efforts to delay it. Tragedy never discriminates; death and serious injury can come to anyone, at any time, anywhere. People tend to do what they want to do and not what others want them to do. The parents of midlife adults age and may need the time and support of their offspring. Also, the world's governments and the relationships among them fail to conform to our standards of common sense.

Learning to let go of things that cannot be controlled, wise adults shift their focus to what can be—either completely or partially. For example, humans can control, or learn to control, their own behavior. They can decide how to treat the people they love and those with whom they associate. In many areas, however, adults enjoy little influence. They cannot stop it from raining during their long-awaited vacations any more than they can prevent criminals from destroying the lives of innocent victims.

Although much of life eludes total control, small actions can influence life. Adults can join others to try to change the conditions that create crime, and they can support legislators and legislation that protect the environment. Money can be donated to help alleviate starvation, and volunteer work often reduces the plight of a few needy adults. Parents cannot control their teenager's behavior, but they can set appropriate limits, provide encouragement, and make judgments that will influence their children's decisions and actions. Rather than control events, seasoned adults learn to influence them.

Events close to home usually present the toughest test of one's power to control life. For example, how much and in what ways can midlife adults help aging relatives without undermining their self-confidence and treading upon their independence? How much freedom can their teenagers handle and how much structure do they need to protect them from potential harm? To each of these questions, as well as to most personal struggles, no perfect formula exists. Therefore, parents struggle along with their families to create the best plan they can. As with all struggle, there is no assurance that their efforts will be appreciated or will turn out for the best. As soon as one strategy is set into motion, it seems that adjustments are quickly required. Everything certainly seemed easier when children were toddlers and their grandparents enjoyed good health. Nevertheless, for adults who recognize the limitations of their own power, the autonomy demands of their growing adolescents will be more easily negotiated.

Some parents in middle adulthood simply do not resolve control issues well. Often, they take extreme stands that represent the most simplistic solutions. Many refuse to acknowledge their limited control over life and others and attempt to overcontrol their children as if they were still infants. In the home, the cost of their inflexibility is frequently observed in the extreme reactions of their children who struggle to create identity. Some children openly rebel, creating havoc and turmoil in the home. Others submit to authority like puppets and, as a result, fail to create their own identities. Often, these conforming youth will continue to be unable to support or control themselves without the help of rigid structure.

Other parents, equally unable to resolve control issues, abandon all responsibility for participating in difficult decision making. Rather than negotiate their children's autonomy demands, they abdicate all control. As a result, their children usually possess more power than they can productively handle. Running full steam ahead, these adolescents may slam into major obstacles such as drug use, early pregnancy, or school failure. Sometimes, however, it is the adults who bear the symptoms of their forfeiture of control. Too stressed to take charge of their lives, adults may disintegrate into alcoholism, heavy drug use, psychosomatic illness or self-destructive pessimism. When not organic in nature, these disabilities become an excuse for failure: How can you expect me to control my children when I have lost control of my life? While adults struggle with diminishing ability to control life, adolescents storm into the scene with their challenges to adult authority.

Teenagers

Never underestimate teenagers' desire to control life. Unlike their parents who are recognizing the limitations of their control, young people are thrilled by their newly found ability to act. As of yet, most have not traveled far enough to run up against their own limitations. For the majority, possibility seems unlimited and any compromise of their wills amounts to an outrageous failure.

Perhaps today's parents and teens face more intense challenges over control issues than families in the past experienced. For one reason, young people live far longer in their parents' homes than did past generations. No longer serving apprenticeships with master craftsman or studying in institutions away from the home, most teens spend these developing years with their families. Having no rites of passage to signal their arrival to adulthood, society offers no exact time to mark the beginning of adulthood. Therefore, adolescents feel suspended between childhood and adulthood and push all the harder to be treated as full adult partners. This conflict often protracts to the college campus, where administrators continue to treat students in their 20s as if they were half-children and half-adults. Young people usually live up to the expectations of those in power. Therefore, a natural tension erupts between teens who seek more control and parents, or other adults, who wish to limit their youths' freedom.

If adolescents live with parents who have learned what they can and cannot control, then families can move more peacefully toward mutually shared power. For example, rules and consequences for breaking them can be jointly created. But when young people live with adults who either overcontrol or abdicate all power, turmoil can be expected.

How well families handle freedom and control issues in the home largely depends upon the adults' ability to use their power and influence wisely. How soundly adults act depends upon their own acceptance of when and how their imperfect ability to control life can be successfully used to influence others. For all parents, however, control issues bring with them many difficult challenges.

VISTA 6: COMMUNITY

Middle Adulthood

The sense of being closely connected to others begins in infancy. In those years children feel close to caretakers who meet their needs. As the years pass, people are added to the sense of community as interests and relationships expand. In midlife, issues of community are reconsidered: Who are the people to whom I feel connected? For whom am I responsible? Answers to these questions cause adults to either broaden their sense of community or severely narrow their worlds.

Through the years adults have felt every emotion deeply: love, hatred, hope, fear, bliss, hurt, loneliness, and togetherness. There is probably no one in this world with whom a middle-age adult cannot empathize. They understand the pain of parents who must watch their children starve. They know the hurt of those who feel rejected and the hopes of those who long for freedom. Their voyages have brought them closer to the billions of men and women who share this small planet. Although they do not know their names or faces, adults often feel a kinship with them that transcends race, religion, and nationality. In middle adulthood, many begin to act in concert with a belief in world community. They care actively for the disadvantaged of the world and work toward the goal of freeing people from discrimination and oppression. Positive adults stress the right of all humans to experience freedom, equality, and the pursuit of happiness. Love and acceptance expand.

However, for many reasons some adults become increasingly self-absorbed. As a result, their worlds narrow rather than broaden. Like turtles, stagnating people pull in their heads and avoid any risk of being open to the disturbing outside world. Mistakenly they believe their shell protects them from harm and obligation. In truth, their self-absorption simply prevents them from experiencing the healing that comes from being part of a larger community. As a result, the self-centered become more isolated and alone.

A few people take a middle path and venture out of their homes to join groups that share common interests and beliefs. Many organizations dedicate themselves to helping groups of needy people. Everyone benefits from their concern and outreach to others. Of course, there are always a few negative groups of people. Basically hostile to those they do not understand, these groups—whether they be countries, religions, or organizations—create increased fragmentation in the world. Fear, intimidation, and hatred usually flow from them.

Children model themselves on their parents' attitude toward others. When young people see openness and caring, they learn to love others. On the other hand, when they see hostility and coldness, they usually fail to treat others as they wish to be treated themselves. Of course, young people are often swayed by other models and events, but their parents' behavior inspires their initial attitude toward those with whom they share the world.

Teenagers

During the teen years, young people look for the first time beyond their localities to the world. Some are horrified by what they see; others simply look the other way. With a critical eye, young people who are loving clearly see the injustices and inequalities that exist throughout the world and demand that change begin to occur immediately. If the times seem to require it, some may, at great personal risk, attempt to force changes in society. Although impetuous and uncompromising, young people who challenge the unhealthy values of their own or other nations will strengthen the values and policies of those countries.

Nevertheless, despite their purity of will, the young suffer from a peculiar vision that allows them to see clearly the faults of others, while remaining blind to their own imperfections. Thus, while loving humanity, they may thoughtlessly join cliques that exclude people who are different. While lambasting the conditions that lead to poverty, they may buy only expensive, brand-name clothes. And while criticizing their parents for not doing enough to change the world, they often ignore the opportunities they have to make a difference in the lives of people in their own homes. The young can in one moment be remarkably sensitive and, in the next, be completely callous to others. For parents who feel like members of the world community, patience is required. By seeing their example, young people eventually will find a positive outlet for their passions.

Not all young people wish to make the world a better place. Some are too busy simply trying to survive in their own lives. Concerned with finding their place in life, they cannot be bothered by the needs of others. If their parents fail to model an openness to others, then the children will be hard-pressed ever to look beyond themselves. At the worst, the young may mirror their parents' involvement in mean-spirited groups that lord it over others.

Who is my neighbor? For the first time, adolescents must answer this question. As a result, the world will become either more open or closed, at least for a time. How will young people respond? Many factors will influence them, but most teenagers have difficulty seeing beyond their parents' vision.

VISTA 7: FAITH

Middle Adulthood

The direction that one's quest for religious truth takes depends, in part, upon the perspectives one has taken on the six preceding vistas. After losing loved ones to death and facing one's own mortality, midlife adults review life's most basic questions with more than an intellectual interest: Does God exist? If so, can I have a relationship with God, or is such interaction an illusion? How can there be so much evil if God is all-powerful and all-loving? If there is a God, does He or She intervene in life or are our lives left in our own hands? Why are there so many religions? Why are so many wars fought in the name of religion? And on and on. . . .

Although answers to these questions vary greatly, the responses often direct the remaining course of an individual's life. At times radical changes in direction are made and, at others, no alterations are forthcoming. Those too frightened to reexamine these basic questions may cling to the answers of their youth. For example, many have invested so heavily in their belief that there is no God that to consider the possibility requires swallowing far too much pride. Similarly, many will deny all evidence that contradicts the narrow religious beliefs that they have always held; the defensive faithful become less and less open to discovery. Still others, who cannot find definite answers, may decide to go through the motions of a formal religion in the hope that faith will eventually come. But many people do change. Some will discover a community of people who will share in their personal search. And some will find truth and comfort in religions that connect them to the generations that came before and to those that will follow.

Religious searches often make people more tolerant and accepting of others' beliefs. For example, many sojourners believe that all religions are true in their own way, that God cannot be captured by the human mind and, therefore, can be seen differently through different eyes. But religious searches can also lead to intolerance and a stance of superiority over others. In their absolute self-assurance, many groups representing a variety of religions deny that any truth could exist in outsiders' experiences, although the beliefs of these enemies of the faith are poorly understood. Declaring their vision of God to be the only true faith, many zealously declare rival faiths or even variations within their own faith to be heretical and simple-minded.

Teens may not understand the depth of their parents' religious convictions, but they do observe how their faith leads them to treat other people. Because young people wish to find their own truth, their quests may conflict with their parents' journeys, at least for a few years.

Teenagers

Their childhood stance toward faith no longer satisfies most teenagers. Those who never entertained the possible existence of God will be confronted with the possibility that God exists. Those who adopted their parents' religion may question whether or not the God of their parents exists. Or, at the least, they may wonder whether or not God exists as they had once believed. No longer accepting a childhood image of God with a long white beard and a palace in heaven, these young people strive to see God more clearly.

Being able to think of limitless possibilities and being critical of all things, teenagers often become disillusioned with the institutional church and its obvious weaknesses. For a time, even the services and symbols that their parents celebrate may seem meaningless. As a consequence, young people frequently rebel against forced participation in formal church activities. Their resistance to participation in formal religion does not indicate that the young deny God's existence. Ironically, many resistant teens are deeply religious. Like many parents, they are seekers of the truth, but they are looking at God with youthful eyes and from a different perspective. Many wish to consider all of the options before deciding the truth for themselves. Eventually these teenagers may make commitments, but until they do, their parents will feel helpless because they cannot directly influence them.

Of course, not all adolescents question faith. Some find satisfaction and meaning in accepting the teachings of their adopted religion or sect. Others may discount religion entirely and attempt to create meaning in a world without God. Religious questioning and the pursuit of truth takes on innumerable expressions. It is not unusual for teens and their midlife parents to be seeking answers at the same time, but different perspectives are as common as they were on the previous vistas discussed. In these times, the different quests for truth undertaken in the family may collide. When they do, the fruits of each member's faith is clearly shown in their treatment of each other.

OUT OF THE NEST: THE 20s

The Mental World

In his book *Transformations* (Gould, 1978), Roger Gould explained his belief that the major task of young people aged 16 to 22 is to progressively move away from their families of origin. At each age in life, myths of childhood are broken down and replaced by more mature beliefs. During the period when one leaves one's parents' world, the myth broken is: "I'll always belong to my parents and believe in their world."

While living at home, most teenagers' identities are still tied directly to their families. Difficulties arising in their lives frequently center on direct or indirect conflicts with their parents. As adolescents leave for college or their first jobs, friends become increasingly influential as parental influence wanes.

In this process young adults become more independent, realizing that they can indeed live without their parents' direct intervention. In the process of separation, young people begin to create their own ideas rather than blindly accepting the beliefs of their parents. By the age of 22, most have developed a healthy independence.

Nevertheless, there remains from 22 to 28 another false assumption: "Doing things my parents' way, with willpower and perseverance, will bring results. But if I become too frustrated, confused, or tired, or am simply unable to cope, they will step in and show me the right path." During these years, young adults discover that "they are nobody's baby now."

Friends, although important, become less central to growth in the 20s. Increasingly, young adults become autonomous, expanding their self-reliance and competence. They also become more realistic about the world. They realize, for example, that life is not always fair to those who work hard. Jobs may not be available for the worthy or promotions may be denied despite one's deserving accomplishments. Parents cannot right all of the wrongs or heal the wounds of their children. Now, young adults begin to seek a life partner to journey with through these challenging years. Increasingly, the family is left in the background as autonomy and love relationships grow.

The Tasks of the 20s

Daniel Levinson (Figure 5.1) of Yale University agreed that between ages 17 and 22 young people make a transition into early adulthood. Relationships from the past must be modified or terminated. Levinson called this process individuation, which involves "becoming more of an individual; we develop a separate and special personality, derived less and less from . . . parents and teachers and more and more from our own behavior."

Entering the adult world requires a longer span of time than most people, including parents, believe. In fact, Levinson suggested that it takes most 17 year olds almost 15 years to find an acceptable niche in adult life. During this period, young adults will make, then reevaluate their initial choices in occupation, marriage, values, and lifestyles. By no means are the 20s an easy time. Levinson reported that more than 50% of young adults feel, at times, that their lives are incomplete.

The major tasks of people in their 20s include creating a dream, searching for a mentor, making early occupational decisions, and selecting a spouse. Although men and women face different challenges and timetables in meeting these tasks, Levinson believed that both sexes share similar tasks.

The dream is a vision of what one hopes to become. It gives a person enthusiasm, spirit, and a destination. It is important that dreams be connected to reality. Youngsters with minimal athletic skills, for example, will not be served well by a dream of being a star in the National Basketball Association. Frequently, those with social and financial advantages enjoy an easier time actually reaching their dreams. Without a dream, people from any background will live without vitality and purpose.

Dreams are crucial to positive development and are connected to the identity formation discussed in an earlier chapter. Young people with foreclosed identities will dream their parents' dreams. Those in identity diffusion may be incapable of creating a dream, while those in moratorium are too frightened to dream.

Figure 5.1.   Daniel Levinson. Courtesy of Yale University.

In careers, the 20s is a time for exploration rather than total commitment. It is the norm for young adults to make several job changes in their 20s. This is also an age when workers are most critical of their jobs, bosses and working conditions. Their criticism helps them rethink certain career options and gives them the impetus to keep searching for the most appropriate occupational match.

Many young adults will have the good fortune of finding a mentor, an older, experienced person willing to guide young adults through the work world. Mentors help young adults strive toward their dreams. They are guides, sponsors, teachers, and counselors. Usually 8 to 15 years older than the young adult, mentors are neither parent nor friend. The relationship is a special, reciprocal one. In return for guidance, the mentor receives appreciation, admiration, respect, and gratitude. Unfortunately, the mentor relationship often ends acrimoniously. After young adults learn the ropes, they may feel that mentors hold them back, and the mentors may believe the young adults are touchy and ungrateful.

Unfortunately, not all young adults will be fortunate enough to find a person to shepherd them through the career world. Women have fewer mentors in the business world than men do, for instance. For women it is easier to find mentors in careers that allowed the entry of women years ago, such as teaching, nursing, and parenting. Possibly time and increased equality of opportunity will help the next generation of women gain access to mentors in a wider variety of careers.

During the 20s, men and women look for a companion who will support them in their life pursuits. Good communications and planning are essential to their future. Many times couples marry before they are sure how their lives will fit together. If their dreams do not match, trouble usually follows, as will be discussed in a later chapter.

By the late 20s, young people usually choose a life structure on the basis of an occupation, marriage, friendships, and religion. In addition, individuals initiate a variety of commitments to civic, political, and social organizations. Levinson believed that as adults near 30, they will review these initial choices. Some will continue on their voyage without making significant changes. Others will make major alterations in their marriages, careers, or other commitments. Two more transitional periods will occur when major changes in one's commitments are considered; one comes during midlife (40 to 45) and another during late adulthood (60 to 65).

The 20s usher in major challenges to young adults. The comfortable myths of their childhood break down. They make major decisions about life commitments, then critically review them as they near the age of 30. Those who believe that the 20s are among the easiest time in life are mistaken. They are years filled with crucial choices that will make the future years either easier or more complex.

Chapter 6

THE INNER QUEST: COGNITIVE, MORAL, AND RELIGIOUS GROWTH

But for the man also who does not so much as reach faith life has tasks enough, and if one loves them sincerely, life will by no means be wasted, even though it never is comparable to the life of those who sense and grasped the highest.

Søren Kierkegaard

Ponderings.   *How do adults and children differ in the ways they think? What problems do these differences sometimes create for parents? For children? For teachers? How might some of these challenges be resolved? What does it mean that cognitive development creates the basis for moral development?*

Is it natural for children to make self-centered moral decisions? When do people begin to make decisions based, in part, on the needs and feelings of others? How do men and women differ when making complicated moral decisions? What makes the moral thinking of famous people (Ghandi or Mother Theresa, for example) different? Does the ability to achieve "higher" moral thought assure that one will act accordingly?

What does it mean that moral development is necessary but not sufficient to assure growth in the stages of faith? Why do you believe many psychologists, until recently, seemed reluctant to discuss faith despite its obvious power for good and bad in the world? Why do people who share the same faith seem to live out their convictions in remarkably different ways? Can understanding people's differences help the world to become more peaceful?

Never in the history of humankind has it been more critical for people to understand the thinking, moral reasoning, and faith of people in distant parts of this world. The very existence of the planet Earth seems threatened at times by intolerance and hatred, but tremendous progress has been made in helping human beings appreciate the different cognitive, moral, and spiritual worlds in which people live.

Although understanding the inner worlds of others will not in itself solve the problems of this world, perhaps it is a first step in becoming more open and accepting of people who think and believe in different ways. Sensitivity to these differences will help us understand why within the same religion, for example, one sect strives for a nonviolent, peaceful world and another seeks to destroy outsiders believed to be the enemy. Possibly an increased receptiveness and tolerance of peoples' differences will help future leaders find more creative ways to coexist rather than discovering ingenious methods for spilling blood and preserving ancient hostilities.

This journey will begin with the stages of cognitive development created by Jean Piaget (Figure 6.1), whose work serves as a foundation for the stages of moral development constructed by Lawrence Kohlberg. Then, in turn, how the stages of moral development become the underpinnings for the ways in which people create meaning, as described in the stages of faith developed by James Fowler, will be examined.

As you read about the different inner worlds that govern people's lives, you may also see yourself as a traveler through many of these modalities. After examining your own growth, it will be easier to be more accepting of those whose ways of knowing and living differ. As philosophers throughout the years have advised, we are indeed more alike than different.

COGNITIVE DEVELOPMENT: JEAN PIAGET

Born in 1896 in Switzerland, Jean Piaget developed the most influential theory of cognitive development in the 20th century. Piaget explained that most people travel through four different worlds of thought during their lifetimes. Each stage or modality of thought is unique and beautiful in its own way. Of course, along with their most charming and distinctive characteristics, people in

Figure 6.1. Jean Piaget. Courtesy of Jill Krementz, New York City.

each stage exhibit specific limitations in their ability to think and reason. In some ways, these very boundaries to thought, particularly in children, become among the most enjoyable features of each stage.

Although the ages at which individuals reach each new world of thought vary, those who share the same stage are remarkably similar in their ways of thinking and knowing about the world in which they live, themselves, others, and the universe. Each stage becomes more complex as individuals develop increasingly complicated modes of thinking and knowing.

Understanding the four worlds of thought allows educators, professionals, and parents to work with children and adults more effectively and with increasing enjoyment. In addition, Piaget's exploration of these four worlds has encouraged theorists and researchers to learn more about how people in each of these stages make moral decisions and think about the meaning of life.

The Sensorimotor Period (Birth to Age 2)

Infancy begins with a baby who seems little more than a bundle of reflexes capable of only sucking, reaching, feeling, and grasping. Yet these sensorimotor abilities will allow each child to learn about and adapt to the world. By physically manipulating objects in the world around them, infants answer important questions about the characteristics of things from baby rattles to the cat's tail. These sensorimotor schemata for learning about the world become more purposive and sophisticated throughout the first months of life.

At no time is growth more dynamic than in the first 2 years of life. In the 1st month children suck and cry without discrimination. For instance, they will suck not only a nipple, but also they instinctively "nurse" on any object that contacts the mouth. During the 2nd to 4th month children begin to gain more control over their bodies and, therefore, their investigative abilities. They can distinguish the nipple from other objects. Now they can coordinate the hand and arm to permit them to suck on their thumbs or to insert in their mouths any object that interests them. Behavior, in other words, becomes more purposive.

Between the 4th and 8th months children will repeat actions that bring about interesting results. They may, for instance, bang their feet repeatedly against the sides of their bed. Also, babies enjoy mobiles without motors because they can kick their legs and watch the figures move. Or, they may toss bowls and cups from their high chair just to watch them fall. Few parents think of these methods of learning as acts of intelligence, but they are. Babies are in many ways like little scientists interacting with and experimenting with their environment. Because they do not understand most words and certainly cannot read, they learn about difficult scientific principles experimentally. For example, they learn about gravity by simply letting objects fall—over and over again. In addition, children begin to anticipate future events. For example, if a baby sees dad put on his coat, the child anticipates that he will leave the house.

Babies slowly learn about object permanence, the concept that objects exist even when they cannot be seen. During the first month when something is out of sight, infants believe it does not exist. Children between the 8th and 12th months will search for things that are partially covered up. However, they will not search for objects they see hidden but that are placed totally out of sight. This is a wonderful period for parents to play peek-a-boo and Jack-in-the-box with their children. When playing, children will be surprised when mom or dad appears from hiding. But as time passes they begin to anticipate their parents' reappearance, just as they begin to realize exactly when Jack will emerge from the box.

During the 12th to 18th month, children begin to find unique ways to explore their environments. Because they can now walk, their curiosity extends to many objects in the environment. They begin to experiment by trying different ways to do things. If children are given a plastic dog that squeaks, they may press it, step on it, jump on it, then sit on it to discover new ways to make the dog bark.

Object permanence continues to develop. Children will look for missing objects in the last place they saw them hidden. However, they will not search for objects that disappear if they did not see them hidden. Toward the end of the second year, children's object permanence solidifies. Now, they will search for missing objects they did not see hidden. For example, they may search the kitchen to find candy their mother bought at the store. It should be noted that new research suggests that an infant's understanding of object permanence may occur even more rapidly than Piaget believed.

Toward the end of this stage, children begin to acquire language and are able to use symbols more fluently. This new-found symbolic ability will propel youngsters into the second stage or Preoperational Period. Because of children's language growth, they can think, reflect, and plan ahead. No longer are Preoperational children restricted to learning by trial and error because now they can remember more, plan better, and anticipate future events. To some parents' dismay, for example, a 2 year old can watch another child's temper tantrum and then duplicate it at home at a later, appropriate opportunity.

It should be noted that current research suggests that children may be able to master some symbols before Piaget realized. For example, 6 month olds with deaf parents are able to use basic signs in sign language (Mandler, 1990). With the use of new scientific testing techniques, researchers are making startling discoveries about children's ability to remember and think.

The Preoperational Period (Age 2 to 6 or 7)

Children who seemed as if they might never talk in complete sentences frequently shock their parents with the burst in language that accompanies the Preoperational Period. Now the same parents who worried about their children's limited speech may wonder if their children will ever be quiet again. Children's spectacular language bursts allow them to expand from the 200 word vocabulary of a 2 year old to a vocabulary at age 5 that allows them to understand an average adult's language. As a result of their language growth, children no longer are limited to learning by sensing and doing. This explosion of symbols (words) allows them to think, reflect, and plan.

The preoperational period may be best known by adults because of the development of animism or the tendency to treat inanimate objects as if they are alive. Teddy bears become friends, dolls talk, action figures engage in combat, the sun and stars listen to children's songs, and make-believe guests attend tea parties. Children's boundless imaginations allow a stick to become a magic wand, a sword, an airplane, or anything else they wish it to be.

If you assume adults outgrow animism, listen to drivers talk to their cars that fail to start, watch golfers wave their arms to try to push a golf ball already in flight onto the green, or observe drink machines dented by the angry pounding of an irate, short-changed customer. Although adults may move to higher stages, they will frequently exhibit traits of earlier stages.

Preoperational children are egocentric by nature. Sometimes it is difficult for them to understand another person's needs or point of view. That is why parents may become frustrated by their children's endless talking at the dinner table. The needs of family members are not easily recognized by preoperational children. Interactions among children reflect egocentrism as well. When 4 year olds play, they do not usually play together. Instead, they play side by side (parallel play), not entering each other's worlds. While they are playing, young children usually talk at the same time (collective monologue), not bothering to listen to others.

For those who believe egocentrism ends in childhood, stay tuned to the next political convention. However, it should be noted that many researchers believe children are able, at times, to understand another's viewpoint. They may be capable, for example, of true empathy for another's feelings. Piaget probably underestimated this capacity in childhood. Nevertheless, he was correct in his observation that egocentrism is naturally its strongest during this period.

Preschool children exhibit a limited understanding of time and space. They cannot save money well for a future trip, for instance. They do not understand phrases such as "wait until later" and they certainly do not think of bedtime and dinnertime as a "time" on the clock. For them dinnertime occurs when they are physically present, sitting at the table with others who are also ready to eat. As long as they are not at the table, children seem to believe they can delay dinnertime indefinitely. Children learn by talking and doing at this stage. They learn little by listening to parents' or teachers' lectures. Parents need to provide experiences through activities, trips, and books that allow children to exercise their newly found verbal and mental abilities. These years are exciting ones for learning because children are interested in anything and everything.

However, there are limitations to children's thought. Between ages 2 to 4, children's thought is preconceptual. In other words, preschoolers' use of concepts is incomplete. They can identity Santa Claus, for example, but they do not understand that the five Santas seen in various stores on the same morning are different. If they see a toy like their own, they may feel it is their own.

From the age of 4 to 7, children's thinking becomes intuitive. They now rely not on logic, but on appearances and perception. They do not realize, for example, that objects do not change in volume or weight when the shape of the container or the object itself changes (conservation). Therefore, they will insist that a taller glass with an identical volume of liquid holds more than a smaller, wider glass.

Likewise, they may realize that two different balls of clay contain the same amount of clay. However, when one ball is flattened out into a pancake, children are mislead by the new appearance and believe that the pancake no longer contains the same amount of clay.

In part, preoperational children's limitations come because of their tendency to center on one aspect of a problem at a time (centering). Any parent who has allowed a child to choose a candy bar has seen how long it takes a child to "weigh" each one. Children who have something on their minds will not easily let go of the idea. When my daughter was 4, we had the following conversation at dinner:

> **Emily:** *"Dad, is this chicken a bird?"*
>
> **Dad:** *"Yes, it is, Emily."*
>
> **Emily:** *"Is it a dead bird?"*
>
> **Dad:** *"Yes, it is, Emily."*
>
> **Emily:** *"Are you eating a dead bird's leg, Dad?"*
>
> **Dad:** *"Yes, I am, Emily."*
>
> **Emily:** *"Are you eating a dead bird's dead leg, Dad?"*
>
> **Dad:** *"No, I'm not, Emily. I'm not very hungry."*

Unfortunately, because of their reliance on their perceptions over logic, children do not understand the complex causes of events. A child, for example, may believe that dad left home because he (the child) yelled at him. Or, a young person may believe that something she did or failed to do—like visit in the hospital—caused the death of a relative or friend. Justice is seen in the same light. When someone is injured, children believe they deserved it or that God punished them. Also, the severity of the punishment defines the wrongness of the act.

Needless to say, adults frequently think in similar ways. A coach, for instance, may wear a lucky sweater that he believes may cause his team to win. Fans thousands of miles away may assume they can influence the outcome of a game by something they say or do even before the game begins. Similarly, adults often blame God for the good and bad events in their lives, from finding a parking place to stubbing a toe.

The preoperational world of children is one of magic, fantasy and imagination. If logic is cherished, one will need to wait.

Concrete Operations (Age 6 or 7 to around 11)

Between 6 and 7 years of age, children begin to think logically about things they can see and touch, but not about abstractions. Now they understand conservation. For example, they know that the volume does not change when liquid is poured from a tall, thin glass to a small, wide one. They are less tied to appearances and are able to think through solutions because they realize there are rules that govern life. Thinking that involves rules is called *operations*. At this age children can use logic to solve problems involving real objects or those easily thought about, as the term *concrete operations* suggests.

Concrete operational children are less egocentric and begin to understand the point of view of others. They do not center on one aspect of a problem, but can find solutions by looking at a variety of variables. By the age of 8, most children can add, subtract, multiply, and divide. They understand more about money, but still have difficulty with distant time, either in the past or future. Therefore, they will have difficulty saving for college, but will be able to save for a trip to the fair next week.

With the advent of concrete operations, parents may mourn the passing of the boundless imagination of the preoperational child. Concrete operational children are literal. Dolls cannot talk. The sun does not listen to songs. A stick is just a stick.

Rules become crucial to school-age children. Therefore, they frequently fight over rules when playing games. At times, they honor one rule more than others: I must win.

Children's mistakes are frequently created because of an absence of rules or the presence of incorrect rules. For example, if children miss a particular type of math problem, their mistakes may be caused by their adherence to an incorrect rule or simply by the lack of a rule needed to solve problems (for example, not knowing to carry numbers in addition). Good teaching and parenting require professionals to walk in the shoes of children at all times.

Parents frequently encounter difficulty with children's lack of ability to think flexibly. For example, it is difficult to help children with their homework because children may believe there is only one correct way to do things. They may say, "Dad, that's not the way my teacher told me to do it."

Also, children tend to think in black and white. People are stupid or smart. Individuals are good or evil, guilty or innocent. School-age children do not yet understand the complexity of life. Unfortunately, they can create rules about themselves or others that are damaging: I cannot succeed in school. I am too ugly to be loved. All Moslems are warlike and dangerous. Minorities are frequently poor because they're lazy. Politicians representing certain parties are "total idiots." Too often concrete thinking leads to an *us vs. them* mentality. Of course, "we" are the good guys and "they" are the bad.

Although the child's ascent into the world of concrete operations brings many new, positive abilities, there can be negative learning that if unchanged can prove harmful to one's self and others. Parents, educators and professionals must always be aware of the potential for both good and bad that occurs because of this expanding but limited world of thought.

Formal Operations (Age 11 through Adulthood)

Although not all people enter formal operations, those who do will travel into a world of complexity, symbolism, and excitement. Young people in this world can think of almost anything. They understand the symbolism in stories, realize that social problems have many roots, and know that few things are as simple as they may appear. Their formal logic allows them to deal with hypothetical situations in addition to those things they can see and easily imagine.

Young people who enter formal operations imagine what the world, their parents, politics, and religion would be like if perfect. Of course, they find all of the above are far from flawless. Teenagers, therefore, may become extremely critical of their parents, teachers, and many social institutions. At times, they may exhibit a righteous indignation that is difficult for adults to tolerate. They may imagine, for example, that they will enjoy perfect marriages and careers untarnished by compromise. They are free to feel superior because they have not yet been bothered by life experiences.

Teenagers frequently argue with their parents, not so much in serious disagreement but because they enjoy practicing their newfound intellectual skills. That is why battles can be fought over seemingly trivial issues. Unfortunately, many of the young can be equally critical of themselves. They are painfully aware of physical changes and appearances that may make them stand out. As of yet, their identities are not strong and they become extremely sensitive to the same type of criticism they may freely dispense.

On the positive side, their critical thinking allows adolescents to dream and eventually make positive changes in the world. Formal logic allows young people to learn about physics, chemistry, and literature. Important advances in medicine, technology, and politics become possible because of their newfound mental strengths. Also, the ability to understand people with a variety of meaning systems frees formally operative people to respect individual differences in people and countries around the world. Adolescence for the formally operative young person is, to borrow from Dickens, "the best and worst of times." But it must be remembered that not all adults move into this world of complex thought.

MORAL DEVELOPMENT: LAWRENCE KOHLBERG

Lawrence Kohlberg (Figure 6.2) of Harvard University based his stages of moral development on Jean Piaget's theory of cognitive development. Kohlberg believed cognitive development precedes moral development. However, attaining higher stages of cognitive development alone does not insure that the higher stages of moral development will be achieved.

In fact, Kohlberg's later research suggested that very few individuals reach the sixth or seventh stages. In addition, peoples' ability to think in sophisticated moral terms does not insure that their behaviors will be consistent with their moral thoughts.

Sometimes people do things they know they should not. A simple example should prove this point. How many people who drive frequently will on occasion drift through a stop sign or turn right on red without coming to a full stop? However, these same individuals would stop if a police officer were at the scene. Perfectly moral people will, on occasions, break well-known laws.

Adolescents or adults who have not yet established sound identities or who suffer from low self-esteem may frequently behave in ways that appear to be inconsistent with their capacity to think morally. Lawrence Kohlberg's work tests people's ability to think morally in abstract situations, not their courage to live up to their moral potential. Nevertheless, studies suggest that individuals reaching higher moral stages are more likely to act morally in difficult situations. After all, one cannot do what one cannot think.

Kohlberg outlined three levels of moral thinking. Each level has two stages. Although Kohlberg hypothesized that a seventh stage exists, it was not well articulated before his death.

The Preconventional Level

In the first two stages morality is external, not internal. Right and wrong is judged by the consequences of one's behavior rather than by one's adherence to an internal code of ethics.

Stage 1: Punishment and Obedience Orientation. In the first stage, individuals believe that any action that is punished is bad. Therefore, what is good is to do what one is told and to avoid punishment. Fear of punishment becomes a primary reason for choosing behaviors.

Figure 6.2.   Lawrence Kohlberg. Courtesy of Harvard University.

Therefore, individuals might not drive after overdrinking, not because of the danger driving presents to themselves or others, but because of fear of being caught by the police. People acting in stage 1 might be the least likely to resist the orders of those who have power over them, no matter how harmful the superiors' instructions might be to others.

Stage 2: Naive Instrumental Hedonism. Good now is symbolized by "what's in it for me?" Rewards are expected for positive behavior and individuals will try to avoid negative consequences. In this stage, people are more likely to be sneaky. They may justify cheating on a test because the assignment was unreasonable or because "everyone else is cheating." People who overdrink at a party will select back routes to avoid detection by the police. They do not seriously consider the potential harm their driving presents to others.

Simple reciprocity also begins in stage 2, represented by the saying "scratch my back and I will scratch yours." Special deals are struck so that everyone can benefit. At its best, this may allow individuals who anticipate drinking too much to pay for the nonalcoholic drinks of a designated driver. The purpose in doing so is not so much to make the highways safe for others as it is to avoid detection and punishment. Reciprocity might also lead students to conform to rules in a classroom with the hope that teachers will reward their behaviors with higher grades or additional privileges. However, if students in stage 2 feel pressured to pass tests or papers, they are likely candidates for bending the rules or cheating.

The Conventional Level

To enter conventional morality requires significant growth in moral thought. People must develop a code of ethics that incorporates others' needs and feelings. A significant movement away from self-centeredness occurs.

Stage 3: Good Boys and Girls. Relationships become the primary consideration in stage 3. People want to be considered good friends, sons or daughters, students, workers, parents, spouses, or citizens. Therefore, they consider the feelings and needs of others. At times, they may forego doing what they wish because their behavior would be detrimental to or even disapproved of by others.

Of course, frequently moral decisions become complicated because there are so many important relationships. For instance, if peers encourage a behavior that would be objectionable to one's parents, an individual may feel torn. For example, friends might challenge a person to drive after overdrinking. Their demand will place in conflict a friend who wants to please his parents, uphold his civic duty, yet enjoy the approval of friends.

People who truly care about others inevitably encounter a string of difficult moral decisions. For example, a mother may worry over the consequences her return to college might have for her children. Or, an unhappy college student might be concerned about his parents' reactions if he were to drop out of school. Such dilemmas pose complex difficulties and can be frustrating because no simple answer or formula for finding solutions exists. As will be seen later, Carol Gilligan (1982) of Harvard suggested that this stage may indeed be higher than Kohlberg realized because his judgments were influenced by his own masculine value system.

Stage 4: Law and Order.   "What would happen if everyone in your situation broke the law because they thought they had a good reason to?" This retort to an explanation for breaking society's laws demonstrates the basic thrust of law and order thought. Indeed, the question is a sound one. The world would be chaotic if everyone simply broke laws because they did not seem to apply to their situation.

Law and order thinking suggests that for peace to occur in this world people must follow principles and laws created by society. Even when one does not want to follow the law, it is one's duty to do so. The law outweighs one's emotional desire to break the law for personal or interpersonal gains.

Stage 4 thinkers believe that adherence to laws will be crucial if there is any hope of achieving world order. For peace and cooperation to occur, people need to trust others to follow the wisdom that guides legislative bodies. The stage 4 insistence on following the letter of the law can lead to unreasonable hardships, however. Because a country's law might dictate that a person's hand be severed if caught stealing, for example, should the mother of starving children be maimed for taking bread?

Postconventional Morality

Few people enter Postconventional morality. Some research suggests that the fifth stage is reached by less than 15% of people and then only after the age of 25. So few people reach stage 6 that it was eventually described by Kohlberg as a "potential" stage. Even those who might be able to think in stage 6 will have difficulty consistently coordinating their actions with their beliefs.

Stage 5: Social Contract.   In the fifth stage individuals realize that "laws were made for man and not man for the laws." Laws are meant to protect individual rights and not to violate them. In other words, specific situations might arise that do not fit the law's intentions. In these cases the laws need to be changed or reinterpreted.

These individuals, however, do not feel free to randomly break laws that seem inappropriate. Although no longer dominated by stage 4 thought, they respect law and order and the necessity of working within the system whenever possible. Therefore, individuals look at every available alternative to help those who might be victimized by the very laws meant to protect them.

Far from an easy stage, the stage 5 thinker frequently agonizes over complex moral dilemmas and works diligently to make society a more just place. Every available option, for example, would be used to help a woman who steals bread to feed her children: What kind of society could allow a mother to be in this position? What can we do to preserve her family and yet let her know that stealing is not the best solution to complex problems? Moving to higher stages may complicate rather than simplify one's life.

Stage 6: Universal Ethical.   In the sixth stage, morality is guided by a set of deeply individual principles. Guiding moral principles rest on the belief that every individual has the right to life, liberty, and justice. Rather than laws, per se, morality is founded upon a set of self-chosen beliefs based on universal principles. The value of a single life becomes more important than the opinion of a majority.

Stage 7.   The final stage is a religious stage that is mystical in nature and cannot be reached until the final years of life. At that time, individuals might see themselves as a small element in the universe. A unity with the universe or God is felt, a big contrast to a child's feeling that he is the center of the universe.

Kohlberg outlined a sequence of stages that is seen repeatedly in developmental theory. There is a movement away from preconventional self-concern to a concentration on one's relationship with others and society (in the conventional period), to a set of self-chosen principles that extend beyond the norms of friendships and society. In a sense there is a movement from inner self-centeredness to an outer recognition of others to an inner choosing of universal principles that govern life.

Ages and Stages

Kohlberg's later research led him to reevaluate the relative ages that people move from one stage to another. Individuals move more slowly than Kohlberg first theorized. Preoperational children remain in stage 1. Kohlberg maintained that 10 year olds were usually in stage 2 or in a transition to stage 2, still making decisions on the basis of their own desires and needs.

By age 13 or 14 when many teens reach Formal Operations, they begin a transition to stage 3, where most stay through early adulthood. During this period, individuals concentrate on doing what they "should do" and being accepted by society. Men in particular seem to move to Stage Four as they begin to emphasize law and order. By the 30s, around 15% of adults move to stage five. Stage 6 was reached by very few people; some examples might be Martin Luther King, Jr. or Ghandi.

Carol Gilligan's Response: The Ethic of Caring

Gilligan, a Harvard professor and former student of Lawrence Kohlberg's, supported Kohlberg's basic ideas, but challenged some of the assumptions that underlie his stages. Kohlberg's initial research, which included only male subjects, tended to support his notion that men more frequently reached stage 4, Law and Order, while women remained in stage 3, Good Boys and Girls. Not only did Kohlberg's research display an element of male bias, contended Gilligan, but the ordering of his stages also reflected a male perspective.

Men and women, generally speaking, live in different worlds of moral thought. Men, as was seen in Chapter 3, tend to stress autonomy over relationships. Men seek to protect the rights of others by focusing on rules rather than feelings and relationships.

Women, on the other hand, emphasize the importance of relationships. They make decisions that avoid hurting others. The emerging differences between men and women can be observed in children's play. Boys prefer competitive games with winners and losers. If a dispute occurs, boys use rules to settle the problem, then continue to play.

On the other hand, girls prefer games that are less competitive and require more cooperation. If a dispute erupts, girls might stop playing the game rather than argue. Or, girls will make accommodations, exceptions, and innovations to allow the game to continue without hurting others. Girls tend to be sensitive to people's feelings and prefer to avoid harming friends.

Those who follow Little League sports may have witnessed situations that support Gilligan's contentions. I once observed the coach of a boy's team yelling at a player who was not playing well. The other boys immediately joined in, "Yeah, Tommy, run harder. You're killing the team."

Days later I observed another male coach yelling in a similar way at a young girl on an all-female softball team. The girl began to cry and all of the players surrounded her to offer support. The entire team refused to look at the coach when they entered the dugout. Dumbfounded, the coach turned to the fathers watching the game and shrugged his shoulders as if to say, "What did I do?"

Girls' sensitivity to relationships can also be seen in most classrooms. A fifth-grade teacher might ask girls: "Who in this class has a crush on whom?" The girls can reply in great detail: "Well, Jane liked Tom until he began ignoring her and then she dropped him for Jerry, but Jerry was rude. Now she likes Mark." The same question addressed to most boys might elicit blank stares or a macho response: "Who cares?"

When it comes to justice, Gilligan suggested that the poignant, Biblical story of Abraham and Isaac represents a paradigm for male morality. When asked by God to sacrifice his son, Abraham built an altar and planned to fulfill God's command. A woman's sense of justice may be better represented by the story of Solomon and the baby. Two women claimed to be the mother. But when Solomon suggested that the child be cut in half, the true mother gave up the truth to save the child's life.

To test her theory, Gilligan (1982) interviewed 28 women who were deciding whether or not to have an abortion. As she reported in her book *In a Different Voice*, Gilligan discovered three levels of moral growth.

The first level is dominated by individual survival, and women's responses are basically self-centered: "I don't want to have the child. The child will ruin my life. I have other needs." In the second level, women become more aware of the needs of others and frequently become self-sacrificial: "I'm not sure I can create a decent life for a baby. The father doesn't want an abortion." Too frequently, however, women give others, particularly males, power over their decisions. In the final stage of nonviolence, women begin to respect their own ability to make judgments. Now they make decisions based on the needs of self and others. This final stage is more complex, but more realistic according to Gilligan.

The differences between males and females frequently is observed in families. For example, when a child violates a nightly curfew, Dad may be more than ready to exact the full measure of the law. However, Mom may insist on hearing why the child was late, then adjust the consequences accordingly. As a result the husband insists: "You're too easy on the children." The wife replies: "But you're too hard and you never listen to them."

Maybe Gilligan is correct in suggesting that one mode of thinking should not be thought of as superior to others. But also, it may be worth considering whether world peace is possible if our leaders exclusively use the law and order orientation that has governed international relations for thousands of years. Is it possible that we need to concentrate on how everyone can live together on this planet without bringing harm to others?

JAMES FOWLER'S STAGES OF FAITH

Basing his research on the work of Piaget and Kohlberg, James Fowler (Figure 6.3) examined the development of faith through stages. Each stage of faith describes a different cognitive and emotional way of creating meaning. Although advancement through cognitive and moral stages is a prerequisite for progression to higher stages of faith, growth in those two domains is not sufficient to insure movement to higher stages of faith. Adults can become arrested in any stage.

Fowler's stages are not linked to a single religion or system of beliefs. Secular humanists, atheists, Hindus, Moslems, and Christians follow identical progressions, for example. Transitions from one stage to another frequently follow internal and/or external conflicts. Transitions involve leaving a more comfortable way of creating meaning to seek new, more complex modalities. As in Kohlberg's stages, it is possible to see oneself in several stages at the same time.

Prestage: Primal Faith (Birth to 4)

As Erik Erikson suggested, the positive outcome of the first stage of life (Trust vs. Mistrust) is a trust that leads to hope. Central to young children is their relationship with their parents. If mutuality develops, children create a sense of trust in others and in life that becomes a firm foundation for faith. On the other hand, negative outcomes in the early years—such as the creation of too much mistrust, shame and doubt, and guilt—can lead children to become

Figure 6.3. James Fowler. Courtesy of Emory University.

isolated, distrustful, and overly self-concerned. These negative outcomes will make the development of faith more problematic.

Stage 1: Intuitive-Projective Faith/The Innocent (Early Childhood Faith, 4 to 7)

The time period for this stage parallels Piaget's Preoperational Period and Kohlberg's first stage of Punishment and Obedience. Children can now use symbols and language to understand the world. Children's imaginations override their limited logical abilities and their view of faith becomes magical.

God is thought of in mostly human terms as one who is capable of performing wonderful feats and who responds directly to children's positive and negative behavior. Modeling and proper guidance from parents is crucial to children during this impressionable period. Parents can become overbearing, thereby crushing children with fear. Or, the great stories and traditions of faith, shared by parents, can open children to a life of wonder. Preoperational children cannot yet understand complex concepts such as spirit, nor do they see that life is more than a string of unrelated events. In this stage, dominated by egocentrism, the innocent child assumes that everyone understands God exactly as he or she does.

Stage 2: Mythic-Literal Faith/The Literalist (School Years, 7 to 11)

As children enter Piaget's Concrete Operations, they become literal in their faith, fascinated by what is true and what is not. Just as school children do, literalists look to people in authority to verify their beliefs rather than examining their own experiences. Those in authority include teachers, ministers, and others who are respected by their parents. In other words, their family and people "like us" are most influential as a child tries to fit into his particular society.

Stories are usually understood literally and offer a sense of comfort for knowing who one is in the world. The symbolism flowing from, for example, the story of Adam and Eve cannot yet be understood. Because egocentrism and centering is still prominent, a tendency exists to believe that God always wants what the child wants and understands the world as the child does.

As in Kohlberg's second stage of morality, reciprocity becomes important. Children believe that God quickly rewards good behavior and punishes bad behavior. By doing extra good things, a child hopes to receive extra rewards. Attending Sunday School might, the child hopes, lead to a victory in an upcoming Little League game.

Although most people make transitions to other stages, literalists are found among many adolescents and adults.

Stage 3: Synthetic-Conventional Faith/The Loyalist (Adolescence)

With the advent of Formal Operations, literalism breaks down and contradictions in stories and teachings are clearly seen. One's allegiance to past teachers may end. Nevertheless, this is primarily a conformist stage and the approval of significant others in life is important.

Relationships are critical. Although loyalists begin to use their own judgment more, they are most influenced by the opinions and beliefs of "selected authorities." Adolescents (and many adults) also exhibit a strong allegiance to several important groups. They feel loyalty to their church, work, school, families, and peer groups, for example. Loyalists tend to think of people not by their individual characteristics, but by the groups with which they are associated. A person is a Muslim, Christian, Atheist, American, or Puerto Rican, for instance.

When demands among groups conflict, individuals may bend their religious beliefs to make concessions to the group most influential at that moment. Their inconsistency displays a lack of autonomy in their beliefs and a lack of knowing how the parts of their faith join together as a whole.

Adults can reside in the third stage indefinitely. On occasion, however, a conflict from within or without will create the conditions necessary for a transition to the next stage. As in Piaget's and Kohlberg's theories, conflict frequently leads to growth.

Stage 4: Individuative-Reflective Faith/The Searcher (Young Adult)

In this stage, young adults begin to take more responsibility for their own beliefs, lifestyles, and commitments. Theirs is more of an examined faith. The searcher is less influenced by what others say is true, particularly past authority figures. As Kohlberg discovered, college frequently provides an organized opportunity for people to examine and question their beliefs and attitudes. This systematic inner conflict usually leads to growth. In attempting to decide what they really believe, searchers examine their own experience or what is true in their personal lives. The searcher's quest is dominated by logic and reason.

Fowler suggested that conflicts at this stage frequently create personal dilemmas. For example, one feels the tension between individuality and group membership, one's unexamined feelings vs. objectivity, self-concern vs. giving to others, and commitment to the relative vs. a struggle with the possibility of an absolute (Fowler, p. 193).

In addition, searchers select groups that will allow them to live out their personal beliefs. Therefore, the searcher may become less defined by the groups and roles that were previously influential. They are now able to see individuals as unique (honorable, impulsive, hard working, perfectionistic) rather than as extensions of the groups with whom they associate.

When a personal faith is established, Joseph Campbell suggested that people become suns radiating their own light rather than moons reflecting the light of others.

Stage 5: Conjunctive Faith/The Seer (Midlife and Beyond)

In the fifth stage, one wrestles with the inner voices of the past that may have been muted in the logical quest of the previous stage. Seers bring into awareness the prejudices and myths that were a part of their heritage. By midlife, individuals take responsibility for decisions that now are irreversible. Having been visited by defeat as well as victory, life no longer seems to fit into the neat packages once imagined. As a result, what occurs is what Daniel Levinson called *detribalization* (1978, p. 242) or becoming less dependent on the rewards and values of the tribe in which one was raised. The movement allows a distancing from a narrow culture and an acceptance of others.

The seer becomes open to forces previously left outside of one's experience. Contradictions in life are accepted rather than shelved or intellectualized away. Experiences from different cultures and belief systems are no longer seen as foreign or outside of oneself. Rather than insisting that there is one single, fixed truth, a strong respect for differing cultures and traditions is felt and lived. In this stage, the person of faith may seem slightly strange or eccentric, as an increasing acceptance of differing cultures and traditions mounts and less allegiance to one's tribal heritage is demonstrated.

As Erik Erikson and Alfred Adler suggested, at this stage a true interest grows in the welfare of others. Justice for all humankind is insisted upon as people become free of the confines of their previously held viewpoints. However, seers live with a certain agony created by the clash between their desire for an inclusive world community and their acknowledgment that it cannot come about immediately.

The strength of the stage is in the realization that any faith contains only a partial understanding of truth and meaning. Within this growth, however, lies the possibility that one will become paralyzed by an inability to possess the ultimate understanding of meaning and reality.

Stage 6: Universalizing Faith/The Saint (Exceedingly Rare)

According to Fowler, reaching this final stage is extremely rare. In this stage one's "ultimate environment is inclusive of all being" (p. 195). As in Kohlberg's sixth and seventh stages, the saints' participation in love and justice can lead them to lay down their lives for others. But one sacrifices not just for others like oneself, but any other. The absolute value of a single, human life is honored. In a sense, the saints have risen above the self-centered notions that in part govern the stages below.

The saints live in the world but are not of it. They are truly genuine and never try to sell an image of themselves. Somehow they seem more human and can relate readily to people of all stages and backgrounds. They feel part of a force that attempts to unify the world. Others may not appreciate the saints during their lifetimes because they frequently disrupt a society that fails to recognize the sanctity of all human life. Examples of universalizing faith are found in Ghandi, Martin Luther King, Jr. and Sister Theresa.

THE PERSONAL QUEST FOR FAITH

> But the highest passion in a man is faith, and here no generation begins at any other point than did the preceding generation, every generation begins all over again. . . .
>
> Søren Kierkegaard

Mythology and the history of the great religions are the stories of quests already undertaken by adventurers, who tell of the discoveries they made and of their encounters in the spiritual world. Many also report on what they have failed to discover. Atheists, for example, are deeply spiritual people who have followed the quest for truth and faith and have concluded that nothing authentic exists beyond the world that can be experienced.

Now, each of us will write our own verse and add a personal story to those the millions have told before. We, as our ancestors did, will pass on our own discoveries and beliefs to our children, to a new generation of seekers.

The Passion within the Search

Struck! Awed by a collision with the mysterious or holy, humans may experience moments when the ordinary, the common, is swallowed by infinity. Once encountered, one rarely returns unchanged to daily life. Rudolf Otto called this encounter the *numinous experience* (Otto, 1958, pp. 5–7). In these moments, we are caught up in something overwhelming, enigmatic yet for an instant partially understood; something infinite, yet for the moment seemingly held; something totally other than us, but of which we seem a part.

Some experience the numinous in nature, possibly when they behold the mysterious mountains of Tibet or the vastness of the Grand Canyon. At night when the infinity of the stars unfold or in the morning when the sun rises over the ocean, the numinous may sweep through an individual. Also, it can overtake one as the fragile perfection of a single flower is beheld or when swarming life is discovered within a single drop of pond water.

Human expressions of the numinous—through art, music, literature, dance or architecture—often transmit the experience. The numinous may strike as a Buddhist temple with its hundreds of years of history is observed, or it may come as one sits within the grandeur of a European cathedral that seems filled with an unseen presence, or when an ornate Mosque, surrounded by thousands of believers, is visited. For others, the music of Handel, the jointly uttered incantation of "aum," a landscape portrayed in Oriental art, or the writings of a Lao Tzu may usher in the numinous moment. Holy people whose lives testify to their faith in a greater reality—whether a Hindu guru, a Buddhist monk, or an evangelical minister—may become guides to the numinous. Most people at some time, in some place, and in their own unique circumstance, encounter that which is transcendent.

After one has felt this, each heroic traveler begins a quest to understand the inner spirit, to define one's place in the universe and the possible relationship a God or gods may share with humankind and this planet. In this search, one will encounter the mysteries of birth and death, good and evil, love and hatred, the eternal and the temporal. This journey will be but one leg in the continuing quest for truth made by millions of individuals who have lived before and millions who will follow. The quest for truth is the authentic last frontier into which each person can immediately travel. Once on the quest, each person's discoveries will transform his/her other voyages through life: the creating of an identity and the experiences of loving others, rearing children, and establishing a career.

TRADITIONAL QUESTS FOR FAITH:
COMMON DESTINATIONS

Even before written history, people appeared to believe in some force or forces beyond those they could see and touch. In placing food offerings and flint for hunting in the graves of the dead, Neanderthal Man apparently believed in an afterlife. Cro-Magnon Man also left behind evidence of his supernatural beliefs, as seen in the use of fertility rites, magic to bless his hunting, and defensive charms to protect him from the dead. In later times, elaborate myths and rituals enriched ancient cultures and now testify to the many religious beliefs that have come and gone. Although many of these religious systems died, their traditions and myths continue to fascinate and enlighten modern men and women.

The major religions of today are so complex that any one of them fills countless library shelves with books and documents. A few of the many beliefs of five of the world's most prominent religions are discussed below. The purpose of this discussion is not to give an exhaustive or even limited overview of each religion, nor is it to champion the truth of any single faith. To the contrary, only a few beliefs that exemplify the rich diversity of faith and expressions of that faith found in today's world will be discussed. In addition, some of the modern movements that have countered traditional religious beliefs will be described briefly.

For most people reading this book, the days are long gone when a person is born into a culture that embraces only one religion. Instead, the world today is blessed by diverse beliefs and practices that are accessible to most people. The more others' beliefs and ways of living out their beliefs are understood, the closer individuals can come to creating a peaceful world. Disciplines such as psychology can no longer afford to separate themselves from other fields of study. The more our worlds are seen as interconnected as professionals and individuals, the more movement can be made toward the possibility of creating a peaceful world.

Hinduism

No expression of faith seems more mysterious, and sometimes confusing, than Hinduism. Considered the world's oldest religion, Hinduism may date back to prehistoric times. Called by some the "Museum of Beliefs" or the "Encyclopedia of Religion," Hinduism includes a wide variety of practices and beliefs, many of which contradict one another.

Having no single founder, no unified doctrine, and no central organization to monitor and promote it, Hinduism has accepted and incorporated ancient and newer religions into its various sects. In fact, hundreds of villages in India possess scores of temples where local deities are worshiped by a variety of rituals and practices. The flexibility of Hinduism and its ability to accept the beliefs of other religions leads to religious sayings such as: "right action and right behavior are more important than right beliefs" and "all religions are one." Hinduism accounts for the faith of 79% of India's population, and in the world Hinduism claims more than 647 million adherents (Bishop & Darton, 1987, p. 214).

With such diversity of belief and practice, it is difficult to discuss a common core of beliefs without noting the obvious: not all Hindus share each belief. But in general, there are some common ways in which Hindus understand humankind and the universe. Many of these are found in the major scriptures of Hinduism that include the Vedas (written about 1,000 B.C.) and the Upanishads, commentaries on the Vedas.

Hindus believe that all things—whether humans, insects, plants, or gods—come from Brahman, the unchanging ground of all reality and existence. Ancient Hindu teachings compare Brahman to a lump of salt, which when dissolved in a cup of water cannot be seen or felt but is prevalent throughout the whole. Thus, in their belief, all life comes from and returns to Brahman.

All living beings are caught in an eternal cycle of becoming and perishing. Thus, the *atman* (the soul within the body) transmigrates from one body to the next, whether the body be that of insect, man, or god. Within the body, the spirit will suffer, decay, die, and transmigrate to another form. The new destination of the soul depends largely on the individual's behavior in the previous life. Good or bad behavior or *Karma* will be appropriately rewarded or punished either in the present or a future life. The belief in the transmigration of the soul has supported the strong caste system prevalent in Indian culture.

Most Hindus are primarily concerned with being reborn into a higher state. Thus, they concentrate on the correct behavior appropriate for their specific position and caste in life. These codes of conduct are called *Dharma*. However, a few people are capable of seeking *moska*, the release from the bondage of *Samsara*, which is the continual wheel of birth, death, and rebirth. Different schools of thought follow different paths to gain release. Most of these paths require asceticism and a release achieved through meditation.

Westerners may be familiar with The Path of Knowledge that leads to moksa. This path requires the follower to concentrate on the unity of Brahman and atman. Different forms of yoga (meaning to unite or to work seriously) are directed by spiritual teachers called gurus. The discipline requires adherence to moral virtues, meditation, body control, and the destruction of sense perception. Yogis, who can alter and even stop their heart beats, achieve difficult body positions, and maintain remarkable control over their breathing, continue to fascinate Western observers. Other features of Hinduism commonly recognized in the West are its strong caste system and its three gods: Vishnu (the preserver), Shiva (the destroyer), and Brahma (the creator).

Buddhism

Opposition to the pessimism of Hindu's endless wheel of existence, severe asceticism, and lack of individuality made the rise and popularity of Buddhism possible. Founded in the sixth century B.C. in India by Gautama Buddha, Buddhism has more than 300 million followers all over the world. Some estimate that Buddhism has as many as 400 sects, many of which vary greatly in belief and practice.

The father of Siddhartha (Buddha's original name), a local chieftain, was told at his son's birth that Siddhartha would become a powerful military monarch. However, the father was also warned that if young Siddhartha was ever exposed to old age, sickness, death, or ascetic existence, he (Siddhartha) would become an ascetic himself. Wanting his son to become a great monarch, the king sheltered Siddhartha from the world. Eventually the young man was exposed to each form of suffering, and as prophesied he chose to renounce the world and to seek a cure for suffering.

After years of searching, Siddhartha finally came to the Tree of Enlightenment, under which he meditated until he became the Buddha (enlightened one). It was there that the Buddha understood the Four Noble Truths:

1. All life is filled with suffering.
2. Suffering is caused by desire or craving, which leads to rebirth and continued suffering.
3. The cure for suffering is to extinguish all desire.
4. To extinguish desire one must follow the Eightfold Path: right views, right speech, right conduct, right effort, right mindfulness, and right contemplation.

If one follows the Eightfold Path, then nirvana can be reached. *Nirvana* (to extinguish) means the cessation of desire and the end of the painful cycle of rebirths. It is impossible to describe nirvana. It is not a place, but a paradox. It might best be pondered by answering the question: Where is the flame when it goes out?

To reach Nirvana one must seek reality and salvation and follow moral requirements that forbid killing (people or animals), stealing, gossip, lying, drinking alcohol, or sexual misconduct. Monks remain celibate and have few physical possessions.

Since Buddha's death, many branches of Buddhism have been formed. The two major ones are Mahayana (the Greater Vehicle) representing northern Buddhism and Hinayana (the Lesser Vehicle) representing southern Buddhism. The Mahayana developed a more elaborate theology that includes their own scriptures, complicated metaphysics, and rituals. In their faith, Buddha is the savior, but many other gods exist as well. Hinayana remains closer to Buddha's original teachings. The Lesser Vehicle is usually observed by monks who consider wisdom to be the key virtue and Buddha to be a saint, not a god. In their beliefs, no metaphysics and very few rituals exist.

Judaism

Most central to Judaism is the belief that God chose Israel to be His people by entering a special covenant relationship with them. Yahweh (the Creator and only God) redeemed Israel from bondage in Egypt and then entered into a covenant with the Israelis at Sinai. The terms of the covenant are found in the Torah (the first five books of the Old Testament), which records the history of the covenant relationship, God's action through many generations of Jewish history, and the ethical behavior God expects of his people. Adherence to the Torah is a sign of the faithfulness of the Jewish people to their God. The rich traditions and history of the Jewish people play a central role in each of its three theological schools: Orthodox, Conservative, and Reform.

Unlike Hinduism's acceptance of many deities or the Buddha's lack of recognition of any god, Jewish monotheism led to a passionate belief in one God, Yahweh. Unlike the two Eastern religions that emphasize otherworldly pursuits, Judaism proclaims a God who acts in the history and lives of his people. In Jewish faith there is less emphasis on metaphysics and doctrines that concern the afterlife than on the daily response of the Jewish people to the special covenant made between God and his chosen people. More than 18 million people celebrate the Jewish faith.

Christianity

Christianity is founded upon the life of Jesus Christ and composes the world's largest religion, with more than 1.5 billion believers. A Jewish man born around the year 7 B.C., Jesus proclaimed that the Kingdom of God was to come in the future but was also manifesting itself in the present. Although seeing himself as the fulfillment of Jewish Old Testament prophecy, Jesus rejected the Jewish expectation of a nationalistic Messiah. Instead, he came to earth as the Son of God, the Messiah who could forgive sins and would serve as the final judge at the end of time. Jesus brought forth a New Covenant that stressed that those who believed in him (and through him the Father) would be saved from death.

The Gospels record the Good News that Jesus, who was fully human and fully God, died on the cross to atone for the sins of his people. After his death and burial, Jesus was resurrected and appeared to many of his followers. Following his earthly appearances, Jesus returned to the Father. Now, the Holy Spirit (the third part of the Trinity that declares there is one God in three persons: the Father, Son, and Holy Ghost) actively works in the lives of his followers. Faith in Jesus Christ assures Christians that their sins are forgiven and promises them life ever after in heaven.

Distinctive in Christianity is the requirement that believers be transformed and follow a stringent ethical message, one that emphasizes loving one's enemies, doing good to those who cause one harm, and treating one's neighbor as one wishes to be treated. Christian ethics require followers to exhibit compassion for the weak, sick, and disenfranchised. Good works on earth are expected by disciples, who out of love for God wish to do his will. Yet all will fall short of perfection and must find forgiveness and eternal salvation through their faith in Jesus the Christ.

Islam

Islam means surrender, or submission to the will of the one God, Allah. Islam's basic creed is: "There is no God but Allah, and Muhammad is the Prophet of Allah." In the year 610 A.D., the angel Gabriel delivered the first of many revelations from Allah to the prophet Muhammad. Eventually the revelations were collected in the sacred scriptures of the Koran, considered to be the literal word of God. The Koran specifically describes the beliefs and moral requirements required of the faithful.

The five pillars of Islam call for a radical obedience to Allah, a faithfulness that permeates each day of a Moslem's life. The pillars include a belief in the basic creed (There is no God but Allah and Muhammad is his prophet); prayer including ritual prayers made five times each day; the hajj or pilgrimage to Mecca, which is expected of all believers; fasting during the daylight hours in the month of Ramadan; and the *zakah*, the tax used to take care of the poor and disadvantaged. Although early groups considered the *jihad* (holy war) to be a sixth pillar, it was never accepted as such by the Islamic community.

Allah calls all people to worship him. On the Last Day the dead will be resurrected and will either go to heaven or be punished in hell. Because humans are prideful and disobedient, Allah has sent many prophets as messengers, the greatest of whom is Muhammad. Nevertheless, Satan still sidetracks many people who would otherwise be saved.

A distinct feature of Islam is its belief in the brotherhood of the faithful who are required to establish social and economic justice on earth. In the early history of Islam, this was often accomplished by the jihad or holy war. The jihad's purpose was not to force conversion, but to gain political control over societies in order to direct them within the principles of Islam. Islam is the world's second-largest religion with more than 840 million believers.

Modern Doubters and Questioners

In modern times, considerable organized opposition has been made to religion. Atheistic communism once represented the official faith of half of the world, and even following the major changes in the communist world begun in the early 1990s, atheism still represents the faith of a large portion of the world's population.

More influential in the Western world are the many varieties of humanism. Although there are tremendous variations in the beliefs of humanists, they basically are unified in their faith in the supremacy of science in determining what is true and real in the world. As a consequence, they find little support for the beliefs of traditional religions in heaven, hell, or in a creator God. Likewise, humanists generally deny the authoritative basis of any of the great religions' scriptures.

Humanists concentrate on the human condition and human behavior. According to humanists, the problems encountered by people on this planet will not be eliminated by divine intervention. Humankind is responsible for using reason, technology, and compassion to help solve the problems faced in this world. Because they feel a belief in God is superstitious, many humanists believe that religions retard or militate against progress in the world. Other humanists called agnostics (meaning "not sure of") do not deny God's existence but believe that such a reality is unlikely.

Existentialism represents a specific type of humanism. Søren Kierkegaard (1962, 1968; Figure 6.4), sometimes considered the father of existentialism, opposed the idea that God could be understood by reason or that God could be reached by elaborate rituals or cumbersome theologies. Kierkegaard maintained that any attempt to reach God by living a perfect ethical or obedient Christian

Figure 6.4. Søren Kierkegaard. Courtesy of the Royal Danish Ministry.

existence would end in despair, because reason and ethical obedience will always fall short of proving God's existence. At the point of despair, a leap of faith must be taken which places a person in relationship with God. Only through one's relationship, where one stands in fear and trembling before God, does the believer truly understand the nature and calling of God.

Jean-Paul Sartre agreed with Kierkegaard's belief that reason could not prove God's existence. Sartre (Kaufman, 1970, p. 294), however, maintained that a leap of faith would be little more than an act of cowardice. He believed, instead, that humans must live with the anguish of wanting God and eternal life to exist, but of knowing the truth that God does not exist and life is finite. Once free of the fiction of God's existence, individuals no longer must live by prescribed roles and moral standards. Instead, people become free to live authentically and make personal decisions about moral issues.

Another modern belief that challenges traditional religions is held by those whom Ninnan Smart (1984) called modern agnostics in his book *The Religious Experience of Mankind*. Smart described them as those who believe in God but do not belong to any religious organization and who believe that formal worship is unimportant. They follow ethics such as the Golden Rule, but reject the rituals of the church. Although they do not pray regularly, they may pray when experiencing stress. Disturbed by the conflicts between creeds and denominations, they separate themselves from the church and are skeptical of dogma. They believe that God created the world, but that the Creator is not closely involved in the daily activities of humankind.

Modern agnostics oppose the formality of religion and the guilt that orthodoxy thrusts upon its believers. Nevertheless, they deeply admire spiritual and moral individuals. Although they hope for an afterlife, modern agnostics do not believe in the division between heaven and hell. In addition, noted Smart, modern agnostics believe in science and have doubts about the divinity of Jesus. Therefore, they dangle somewhere between atheism, agnosticism, and traditional religious belief (Smart, 1984, pp. 515–516).

THE DRAGONS

The Rush and Religion

It is so simple to ignore religion these days. Rushing back and forth from task to task, from obligation to obligation, from recreational event to recreational event, from social commitment to social commitment, and from problem to problem, the soul is easily smothered by daily routines. Aware that eternal questions exist, most Westerners intend to examine them seriously, at least someday. But they are so caught up in their own motion that no time remains to wonder, ponder, or participate in any reality beyond the self. Potential rhythm with the universe is lost amidst the sporadic cadence drummed out by daily necessity. Quite naturally, serious religious commitment often seems to interfere with the pursuit of personal ambitions and the fulfillment of the secular world's overwhelming requirements. What is more, the self that in The Rush increasingly becomes the center of all existence cannot risk encountering, much less admitting, its own weakness or finitude. Possibly Allan Bloom (1987) had this in mind when he wrote:

> . . . the dreariness of the family's spiritual landscape passes belief. . . . (Parents) have nothing to give their children in the way of a vision of the world, of high moral actions or profound sense of connection with others. The family requires the most delicate mixture of nature and convention, of human and divine, to subsist and perform its function. (p. 57)

Eastern religions that require adherents to take time to meditate and center themselves are intriguing to those living in the Western world. How foreign yet appealing it is to observe a Buddhist monk meditating for hours on a single flower. To many in the West, religion constitutes yet another time-consuming commitment and potentially uncertain relationship. Westerners frequently wonder how people can keep up when they spend hours in meditation or prayer. Religion and The Rush often seem to be heading in opposite directions.

When adults create little time to search for truth, their children will certainly follow their example. Young people already have too little time to discover themselves and even less time to examine eternal questions seriously. Even in sports, which used to be played for fun, the same message of The Rush is heard. When speaking to basketball stars who were participating in the McDonalds' All-American game in 1990, sports commentator Dick Vitale warned players: "Don't forget your work ethic. While you were sitting here being honored, there were hundreds of kids out on the playground." Of course, he is correct. To stay ahead one must rush ahead.

Children need more from their parents and elders than to inherit the wisdom of The Rush. They need to know that the thrill of advancement in professions, or victory on the athletic fields, fade swiftly and pale dramatically before the excitement of confronting the ultimate questions about the meaning of life in this universe. Children need parents who search for the truth, discuss their search openly, and encourage their children to invest in a similar quest.

The Crompton family proves to be a case example of a family devoid of religious passion. Living a day-to-day existence, the Crompton adults never took time to ask about the meaning of life. For Charles Crompton, life's highest moments come on the golf course. For Emily Crompton, life's goal seems to be in keeping her family from falling apart. As a result, the Crompton children are raised in a passion-free atmosphere that at times seems pointless.

If the Cromptons begin to ask serious questions about the meaning of their lives, they will embark on the great quest of faith. Even if they decide that the world's great religions are meaningless, their quest itself will transform their lives and the lives of their children. As Kierkegaard suggested, they may not become knights of infinity, but at least they will not languish without passion against the wall:

> Most people live dejectedly in worldly sorrow and joy; they are the ones who sit along the wall and do not join in the dance. The knights of infinity are dancers and possess elevation. They make the movements upward, and fall down again. (Kierkegaard, 1968)

Without intending to do so, many busy adults will be fortunate enough to rush to the edge of the abyss. There they will stop abruptly, awed or frightened by what they see. Once they look over the edge, life will never be the same for them or for their children. They will understand their finitude, their years that account for less than a second in the endless plane of time. Questions about life's meaning will pour forth, either in their waking or sleeping states: Do I have a spirit that will persist or will I perish when my heart stops beating? Is there a greater being? If so, how do I achieve harmony with this being? What is demanded of me? What can I give? Only when one asks these questions of ultimate importance does the quest for faith begin. And that quest will carry the power to transform families.

A temptation exists to sit on the dock and watch others embark on and return from the great voyages of life. This kind of temptation has always existed in many fields. For example, some find enough satisfaction in simply hearing about others' challenges with marriage and raising children. The quest for faith and truth offers each of us the same option: Will I be an observer or will I be a participant?

In some ways, it's easier to survey the doctrines, rituals and ethics of the major religions and humanistic movements than it is to bet one's life upon the truth of a single one. To be a judge rather than a participant offers safety, if not a trace of fictive superiority.

But nothing substitutes for the personal voyage. To feel the salt breezes blowing, to do battle with the dragons, to validate one's beliefs and to follow a personal quest no matter where the journey ends is to be a hero in the search for truth.

CONCLUSION

A narrow ledge separates our short lives from the infinite. Both Søren Kierkegaard and Jean Paul Sartre stood upon that strip and wondered if life extends into the infinity beyond or if life instantaneously ends when the body dies. Knowing that reason could never lead to a belief in God, Kierkegaard took a leap of faith over the abyss and into Christianity. To the contrary, Sartre refused to leap; he backed away, deciding to live in a world he believed could rely on no divine being, order, or justice.

At some point most reflective people stand upon that same ledge and look with awe and alarm into the abyss. These are among life's greatest moments, when one confronts the meaning of existence and asks questions about the nature of human life and the universe. At some juncture in life, each traveler clearly sees the frailty of his or her body and hears the rush of the years passing. In these moments, the body seems perishable, yet the spirit appears to be indestructible. But is it? Or, is the soul simply awaiting the same death that will come to the body that encompasses it?

Like Kierkegaard, millions who have stood upon the ledge and peered into infinity have leaped into one of the world's major religions. There they live by faith, unable to *prove* the truth of their convictions. Likewise, millions have stepped away from the ledge, choosing to create meaning in a world without the comfort of God, Nirvana, or the reincarnation of the soul. They too cannot prove to others the truth of their beliefs. This ledge on which millions have stood is always, and will always be, crowded with new individuals who seek eternal truth.

Chapter 7

WORK AND CAREERS:
THE PERILOUS VOYAGE

For such men as Jung, Adler, Sullivan, Rogers, Goldstein, Maslow
and Gardner the supreme goal of man is to fulfill himself as a creative, unique individual according to his own innate potentialities
and within the limits of reality. When he is deflected from this goal,
he becomes, as Jung says, a "crippled animal."

Frederick Herzberg (1966, p. 56)

*Ponderings. Why do people work? Describe people who love their work.
How can the meaning of work vary depending upon a person's job or career?
How have men's and women's work patterns differed traditionally? Do workers
in their 20s usually stay with one job or do they experiment with a variety of
possibilities? What special challenges do dual-career couples face because of
the present structure of society? What difficulties do the poor encounter in
finding employment? What happens to families when one parent becomes overly
involved in a career? What challenges do couples face who hope to nurture
careers, a marriage, and children? What crucial topics do couples need to
discuss to prevent their dreams from clashing or ending prematurely? What
policy changes are needed to help everyone in America enjoy an equal opportunity to engage in meaningful work?*

Through work, as Frederick Herzberg suggests, individuals can find opportunities for the ultimate expression of their unique abilities. Work carries the
power to add meaning and to provide the basic necessities that can significantly
increase the quality of individual and family life. However, as with anything

157

powerful enough to fulfill life, complications surrounding work also can frustrate, dehumanize, and even destroy the lives of adults and their families.

This chapter examines the positive and negative potential of work in the lives of Americans. Particular emphasis will be placed on how couples can integrate work into their lives in ways that allow individuals and families to grow. Special consideration will also be given to the challenges faced by dual-career couples, the poor, and those who become overly committed to their careers. The world of work provides one of the greatest adventures in human development. The rewards are as vast as the challenges are difficult.

WORKING TODAY:
MEANING, PATTERNS, AND CHALLENGES

The Meaning of Work

One of the blessings of work is that it provides an opportunity for individuals to develop their native abilities and to express themselves. Recently, management abroad (notably in Japan) and in the United States has rejuvenated employees' commitment to work by involving them in business decisions and by increasing their feelings of control and autonomy on the job. By helping develop their workers' abilities, economic institutions meet the expectations of the economist Frederick Herzberg who wrote in 1966 that "the primary functions of any organization, whether religious, political or industrial, should be to implement the needs of man to enjoy a meaningful existence" (1966, p. X).

Work also allows individuals to contribute to others and to improve the lives of future generations. Erik Erikson (1964a) frequently wrote that the major task of adulthood is generativity—giving to others. There are many ways one can contribute. Some give directly to others by nurturing children, or by teaching, counseling, nursing, ministering, or providing other direct services. Many indirectly serve the community through work that contributes goods, products, or artistic accomplishments that improve the quality of life.

In addition, many workers' concern for others transforms a potentially mechanical routine into one that enriches everyone contacted. Each reader knows people who transform their jobs into true service to their communities. These people make life better for others rather than simply doing what is required. In addition, they teach each of us how much everyone profits when individuals truly love their work. For example, two people who work in Lynchburg,

Virginia, provide wonderful examples for residents. A mail carrier for many years, Marvin Clark, does not deliver the mail; he serves it. Marvin knows every person on his route. Children in the neighborhood greet him at the door with anticipation and joy.

Marvin always inquires about the health and activities of those on his route. On one occasion, Marvin noticed that an elderly woman failed to greet him at the door as was her custom. He returned to the office and called her daughter. His call may have saved the woman's life. She had fallen and broken her hip and was unable to reach a telephone or to reach anyone to ask for help.

Occasionally, Marvin is temporarily replaced by a fast-moving mail carrier who scampers through the route and returns, no doubt, to brag about the speed of his delivery. But efficiency does not always lead to generativity. Marvin Clark makes the lives of people richer because he cares about the people he serves and takes the time to improve their lives. By transforming the ordinary into the extraordinary, Marvin Clark is a heroic figure.

Many people hold doctorates in early childhood education or child development, but few understand children better than the manager of a Lynchburg convenience store. Carolyn Brimm, a grandmother of five, may be as good with children as any person anywhere. She knows when to crack down and when to let up. Several neighborhood children learned their most important lesson about private ownership from Carolyn from an incident in her store.

Wanting baseball cards and not having enough money to pay for them is a crisis in any child's life. On one occasion a couple of boys lifted the cards and Carolyn knew it, the way people who are good with children just know. With firm kindness, Carolyn confronted the children, had them replace the cards, and remained a person they greatly admired. As a result of her reasonable, caring intervention, these good-hearted children may never steal again. On another occasion, a young customer backed into Carolyn's car. In tears, the teenager needed comfort. Who was the first to console her? Carolyn Brimm. She is a master. Her love of life and her artistry with children shine through every encounter. To these children, this teenager, and to scores of customers, Carolyn Brimm is heroic. Others conduct business; Carolyn orchestrates life.

Of course, work does not bring the same rewards or satisfaction to everyone. For example, William Roth distinguishes between those who are employed at subsistence-level work—just trying to pay the week's bills—and the majority of people whose goal in working is to improve the situations of their families. Subsistence-level work often is repetitive, dull and unchallenging. One's contact with others can be superficial and infrequent and is usually without opportunities for advancement, creativity, or self-expression. (Roth, 1989) With the high demand for unskilled jobs, any expression of discontent with their work can lead to unemployment. Under such limited conditions, it is difficult for workers to either self-actualize or to feel they are significantly contributing to others. It is against great odds that the poor accept life's major challenges.

Better opportunities in the workplace allow parents to insure an education for their children, build bigger homes, own nicer cars, pay for interesting vacations, and, generally, to experience a higher standard of living. In addition, a growing number of people work primarily to express themselves, to develop their talents, and to make a direct or indirect contribution to the world. Their motivation to work comes from within and the material rewards earned are of secondary importance (Roth, 1989).

Whether the need to express one's self through work represents a natural urge as humanists suggest or is a trait learned through generations of socialization remains a seriously debated question among career specialists. But no matter what underlies people's love of work, their desire pushes them toward a human experience that, at best, adds meaning to life. In a frequently cited older study, 80% of Americans surveyed reported they would continue to work even if they were given enough money to live comfortably without laboring. It seems likely that this 1973 study by the Department of Health, Education and Welfare, if repeated today, would find similar results.

Alfred Adler (1964) maintained that a healthy person is one who contributes to others whether he or she wills it or not. Through their work, people can survive, improve their quality of life, express themselves, and self-actualize. In addition, they may give to others, prepare new generations to live well, and make this planet a better place to live.

Patterns and Trends in Careers

Trends indicate that the average American man will spend from a third to a half of his waking hours at work over a 40 year period. The average woman born in 1980 will work for an average of 29.4 years outside of the home, more than double the number of years (12.1) worked by women born in 1940 (Spenner, 1988).

Traditionally men and women's work patterns differ. Typically men are more likely to enter the workforce and stay there until retirement (66% of white men and 76% of minority men). Women's work is characterized by more interruptions, usually to accommodate their families. Only 20% to 25% of women work continuously until retirement, even during this era characterized by significant change. Single parents, the poor and those philosophically committed to careers comprise the largest groups of women working without interruption (Concoran, 1978).

Men and women who work continuously generally ascend higher on the career ladder than those who do not, with most advancements generally occurring early in the career. By the age of 40 or 45, most adults entering the workforce early and remaining there have reached or are close to reaching their highest rung on the career ladder. Research by Daniel Levinson (1978) and others provides a pattern or stages leading up to this point.

In the "establishment stage" (up to age 30), young adults strive to match their own personalities, dreams, and abilities with a job or career. Although important, rarely are early decisions permanent. In fact, the norm for workers in their 20s is to change jobs frequently as a search for the "perfect" fit begins. Searching for the best fit may account, in part, for the fact that young adults, as a whole, are more critical of their jobs and bosses than workers of other ages. Older workers, of course, generally enjoy greater job satisfaction because they have successfully passed through this stage of trial and error and receive higher wages and better benefits.

Levinson, as mentioned in a previous chapter, believed that in the 20s individuals need to create and pursue a dream. For those who are fortunate, mentors help speed their understudies along a fast career track. After initial decisions are made, adults between the ages of 28 and 33 reach a period of transition. Some time during these years they review their early decisions concerning careers, marriage, and other major commitments. While many make major changes in the structure of their lives at this juncture, others review and continue without making major alterations.

Between 33 and 40, Levinson's studies (1978) suggest that men either make it or falter in their careers. This is a period of intense commitment to the job, which frequently ends with the desire to become one's own man or to be less dependent on others. Adults who make major life changes such as divorce or career shifts during this period when intense commitment to work is the norm may require years to recover from their loss of focus.

As men approach midlife (40 to 45), they again review their commitments. Usually men have almost reached their highest stage of power and influence, or they know what that level will be. Their careers hit a plateau and few will make rapid, unexpected advancement. In their 40s, men usually adjust their career goals, particularly if it becomes evident that their early dreams will not be reached. After a period of difficult introspection, men in their 50s finally enjoy the peak years of influence and power. Satisfaction increases, as does a sense of faithfulness to employers.

Other changes also occur. During their 40s men who have worked throughout their adult lives frequently find that their careers are less central to happiness. Many become more caring and helpful to those with whom they work rather than competitive and aggressive. They may, for instance, become mentors to younger workers, better fathers, and more sensitive husbands.

As a whole, women's patterns of work are more complicated. As will be discussed below, married women with young children constitute the largest increase in the labor force. Although women as a group still have more interruptions in their working years than men, many women are committed to full-time work and take on the traditional male work pattern described above. Others begin careers before their children are born and stop after the birth of their first child. Still others do not begin careers until after their children reach school age. Unfortunately, most research on careers has focused on male work patterns. Although it is known that women who work without interruption enjoy more success than other working women, little research has been conducted on women's work patterns that are suspended because of full-time work in the home.

It is possible, however, that Levinson's stages, with its periods of stabilization and transition, are dependent more upon the years workers have been on the job than their chronological age. Therefore, a woman's journey through the world of work may be similar to a man's, only proceeding on a different time table. Until further research is reported, our knowledge of women's work patterns is disappointingly meager.

Three Challenges to Society

All activities are subordinated to economic goals, means have become ends; man is an automaton—well fed, well clad, but without any ultimate concern for that which is his peculiarly human quality and function. If man is to be able to love, he must be put in his supreme place. The economic machine must serve him, rather than he serve it. He must be enabled to share experience, to share work, rather than, at best, to share in profits. Society must be organized in such a way that man's social loving nature is not separated from his social existences, but becomes one with it.

Erich Fromm, 1956, pp. 132–133

Two Modern Sojourners.   When the traditional family unit (wage-earning father, mother working in the home) left center stage and became a minority family form, two new movements swept across a nation unprepared to accommodate them. The first, women engaged in full-time work and careers, became a bright symbol of American freedom, ingenuity, and productivity. It did not matter that most families with dual-income parents lacked the proper social supports to flourish. Still, American businesses needed women's productivity. Dual-income families were thrust into the spotlight. National leaders in government and in the private sector accepted the stress, the pain, and the frequent disintegration that these emerging dual-income families experienced as the price that must be paid for the slow pace of social evolution.

The statistics that document family changes are well known. In 1940, only 9% of mothers who had children under the age of 18 worked in the labor force. Today that figure has reached 64%. One half of mothers with newborns remain in the workforce, and 62% of mothers with children between the ages of 3 and 5 work outside of the home. In addition, one fourth of mothers who stay at home would work if they could find acceptable day care, according to a report sponsored by the Ford Foundation (1989).

Clearly, the average American home has changed, and families with a mother working outside of the home will continue to typify the majority of American families. Women enter the workforce for many reasons. Some labor in order to bring financial security to their families, as well as hope and opportunity to their children. More than 50% of working women are married to husbands who earn less than $20,000 per year. Buying a home, paying monthly bills, and preparing to finance their children's education require more than a single income for most families. In addition, many women's careers become catalysts for self-actualization and self-expression. The benefits they discover through work include not only financial support for their family's basic needs but also the satisfaction that accompanies personal expression and professional achievement.

Only 10% of American families reflect the norm found three decades ago when a man's income could support the average family. In these two-parent, one-income families it is generally the man who pursues a career and the woman who strives to experience personal fulfillment and self-actualization through nonpaid work. Contributing to society in creative ways and being ever-present for their children brings contentment and a sense of meaning to many women. As in any profession, many unpaid mothers experience frustrations and psychological challenges, not the least of which includes the self-doubt felt when outsiders insist they should develop themselves as the majority does through paid work.

For those happy within the traditional family, however, the structure offers many advantages to parents and their children. Nevertheless, women who do not work for financial rewards (although they are an important part of American life) now represent a minority of women. The new American majority features a single mother (unmarried or divorced) or dual-income parents actively involved in the labor force.

A second America proliferates as rapidly as the first, but the poverty that besets them proves to be an embarrassment to a free, democratic nation. Children, now the largest group to live in poverty, have been hustled along with their families into the wings of the American stage. Although they have found many spokespersons to champion their causes, nowhere have they discovered liberators. Possibly Neil Postman (1982) was more correct than Americans realized when he observed that, "We have reached the point of not needing children, just as we have reached the point (although we dare not admit it) of not needing the elderly" (p. 142).

"Today, children are the poorest Americans. One in five lives in a family with an income below the federal poverty level. One in four infants and toddlers under the age of three is poor. Nearly 13 million children live in poverty, more than 2 million more than a decade ago" (pp. 7–8), according to a 1991 report made by the National Commission on Children.

Many poor children live in America's fastest-growing family unit, the female-headed house. At least, 23% of American families are led by single females, and 43% of these female-headed families live in poverty compared to 7% of two-parent families (p.8), according to the Commission. This situation has led to the frequently used term, *the feminization of poverty*, that refers to the plight of poor, single mothers in America.

The Commission's report continues: "Most poor children in America are in double jeopardy. They experience the most health problems but live in the least healthful environments and have the least access to medical care. They are at the highest risk of academic failure, but often attend the worst schools. Their families experience the most stress, but have the fewest social supports" (1991, p. 11).

Thus, two Americas have emerged: One is a promising light unto the world and the other is a black hole of poverty that threatens to consume the very children who represent its future.

The Interim: While the Earth Is Still Square.   The Interim is the uncertain, painful time that connects the old and the new, a period when emerging lifestyles receive limited help and protection from the government and business. The original influx of dual-income families signaled the approach of a new day in America. (In the remainder of this chapter, the term *dual-income parents* is used in a narrow sense, meaning two parents engaged in full-time work outside of the home.)   Despite the fact that many women worked only because of financial necessity and that their labor was welcomed by business, they were originally made to feel like the untouchables of modern society. In fact, the shock of the first use of full-time day care by middle-class parents rocked psychologists and pricked the moral sensibilities of the nation, a nation largely undisturbed by the previous decades of day care use by the poor.

Prophets of doom arose on every front to forecast the demise of children and the family. But as the years passed, many leaders (Kagan, 1984) who originally feared day care's potential harm to children reversed their stances, discovering, to the contrary, that high quality day care can often be helpful to young people. Nevertheless, other psychologists (White, 1975) remain honestly skeptical and a few remain openly critical, as are many people who believe that mothers should remain at home during their children's formative years. A 1993 poll conducted by the Wirthlin Group demonstrated that 54% of married adults without children and 74% of married adults with children believe that a preschool child's mother should stay home if it is not financially necessary for her to work. As a result, two factions—both of whom support the family but who disagree on how to do so—lobby Congress and attempt to influence the business world's decisions concerning family issues such as the assurance of unpaid emergency leave, quality day care, and family health insurance.

The families who pay the greatest price for living in the Interim are dual-income families. Without the proper social and financial support to help their families succeed, many experience difficult, debilitating challenges. The extreme advocates of traditional family forms use any failures of these families as evidence of the depravity of new family structures. The vicious circle that results (dual-income families—lack of support systems; stress and occasional failure; more criticism of dual-income families; continued lack of support) lengthens the Interim and the pain for those who through necessity or desire find themselves on the front lines of change.

As a result, The Rush (the frequent enemy of self-actualization and personal expression), reaches its highest speed in dual-income families. Without the necessary support of society (and lacking an edifying tradition of harmonious communications, cooperation, and values), too many dual-income couples are so rushed and overburdened that meeting any of life's most promising opportunities becomes problematic. The result, at worst, can be a life lived frantically without adults or their children appreciating the quality of life for which they strive.

Because family stress and poverty often lead to divorce, many people suggest we live in an era of family crisis, a time when love and loyalty are no longer cherished. This misconception may serve to justify the lack of family support given by the government and the business sector, but it is false. In truth, American men and women do not love less passionately, nor do parents yearn for their children's future fulfillment less ardently than did the generations that came before. Instead, it is the United States of America that suffers from a crisis of values, a nation that now struggles to answer an age-old question: Who are my brothers and sisters?

In a perfect community, people's choices would be supported at a level that denies no one access to the celebrated quests of life. A husband or wife who found fulfillment raising children and working in the home could do so. Similarly, men and women who wished or needed to work outside of the home while raising a family could succeed without risking the stability of their marriage or children. But in the Interim, any decision too often brings The Rush and a parade of unhealthy challenges into a family's life.

For dual-income families, the dawn will one day break and the Interim will end. The United States will eventually support, to the best of its ability, the healthy choices of its people, but evolution is slow. Painful decisions must be made that balance an adult's freedom of choice with an economic system that values the bottom line. The rays of that dawn in America's discussion and debate over family issues can now be seen. For example, in 1993 The Family and Medical Leave Act finally allowed parents in workplaces with 50 or more employees to take 12 weeks of unpaid leave for the birth or adoption of a child. Yet the darkness still lingers, and families struggle and too frequently suffer because of the painfully slow pace of evolution.

The future of the poor would seem to be less optimistic for they too live in the Interim. For them, there are few signs of a new dawn. Housing becomes more scarce, public assistance buys less, and unskilled jobs are sparse, particularly for undereducated males. The poverty cycle continues to churn, while the historic wars on poverty fade from memory and the national restructuring of schools to meet the needs of the poor remains at best a distant dream. Despite momentary feelings of concern, such as the ones that followed the Rodney King verdict in Los Angeles in 1992, much of the public seems entrenched in the belief that the "poor will be with us always" and, therefore, they must survive as best they can—at a safe distance from middle-class neighborhoods.

Unfortunately for families who live in the Interim, a transformation in values and an influx of support will not come in time to help this, or possibly the next, generation. Therefore, they must accept the heroes' challenge: to meet (as individuals, couples, and families) the challenges of the workplace and to overcome its power to destroy marriages, families, and the nation. Not only must these heroes survive the Interim with little assistance, they also must help the nation to understand that a house divided cannot expect to flourish forever.

Careers Out of Balance

> The midlife man may discover his ladders against the wrong wall.
> Joseph Campbell

Most men and women wisely and painstakingly balance a career with the needs of a marriage, children and the inner self. In an earlier chapter, Alfred Adler and Rudolf Dreikurs compared a human being's psychological stability to a chair with four legs. Under the best conditions the four legs—love and marriage, work, friendship/community making, and faith—support mental health. Remove one leg and the chair will wobble. When two legs are taken away, one's psychological health balances precariously. When deprived of three legs, balance is lost as the lone remaining commitment rules life.

Those who become overly committed to their work lose their balance. They sacrifice endless years of labor in order for their lives to be filled with promotions, raises, and recognition. But, returning home they become empty, disconnected from their children, lacking a spiritual union with a spouse, and often suffering from debilitating feelings of inadequacy. Keen of sight in the world of work, their uncanny vision enables them to cut lucrative deals, to settle difficult personnel problems, and to travel nimbly through the maze of work. But at home they are blind to the worlds of their family members. Only the most severe crises can capture their attention as they stumble over delicate and neglected relationships.

Celebrated at work, many adults climb to the summit of their profession and become larger-than-life models whom young employees admire and emulate. In the home, their presence and influence become minuscule. Their spouses learn to manage without them and their children seek role models in the outside world. Soon, the powerful voice that captivates and sways colleagues becomes an inconsequential whisper to their families, the voice of a stranger who was not there to cheer on their childhood games or to ease their disappointment and pain.

To lose balance turns life into a single voyage, only one experience of being human. Individuality is stressed over community and solitary life over relationships. A myopic view of life's purpose replaces a deeper search for meaning. True, often much good is accomplished on the one voyage; others may benefit enormously from one's contributions. But the single leg of the chair, no matter how successful, rarely supports the needs of modern family members.

The Crompton family proved to be a case example. Charles Crompton abandoned his family to pursue a single voyage. In order to save the family, Emily Crompton denied her emerging growth needs that might have led her into a new career. Not being together psychologically, the Cromptons soon became a family in crisis.

However, each person's life situation is unique. If the decision to dedicate one's life to work is consciously made by an unattached person or is jointly agreed upon by couples who can make the necessary adjustments to support this decision, then the choice can be a responsible one. But when one unconsciously drifts into a single life experience or decides to venture there without the agreement of a spouse, then the determination may do violence to the rights of others who, as a result, may be prevented from meeting their own needs and are, therefore, obstructed from enjoying the opportunities life offers.

A program paper of the Ford Foundation (1989) observed that "loyalty and commitment to the company are measured by willingness to work long hours, overtime, at night, on weekends and on holidays" (p. 14). Hindsight allows us to see clearly the complications caused when past generations of fathers who headed traditional homes became out of balance. Those who committed their lives solely to work joined a lost generation of fathers. However, in that era, most wives worked in the home and many were willing and able to balance life for the family. Possibly, most did so happily. After all, it was a different period of history that should not be judged harshly by contemporary standards.

Nevertheless, in many instances wives were abandoned by their husbands to a suburb where women found little family or social support. To counter their husband's affair with their work, many women became overly involved with their children. Their lives centered on the home. For some, unhappiness and a lack of fulfillment resulted. As Betty Friedan (1963) in *The Feminine Mystique* explained:

> The problem lay buried, unspoken, for many years in the minds of American women. It was a strange stirring, a sense of dissatisfaction, a yearning that women suffered in the middle of the twentieth century in the United States. Each suburban wife struggled with it alone. As she made the bed, shopped for groceries, matched slipcover material, ate peanut butter sandwiches with her children, chauffeured Cub Scouts and Brownies, lay beside her husband at night— she was afraid to ask even of herself the silent question—"Is this all?" (p. 13)

Valium may have temporarily lifted homemakers' spirits, but it could not mask their emptiness and dissatisfaction. Children usually grew up without a real sense of who this powerful and distant father was. By tradition, they realized that he could not often be close to them either physically or emotionally. They understood, or so it seemed.

Today, both men and women struggle to remain balanced. Most women pursue work or a career in addition to being a wife and mother. Unfortunately, a few follow the example of the men of a generation past, possessed by what one observer termed "male clone careerism." As a result, at this moment in history a family may have two parents who are out of balance, each taking a single voyage in life, each largely abandoning love and marriage, children, friendship, and spirituality.

As a result, the pills are not taken by housewives, but by the children, the Samuel Cromptons of this world. Parents who lose balance may observe their children spinning like tops, bouncing from wall to wall in search of a place of significance and security in life. Too often their wild motions whirl them through drugs, school problems, delinquency, and emotional instability. They search for a group that will accept them, and they are willing to pass any test or requirement for admission.

The price paid when one concentrates predominantly on the work experience in life can only be partially understood by studying the resultant statistics. Certainly there is an astronomical divorce rate and a high percentage of children who are not able to discover positive identities. But these figures do not describe the emotions of emptiness, guilt, and failure experienced by the parents who become trapped by their decisions. What is also lost are the feelings that never had an opportunity to develop—feelings of closeness to others, being connected to past and future generations of the family, sharing a vital relationship with growing children, or experiencing a spiritual union with one's spouse.

Madcap careerism consumes rather than enriches other life experiences. Gifts of creativity, meditation, introspection, artistry, physical ability, and the spirit fail to take root. Many of the great voyages are tossed overboard. For example, Daniel Levinson (1978) in *The Seasons of a Man's Life* discusses the loss of friendship in men's lives:

> A man may have a wide social network in which he has amicable, "friendly" relationships with many men and perhaps a few women. In general, however, most men do not have an intimate male friend of the kind that they recall fondly from boyhood or youth . . . (and) most men have not had an intimate non-sexual friendship with a woman. We need to understand why friendship is so rare, and what consequences this deprivation has for adult life. (p. 335)

Also routinely dropped is the quest for faith and truth. It is extraordinary that almost none of the best-selling self-help books discusses the most ancient quest: the spiritual voyage that seeks ultimate truth and meaning. Instead, these books continue to fragment humans by discussing how to successfully take a single voyage toward love, parenting, or improved career making. Possibly the writers fear the warnings of the great teacher, for few understand better the Buddha's teaching that "All existence is suffering" than those whose blind servitude to work led to their family's dismemberment. And none knows more poignantly the following painful lesson taught by Jesus than those who have spent their life force on careers: "What profit a man to gain the entire world and to lose his soul" (Luke 9:25). Maybe religion and other quests for truth are carefully avoided because authors fear being identified as extremists. Or, maybe the spiritual quest is ignored because it creates uncomfortable inner conflict; ironically, this is the type of crisis that leads to transformation and balance.

Must life continue this way? Contemporary heroes are beginning to say *No!* No longer must individuality outweigh togetherness; balance can be achieved. Not only do more adults want to experience each of life's journeys, but also they want their children to live balanced lives with all four legs of the chair in full support of their psychological and spiritual weight.

Healthy signs are emerging that heroes are taking charge of their lives. More are disputing the truth of what writer Brian O'Reilly (1990a) called the 11th Commandment: Thou shalt work without limitation. As a result, adults are beginning to make judgments about what they value and what price they are willing to pay to support their beliefs. In an article entitled "Why Grade 'A' Executives Get an 'F' As Parents," O'Reilly (1990a) noted that 36% of the executives studied had children in outpatient treatment for psychiatric or drug-related problems. In a later article, O'Reilly (1990b) observed:

> Hard work is not inherently good or moral, but only as noble as what you're striving to achieve. Working so hard that you're a dismal parent is wrong; working hard so you can be filthy rich is merely greedy. Working overtime because your boss is too dim to let you do meaningful, efficient work is foolish. . . . (p. 46)

New sojourners are realizing what many discovered in ages past: True treasures are not the riches found on a quest far from home but the wealth discovered within oneself and within those whom one cherishes.

Other positive signs indicate that new generations seek balance. Although 30% to 40% of employed men and women experience conflict and guilt about their dual roles (work and parenting), 25% declined jobs, promotions, or transfers in order to spend more time with their families, according to a Ford Foundation report entitled *Work and Family Responsibilities* (1989). Clearly, difficult decisions and sacrifices are being made by individuals as they seek the enrichment of their families. The British author, R. E. Pahl, noted that decisions to pursue balanced lives are being made by males and females of all ages—people who want to work rather than to be worked. Pahl (1988) observed:

> The manager who prefers to stay amongst friends rather than accept promotion elsewhere, the teenager who rejects a boring and monotonous job, the self-employed carpenter who turns down work because he wants to go fishing, the professor who rejects the offer of being chairman of his professional association because it would take time away from his gardening (or even his research), will all discuss their decisions with their friends and will receive at least as much sympathy and support as criticism. Increasingly, people are facing personal decisions about degrees of involvement in employment or self-employment. (pp. 2–3)

CAREERS AND FAMILY

The Importance of Communications

As discussed in the earlier chapter on marriage, the key to most choices of marital partners is timing. In other words, people tend to marry the person they happen to be dating when they decide it is time to marry. Usually, that person is physically attractive to them and generally shares their political and socio-economic background. Beyond these qualities, everything remains mysterious.

As observed earlier, on courtship's moonlit nights couples ask the wrong questions if in their passion they make any inquiries at all. Young love assumes that everything will eventually work out well for those who are filled with emotion. However, the sweeping passions that carried a couple through court-ship seem irrelevant 5 years later when their sick baby awakens them at 3 a.m., a few hours before both partners have important business meetings scheduled. In the middle of the night, questions long ignored quickly spring forth. For unprepared, sometimes unsuspecting couples, answers to these questions can crack the weak foundations cast on those tender, moonlit nights.

These are perilous times for couples. The problems they face in the In-terim, while the nation is not yet family-friendly, are powerful and unrelenting. To flourish as a family, each couple must come to an accord on which voyages he or she values in life and how they will specifically help each other reach these goals. To begin this process early in a relationship is best.

It is amazing to see how ready college students are to succeed as in-dividuals in the world of work, but how poorly prepared they are—men in particular—to marry, nurture children, and succeed in a modern family. Fortu-nately, many women now realize that without agreements made in advance, the probability is high that when a crisis of values occurs, a sacrifice of dreams will be made by the one most sensitive to relationships. Because that per-son more often than not is the wife and mother, women are beginning to com-municate more openly and effectively before committing themselves to mar-riage.

One of the major obstacles to communications for college students is that everyone has learned to speak the language of mutuality. When asked value-loaded questions, replies come as if by reflex: "Sure, my future wife and I will pursue careers." "Yes, I want children." "We'll share parenting responsibili-ties." "Of course, we'll divide housework equally or hire a domestic to do the work." "I don't know where we'd move if we're both offered jobs in different cities. We'll decide as a couple when the time comes." "Religion? It doesn't really matter." What flows easily from the mouth in times of light discussion does not always pass the test when crises arise. In reality, most couples talk about honest communications but few share them until a conflict besieges the relationship. Without the practice needed to make tough decisions, few couples in crisis communicate well.

Ideally, before marriage is the time couples should begin to ask and answer those questions that will prepare them to succeed as individuals and eventually as a family. For couples who are already married, undertaking the process now may still prevent unforeseen shipwrecks.

Are We Kindred Spirits?

Psychologists share many tools to help couples understand their marital problems and to predict challenges that might be faced in the future. One such exercise, based on the Individual Psychology Priorities Chart, lists four characteristics that usually motivate people's behavior. They are the need to be in control, the need to please others, the need to be comfortable or relaxed, and the need to outdistance others. The motivational theory maintains that most people organize their lives around one of these four motivators.

For example, a person who needs to be in control will take charge of most situations, often challenging others in the process. Usually, they have an answer for every question and a solution for each problem. Their need to be in control causes them to be outraged by the mere hint of humiliation. Those motivated by the need to please will rarely confront others or even state their beliefs and preferences. They are enjoyable companions for they wish to have the approval of everyone. Often, however, pleasers fail to take the risks that lead to self-growth. Those most interested in comfort will be laid-back and easygoing, the perfect party animals. But frequently their work piles up and their lack of ambition begins to irritate their companions or co-workers. If outdistancing others is one's major motivation, then both work and play become highly competitive. Often their accomplishments astound people who focus on different priorities. Usually, outdistancers find it difficult to relax and let go of their competitive spirit or their need to achieve. Also, they can be anxiously silent when asked questions about life's purpose and meaning.

By giving thought to the priority of each partner's need to control life, please others, be comfortable, or outdistance friends and competitors, couples can predict potential areas of conflict. For example, two people who share a high need to control life events and situations will experience many more conflicts than a couple with one partner whose need to control is balanced by another's whose need is to please. On the other hand, a couple who shares a high need to please may struggle to make the easiest decisions. And anyone married to an outdistancer must be prepared to spend many hours alone and to feel unproductive in comparison. Each combination of priorities gives a couple strengths to enjoy and challenges to overcome.

Adults change. Couples need to be aware that individuals change through-out life, usually stressing parts of themselves previously denied. Change in one spouse may throw a marriage temporarily out of balance. However, marriage becomes stronger and more vivacious when a spouse encourages rather than resists a partner's urge to grow.

In fact, failure to grow in adulthood can create marital problems. Psychologists believe that the attribute that first attracts one person to another is frequently the quality that later begins to separate them. For example, a person may have been first drawn to a controller because the individual seemed to know the correct way to handle any situation and the best answer to most questions or problems faced. But eventually the controller's same behaviors may begin to seem pushy, insensitive, and suffocating. Particularly this is true when the partner of the controller is inwardly pushed to become more assertive in life. Similarly a person attracted to a pleaser—who in courtship always listened well, was quiet and totally agreeable—soon may complain that the once-pleasing spouse is now unchallenging and unable to think of original ideas. Those easygoing individuals interested in comfort may eventually be seen as lazy underachievers. And outdistancers who are always accomplishing great things may never spend enough time with the family. Adults change. What once seemed attractive can later repel. Couples need to work together to insure that changes enrich rather than endanger marriages.

Me, Thee, or We?

Many couples' most important decision is: Who will make the family's decisions? In the past, many women modified and eventually surrendered their hopes and dreams in order to maintain family harmony. By generally accepting their husbands' wishes, women neglected to use their own voices. Today's families will be better served by realizing Martin Buber's (1970) dream that families (and all people) engage in relationships that equally honor the needs, desires, and goals of each person. Buber called interactions that reflect mutual recognition and respect an "I-Thou" relationship. This bond replaces the "I-It" relationship characterized by one person's will dominating over another's. For example, when a man or woman assumes that the spouse must always concede when conflict arises, then the partner is being treated as an object (an It) rather than a person (a Thou) who has opinions, needs, and aspirations. Similarly, when parents consistently ignore or fail to fill the needs of their children in order to meet the demands of adult schedules and personal goals, an I-It relationship prevails.

Who makes decisions? Is it me, thee, or we? Families can survive when I-It relationships dominate, but usually someone must always give in and sacrifice personal growth. In modern families, true mutuality creates an atmosphere of respect, support, and compromise. Only when the smallest voice in a family is clearly heard can all individuals pursue their chosen adventures.

Deadly Expectations: The Invisible Enemy

Long before marriage, each individual creates unwritten, unspoken, and often unrecognized expectations for who will complete tasks in the home, yard, and community. For example, each partner harbors an expectation for who will clean the bathtub, pay the bills, wash windows, mow the grass, and fix the car. In addition, each has a preference for how to celebrate and where to spend religious celebrations, Thanksgiving, and other family holidays and vacations. Literally, hundreds of invisible presumptions are capable of creating hurt feelings and controversy. Wise couples prevent controversy when they list the multitude of jobs that must be performed and responsibilities that must be accepted and then reach a satisfactory agreement about the division of labor.

Expect surprises. When asked about the division of labor in their future families, college students frequently offer socially expected responses such as, "We'll share work in and out of the house." But invisible expectations arise when specific questions are asked such as, "Who will clean the toilets, fold and put away the laundry, pay taxes, stay up with a sick child?" Frequently, for example, a man somewhat humorously replies, "I do taxes, but I don't do toilets and laundry." Beyond the levity, one sees the demand: "You do the dirty work." For each of the hundreds of tasks awaiting couples, each partner carries a preconceived notion of who will do specific jobs. When these invisible demands are not met, feelings are hurt, anger arises, and a little sand drifts away from the marital foundations. Good communications make the invisible visible.

As a part of early communications, couples need to discuss preferred family size, when to have children, and the specific changes each expects additional family members to bring. Early disagreements over job sharing, child care, discipline, and parenting issues must find resolution.

Opportunities to feel guilt and inadequacy seem to abound after the birth of a child. In addition to the work overload that accompanies an expanding family, children's needs are more constant and pervasive than couples ever anticipate. Appropriate day care for preschoolers and afternoon supervision for school-age children must be secured. Unexpected illnesses and special transportation requirements create havoc with carefully planned schedules. Additionally, school plays, athletic events, and special presentations are times when children not only welcome but also need a parent's support and encouragement. These occasions arise in addition to the informal hours needed for parents and their children to enjoy playing and talking together. To enjoy life's adventures, couples and families need to take time to meet, distribute work, and create schedules that protect them from a frenzied life. Each individual in a family needs to grow, be heard, and be supported. Invisible expectations should not be allowed to throw the voyage off course.

Selecting Compatible Dreams

In this book, a case has been made for the value of many adventures: love, the nourishing of children, the quest for faith, and self-actualization through work that contributes to the general good of others. Any one of these voyages can bring a lifetime of challenge and meaning. Each individual needs to decide which opportunities he or she values; then the choice of a marital partner whose goals and values are harmonious can lead to fulfillment.

To select life goals is not easy. Every generation faces the tyrannical shoulds imposed on them by current movements, governments, religions, educational institutions, their families and the workplace. For example, in this era women face endless and opposing advice: "You should have it all: career, marriage, children, friends, and time for self-expansion." Or, "You cannot have it all. You should reduce your career ambitions and nourish the next generation more carefully." Or, "Compromise with your spouse. Both of you should give up something so you can enjoy a little of everything."

Not surprisingly, men and women look for role models to guide them through the labyrinth of modern possibilities. But in the Interim, few models are found, particularly by women. The heroes of past generations journeyed through a different world and overcame the obstacles of their time. Modern couples are pioneers in a new world. Without admirable models to emulate, individuals are particularly vulnerable to the influence of the "shoulds" in life. But life is too brief for one to live out another person's expectations and dreams for one's life. The mature adult must know his or her own heart and then pursue personal (and mutual) dreams wisely and without undue trepidation.

On those moonlit nights to come or in one's present situation, the major questions should be asked first: Which voyages are valued most? What priority is given to careers, marriage, nourishing children, friendship, spiritual quests? The familiar counseling questions should be asked: What are one's hopes for life in 5 years, in 10, in 15? If differences arise in values and dreams, a major step has been made toward avoiding the perils that can dismember couples.

Dual-career Couples: Common Sense

In her book entitled *Dual-career Families*, Uma Sekkaran (Figure 7.1) offered a helpful exercise for couples who wish to learn whether or not their career and family ambitions will mesh. She stressed three central life-interest orientations (career/family/both) and three sex role identities (masculine/feminine/androgynous) (Sekkaran, 1986).

To begin discussion, each partner needs to identify his or her primary goal in life. Is it to: (a) enrich a career, (b) nurture a family, or (c) balance the demands of a career and family? Priorities can change as time passes; therefore, a present priority is not unalterable.

Stereotypical masculine roles include such characteristics as being analytical, competitive, individualistic, unemotional, and career oriented. A person with a stereotypically masculine role identity generally would not enjoy cooking, washing dishes, nurturing children for extended periods, or working inside the home. Stereotypical feminine characteristics include being affectionate, nurturing, tender, understanding, compromising, and sensitive. If a man or woman adopts a stereotypically feminine role, then working in the yard, fixing cars, repairing gutters, and engaging in physical labor would not be appealing. Of course, an androgynous person feels comfortable expressing emotional characteristics of either orientation. Also, he or she would feel equally at ease with most home job descriptions (Sekkaran, 1986).

A couple's compatibility and future happiness may well depend on how their life interests and sex role orientations blend. For example, when a couple shares a primary interest in career and family and an androgynous sexual role, they are often content and successful. Neither may be a career superstar because each is equally interested in spending time with the family. Because of their androgynous roles, both share in the work at home and pitch in wherever needed. On the other hand, many couples have different preferences but achieve a balance that allows each to reach personal goals. A woman or man whose major interest is in a career can be balanced by a spouse whose highest priority is the home. If both share an androgynous sex role identity, then cooperation and personal satisfaction will be enhanced.

When mismatches occur, one or both individuals may feel overworked and underappreciated. For example, if a woman with a career orientation/androgynous sex role identity marries a man with a career-orientation/masculine sex role preference, then problems are likely to occur. Predictably, the wife will feel overburdened at home and the husband may believe she is a poor

Figure 7.1.   Uma Sekkaran. Courtesy of Southern Illinois University, Carbondale.

homemaker and mother. Sometimes through discussions and compromises, couples overcome mismatches, but often the individual who compromises the most may become too hurt and angry for harmony to prevail.

Serious communication is essential, particularly when spouses enter unchartered territory. Adults' rules from the past for what "good" wives, husbands, mothers, and fathers must do are sometimes narrow and unreasonable. It is not a sin to do things differently (or similarly) than one's parents did. Sometimes it is hard to escape the mythology of one's past.

Some situations, however, should signal alarm. For example, whenever both spouses emphasize their careers first, a caution flag should wave. The question emerges: "Who will care for the children?" To solve the dilemma, many modern couples who stress careers first make a responsible decision not to bear children. This decision is now popular enough to earn the acronym *DINKS* (dual-income, no kids). Other career-first couples struggle, with varying degrees of success, to pay for outside help to balance the needs of the family.

Even when one spouse places a career first, couples need to explore the ramifications of this choice for raising children. Whenever one voyage in life becomes dominant, balance may be lost and the other voyages will receive less attention. To reestablish balance requires one's partner to be willing to provide whatever is missing in work and relationships in the home. Similarly, if a rigid sex role identity is expressed by one partner, the consequences for the other are significant. Despite the premarital exchange of rhetoric, many individuals cling to rigid sex role identities, although they may occasionally display an androgynous preference. Sekkaran's early research suggested that the flexibility provided when couples share an androgynous sex role identity will enhance the home life of couples and allow each member more freedom to alter or change career goals.

In an era when everyone talks a good game, it is essential to discover who the players really are. It is necessary, but not sufficient, for couples to decide on the adventures most important to their lives. They also need to honestly compare their ambitions and role identities. Will each help the other to reach personal goals or will the two be working against one another? Is a spouse flexible enough to allow his or her behaviors and preferences to change in response to a partner's changes and needs? Exercises such as Uma Sekkaran's can help couples make these judgments. It is preferable that these evaluations be made before marriage, but differences will continue to emerge and can prove to be healthy starting points for productive discussions.

THE TAMING OF AMERICA:
TEACHING THE STRONG TO LOVE

Women have revolutionized the workplace, and now men must join them to transform it. The victory for equal opportunity and equal pay will surely be won. Yet if the revolution fails to transform the business sector's attitude toward families, American children may become the greatest casualties of change. If the corporate world seduces both parents away from their families and into an archaic, competitive, and individualistic system that creates parental overload, anxiety, and guilt, then evolution will lead to family destruction.

Men and women must continue the push for legislative and private sector reform that will make businesses family-friendly. Morality traditionally associated with women—that which emphasizes caring, connectedness, warmth, and compassion—must not be abandoned or left in the home. Instead, these attitudes that can foster a supportive, loving community must balance the current values based on separation, detachment, and cold-blooded competition. When needed change finally comes, couples and their children will no longer be at risk. Eli Ginzberg (1989) observed:

> The development of children has been a shared responsibility between family and society for centuries, ever since publicly financed education was first established. As work and lifestyles shift, the nature of this societal responsibility must also shift. The proper care for and the development of children remains a primary responsibility of parents, but not of parents alone. Only a society that has lost its bearing would risk neglecting to contribute—and liberally—to ensuring that the ongoing generation has the benefit of a good start in life. (p. 123)

The United States government and the private sector have been slow to respond to the needs of families, slower than most other Western nations. Leaders have taken advantage of the employment of women and of outdated policies, both of which temporarily increase their profit margins. Families changed, and until now they have paid the financial and emotional costs required by an evolving society. But the burden will be too heavy for future generations to bear. If healthy families are to survive, they must receive just and generous assistance.

Many of the needs of modern families are well known and have since the mid-1990s received some national recognition: higher quality day care, part-time return to work for parents of infants, unpaid leave to respond to family emergencies, health care insurance for all families, and a cafeteria-style benefits plan. Other creative policies also can be explored. In the future, there may be opportunities for job sharing, flexible work schedules and career ladders, sabbaticals for long-time employees, a shift in the site of work to computer-equipped home offices, and shorter work weeks for many jobs.

Businesses that offer attractive possibilities for parents will attract high-quality workers. Contented and happy employees will reduce absenteeism and tardiness while producing work of a higher quality. For this world to survive and thrive, however, families and volunteers cannot be the only ones to value a national and world community. When families in the world's wealthiest nation must struggle on and even abandon one or more of life's great adventures, something is terribly wrong. A crisis of values confronts American leaders. Either they must support a national community of families as well as of individuals or risk implosion as family life withers. It is time for national policy to catch up with national rhetoric.

Single Parents

Being a single parent may be the most difficult job in this world. This chapter concentrates on the difficulties faced by dual-career couples, but not all single parents remarry or marry. Many live in a world filled with obligations, responsibilities, and duties that can overwhelm the most heroic figures.

That societies and communities need to find ways to support single parents has become obvious to most Americans. Many books are now available that address the challenges single parents face. In this brief chapter, no attempt will be made to address this crucial and complex issue. A cursory examination of problems and possible solutions would be a disservice to this growing population. Nevertheless, it should be acknowledged that many of America's truly great heroes are the ones who captain the family ship alone through life's most turbulent seas.

Helping the Poor

What most terrifies compassionate people in our nation may be the hardening of the American heart toward poverty and homelessness. The haves seem less and less willing to help the have-nots journey toward a better life. Elected representatives bemoan the country's social problems but will not risk the election day consequences of supporting substantial programs to help the poor. Have the warm hearts that once began the war on poverty been replaced by broom leadership, content to voice concern for the plight of the disadvantaged before they sweep programs, benefits, and reform under the proverbial rug?

Truly, the poor challenge the values of America as a nation. With one out of five children living in poverty, including one half of all black preschoolers, the alarm sounds. Nowhere is the crisis more striking than in poor, minority communities. When black men are faced with ever-dwindling opportunities for employment, they are less able to function as fathers, husbands, and providers. Black women now realize that the benefits of marrying struggling men are less attractive than heading a house alone. Is it consistent with the American dream that 87% of black children will be raised for much of their youth in a single parent home?

Increasingly, the poor feel less and less connected to mainline America. Clearly, their departure from a feeling of community can be seen in the statistic reported in *Time* (May, 1990) that "nearly one in four black men, ages 20 to 29 is in jail, on probation or on parole."

It is no wonder that Los Angeles in the spring of 1992 was a bomb awaiting detonation. The first Rodney King court decision signaled poor America that there is neither justice nor compassion in mainline America. Whether or not that assumption is true can be debated. But the perception, and possibly reality, that America does little to help its poor makes the inner cities of this nation always a crisis away from rebellion and anarchy. It is not enough to show empathy for the poor; substantive change in American policy is needed.

Not only are the jobs that were once available to the poor shrinking in number, but also much of the work provides neither a challenge nor a forum for self-expression. Nevertheless, a job is often all that shields the poor from the specter of desperate poverty and homelessness. In his book *Down and Out in America*, Peter Rossi (1989), described the precarious position of an employee living in poverty:

> . . . for the extremely poor, with no reserves of savings, no safety net of entitlements, and no credit cards, losing a few days wages or catching a severe cold can mean losing a job, going without adequate food, or getting evicted. (p. 9)

Rossi explained that a thin line separates the housed poor and the homeless. Often those who lose their homes are the chronically disabled who are suffering from alcoholism, drug addiction, mental illness, or a criminal record. Falling through the safety nets provided by the government and extended families (most of whom are poor), they eventually fall onto the streets of America (Rossi, p. 179).

Voices in the Wilderness

While governor of New York in 1985, Mario Cuomo warned the nation of what the future might hold if Americans did not stop preaching about the family and begin acting like one. In a speech to the Children's Defense Fund, Cuomo looked to the future:

> If we deny poverty and the children of poverty, then we understand that we will have to pay to maintain a growing number of people at subsistence levels, to spend more on jails and police, to take money we could have used for schools and day care centers to build prisons instead. We will live amidst increasing social disorientation and in fear—with bars on our windows and in suburban enclaves walled off from the cities they surround. (1987, p. 27)

Of course, the fulfillment of this prophecy is documented daily on the front page of every newspaper. In addition to the financial cost, the human cost of poverty is immense. Teenage women try to feel significant by giving birth to children, because no other avenues to fulfillment seem open. Children and teenagers become deeply involved in a drug culture that offers quick financial gains and a position of prestige in the Other America. Unable to find jobs or to properly support their children, young parents return to the home of their impoverished parents to turn the gray years of grandparenting into troubled times. Wanting the riches they cannot afford, unemployed young adults of able mind and body take from the rich and the poor and give to themselves. Response to these trends is what Cuomo feared it would be: bigger prisons, more fear, increased desperation. The failure of the war on drugs is a symbol of American policy to handle social problems with a big stick and a small heart. Clearly, the United States has not faced the internal problems that create the demand for drugs nor whittled at the growing, seemingly endless list of street soldiers willing to battle in the drug wars.

Can the United States survive as two nations—one of opportunity and the other of poverty? Would the founding fathers advise Americans today to accept attitudes and policies that largely ignore the basic problems of the poor? Certainly they would be as divided as people are today in creating a plan to address the situation. Nevertheless, they likely would meet the situation directly and work until a coherent strategy was formulated that would allow each citizen to seek life, liberty, and the pursuit of happiness.

Where would reformers begin? For pregnant teenagers, they might provide job counseling, child care, and improved transportation to help them escape from their dependency on welfare. Education for preschool children, age 2 through 5, could increase young people's later chances of competing in the academic world and eventually escaping the poverty cycle. The poor who hold jobs could be given unpaid leave to handle emergencies with the assurance that they would have jobs to come back to when their leave ended. The founding fathers would expand the job market and job training, particularly for minority men. Without the hope of jobs, crime and escalating welfare costs will continue to skyrocket. Also, increasing the feasibility of building housing for the poor by making it profitable for builders to enter the market would insure adequate housing for the poor (Rossi, 1989).

So many possibilities exist for the United States to help families and to eradicate poverty. But until the United States government resolves to care for each of its members, families of all socioeconomic levels will suffer.

Conflict leads to transformation, but only when individuals, families, or a nation face their challenges until solutions emerge. The United States faces a crisis of values, and the resolution of that conflict will allow America to continue to be the leader of the free world, a nation that holds "these truths to be self-evident . . ." for all people.

Chapter **8**

THE FINAL DAYS
OF THE HERO

Healthy children will not fear life, if their parents have integrity enough not to fear death. . . .

Erik Erikson

Fear of death is a young man's disease.

Rollo May

When an old person dies, it's like a small library burning.

Alex Haley

Ponderings. *Why is it important for the elderly to talk about the past? Why does crisis frequently lead to growth? Have there been unwanted challenges in people's lives that eventually made them stronger, wiser, or more sensitive? What do Americans today have in common with individuals who live in countries plagued by starvation and warfare? Why might it be a sign of positive mental health for adults to contribute to future generations? What is life like for older adults who feel despair because of their personal failures in life? What are the characteristics of older adults who feel good about their lives? What does it mean to "die a good death?" While dying, what gifts can the elderly bestow upon the generations they leave behind?*

Life's final trial will play before an empty courtroom, for each of us as aging travelers will become our own prosecution, defense, and judge. On trial will be the quality of our lives. Evidence will pour in from the great quests accepted or refused: love and marriage, career, friendship-community, and spiritual adventures. Recalled will be the victories and defeats, adjustments to unexpected storms, struggles with inner conflict, and battles with life's relentless dragons. A review will be made of how well we reacted when life said, "*NO*, you cannot have it this easy way forever." For all voyagers, self-examination will evoke both disappointment and regret as well as satisfaction and pride. The key to handing down a final verdict of self-acceptance will be the courage to face our own imperfections and our evaluation of whether or not our adventures contributed positively to the world community.

THE COURAGE TO BE IMPERFECT

Neurosis is living yesterday as if it were today.

Erich Fromm

People who want to be perfect will become perfectly miserable and a perfect nuisance. Perfectionism dooms a person to be his or her own worst enemy. Life brings with it too many crises and requires far too much risk taking for one to harbor the unrealistic desire to be infallible. God forgives; perfectionists never do.

Rudolf Dreikurs (1971), a founder of modern parenting movements, advised his students to develop the "courage to be imperfect." In order to adjust to inevitable disappointments and failures, individuals must accept that life will not cater to their wishes nor conform to their demands. Therefore, when obstacles obstruct their paths they need to respond freely by traveling uncharted courses and by accepting risks that can lead to transformation. Without the courage to be imperfect, people will needlessly condemn themselves for shortcomings; depression and illnesses will be suffered, and they will be less willing to take risks that lead to self-growth but can lead also to possible failure. Epictetus once observed that "all unhappiness arises from attempts to control events and other people over which one has no power" (Siegel, 1986, pp. 190–191). Sooner or later most people learn when to fight the storms of life and when to pull in the sails and ride them out.

Our lives rarely turn out the way we plan them. Our dreams often are dashed, sometimes early in life, sometimes later. For example, I'm not the person I dreamed I would be. Who of us ever is? I never played tennis at Wimbledon. I didn't marry my college sweetheart. I didn't become a well-known poet. As a parent, I never became the ideal father modeled by my favorite character Atticus Finch, the perfect, patient parent in *To Kill a Mockingbird* (Harper, 1960).

I was blessed to experience several severe crises in my early 20s. I was fortunate because these challenges came after childhood's formative years and before my course in life could be prematurely set. My challenges were far less threatening and were more helpful than those faced by most of the families with whom I work. Also, I was fortunate to have many crises occur in a short time. Therefore, I was forced to reevaluate life and make major changes in its course before I began a family. However, my present appreciative attitude is far from the one I held in those dark and hurtful years when no light appeared beyond the dark shadows.

Each of my youthful dreams ended in crisis, a conflict seemingly so hurtful and dark that I often floundered in an angry sea. There was the ignominious defeat at the hands of a Clemson University tennis player that ended my professional tennis dreams. Then one day, a routine phone call to my college sweetheart resulted in the discovery that she was in Philadelphia with a new boyfriend; my innocence ended. Polite notes accompanied the rejection letters from editors who explained that poetry by young unknowns does not sell. Then held hostage for 24 hours in our home by an armed and crazed stranger, my mother and I awaited our certain deaths. Fear left me, but also with it fled my childhood faith.

My life was in disarray. I reeled violently as the passage to my childhood dreams closed. The now familiar Interim between crisis and its resolution was filled with confusion and despair. As my imperfections overshadowed any perceived attributes, I searched in vain for daylight. Rarely do new pathways materialize on demand; insight usually emerges when it is least expected.

Time passed and the tributaries to human development's greatest adventures slowly opened. Graduate school and a new passion for learning replaced sports. Years later, Patty entered my life and I began to understand and cherish life's most exciting adventure. A poetic heart led me to counseling, teaching, and the resulting joy of being a part of others' transformations. With the end of my childish belief in a Santa-God, whose task was to minister to my needs, came the beginning of my most challenging quest: the search for truth and faith. I was fortunate to be diverted from an unexamined life, but I was not heroic, not like so many others. Many people—the bravest heroes—suffer crises in early childhood or during the midst of their voyages. For them the seas rage; the challenges magnify. Yet they respond to life's calls.

"*Everything* turns out for the best" is not a motto to be believed. This is a motto reserved for those who have been spared horrendous disasters. However, I find remarkable the number of courageous people who face severe challenges, even tragedy, and transform them into positive passages and possibilities. The world of mature men and women is one of imperfection and overcoming, not perfection and security.

People never request crises. No one wants to become discontent with marriage; single parents never wish to nurture their children alone; no spouse longs to be married to an alcoholic or an abusive mate; disabled children are never planned; parents cannot foresee that their children will develop psychological problems; workaholics do not accept jobs anticipating that their labor will drain them of vitality and energy; people never long for the doubts and struggle that a spiritual quest brings; no one asks to be depressed and lonely or to adjust to the death of loved ones. In ancient myths, Ulysses fought the cyclops, Seirenes, and a horde of parasitic suitors who invaded his castle. Modern men and women fight different foes, but each is as dangerous and as potentially destructive. Perfect? Not our lives!

True, not all people who are challenged react courageously. Some refuse to face the dragons. They deny inner feelings or ignore the pain of others. They see themselves as pawns on a chess board, manipulated by life, out of control of their destiny. Inaction becomes their favored response and complaining is their battle cry. When close to them, one will sense their stagnancy and tire of their games of "ain't it awful" or "under these conditions what can you expect from me?" Possibly the lessons they learned in early childhood were negative and now discourage them from risking more disappointment. Nevertheless, those who have delayed action can still experience life's greatest adventures. The first step toward freedom will be the most courageous.

But, more often than not, people are valiant. They do not avoid trials nor the struggle to create solutions. Crisis symbolizes an end and a beginning, for the familiar that imprisons travelers must die as change liberates one's passion for growth. Therefore, couples admit their problems and enter counseling, addictive and abusive relationships end, single parents somehow provide for their family's needs, tough decisions limit intrusive jobs, families help discouraged children create positive identities, and individuals search for religious truth. On each of these voyages, pain and loss, failure and setbacks become familiar obstacles, but they fail to paralyze the courageous. Heroism arises precisely because of imperfection, and the courage to be imperfect allows people to transform their lives and continue to brave the hazards inherent in living well. Perfectionists are only heroes of their imaginary worlds.

SHARING THE HUMAN EXPERIENCE

Wisdom is the ability to look lovingly at others.

Erik Erikson

As men and women mature, they extend themselves beyond personal, family, and tribal concerns to share feelings and understand the needs of all citizens of the planet Earth. To transcend one's immediate boundaries, one's heart and mind must unify in a desire to join the world community. Until that unity occurs, one may feel emotionally separated from others or lack the commitment to contribute to people who may seem too "different" or distant. Some people become world citizens early in life. However, years of struggle and experience are necessary for most of us to become a part of the human experience. I am one of those slow learners.

As a young man, I became an intellectual citizen of this planet but not a full emotional participant. I believed it was my duty to serve my fellow man, to help the disadvantaged, comfort the ill, and give hope to others. There was, after all, ample support for this stance.

Born into a Christian family, I was raised to feed the hungry, clothe the naked, and return good for evil. Later, as a doctoral student I admired Alfred Adler's (1958) philosophy that a healthy person is driven by a desire to give to others and to solve problems in the best interest of the community while, conversely, the neurotic always attempts to solve problems in his own self-interest. Most developmental psychologists I studied differed in details but agreed that the quality of caring for others is basic to positive mental health. Despite hearing the frequent disagreement voiced by psychologists who espoused a "to do what's good for yourself is to do what's good for others" philosophy, I remained faithful to my belief in the necessity of contributing to others. But emotionally I remained outside of this needy world.

Siegel (1986) observed that the longest trip in life is from the head to the heart. Life experience allows most of us to complete this trip. For slow learners, life offers the perfect lessons. Seeing my children born, experiencing the transformation of marital love into deep companionship, watching the eyes of students sparkle as they begin to understand their thoughts and feelings, hearing my children laugh at their own jokes, seeing their grandparents' satisfaction and approval—these are joys that arise from being a part of something larger than one's self.

Life teaches us about other feelings as well. We all face so much loss. Time heals wounds, but it does not fill emptiness. My father, the man I most admired in life, died suddenly some years ago. Still I hear his laughter, feel his hand upon mine, and see him digging in his garden and moving gracefully on the tennis court. I feel his presence on major holidays as I recall big family celebrations when grandparents, uncles, aunts, and cousins scurried about in excitement. Those days are no more and the giants I loved as a child have one by one left this world. Now my children are at the age when my wife and I appear to be bigger than life, eternal anchors in their lives. As of yet, they do not understand the continuity of life, that all things human begin and end, that they soon will take our place.

In these years on the open seas, there are no feelings that are not experienced as friends, lovers, parents, workers, and spiritual men and women. When the trip from the head to the heart is concluded, we are no longer outsiders dutifully giving to people unlike ourselves. We *are* those people. We are the mother standing over her slain child, the orphan sitting in the rubble of a bombed building, the father unable to provide food for his starving children, the terminally ill saying final farewells to the family. We know their feelings: joy and hope, pain and sorrow, hurt and loss. For we now share one pair of eyes, grieve with a single heart, and hope with a common soul.

As our world grows smaller, we observe daily the plight of fellow travelers and we feel kinship with them. The children of the poorest nation breath the same air as the children of the richest nations. They will embark upon the same great voyages and feel the joy and sorrow shared by each generation. But for many in the world, opportunities for success are few, and life may prematurely end. Until the earth becomes a home where each child who hears the call to adventure can journey without being hampered by war, starvation, polluted water and air or extreme poverty, our mission, our children's and our grandchildren's will not be complete. The dragons that beset us under the best of conditions are formidable enough. We cannot allow new generations to enter a world where victory for them will be impossible.

It requires time to become human, to learn that we live in a family of families. In today's small world, any child's cry should awaken all who care about the future. It is not enough to transform American families and the nation; the incredible must be attempted: to transform the world into a community where everyone can experience the greatest adventures in human development equally.

THE HARSHEST JUDGE

> Life can only be understood backwards, but it must be lived forwards.
>
> Søren Kierkegaard

Time may be infinite but life is short. Unlike other animals, human beings understand that they grow old and they await their coming deaths. As the end nears, individuals review the great voyages of life, the successes and tragedies, broken and/or enduring relationships, dreams both achieved and lost, and contributions left or not left behind. If people remain faithful to their chosen quests, have the courage to be imperfect, and contribute to the world community, then they achieve what Erik Erikson called *integrity*, a final blessing given to life.

People with integrity continue to give to others, even in their last days. They are optimistic and supportive, knowing that the great adventures of life are worth undertaking. Having searched for truth, they feel comfortable with their faith and with their standing in the universe. Therefore, death is not so feared. Concern for the lives of others continues and is frequently seen in the love of mature adults for the young. Children are drawn to these accepting and encouraging men and women, and in the eyes of the elderly the young can do little wrong. Most of the aging who achieve integrity are heroes, although they may not think of themselves as such. By accepting their shortcomings and by showing continued enthusiasm for life, the elderly encourage their children and grandchildren to meet life with equal zest and courage.

For the elderly who failed to face life's challenges or could not succeed in the great adventures in human development, life's review brings unhappiness. They dwell on what is missing and regret the broken relationships, the stagnant years that passed without productivity, missed opportunities, the voyages never undertaken. Time is much too short now to begin the great quests or to correct major errors. If, in addition to other failed voyages, the quest for truth was not taken, then death becomes an enemy that too soon will overtake them. As a result, unhappy sojourners become filled with what Erikson called *despair*.

Complaining becomes the major characteristic of despair; nothing seems quite right. The room is too cold or too hot, the food is too spicy or bland, children are too loud or noncommunicative, loved ones appear to be uncaring, and the new generation seems hopelessly lost. One writer called this misery "a thousand little disgusts." What is passed on to the next generation is an unpleasant feeling for aging and for life's final trial. Children dislike visiting their discouraged, negative elders, whom they sense they should respect and love but do not. From my childhood, I recall an elderly couple who stood outside their home each morning to yell at any unfortunate school child who passed too close to their yard. People who feel small and defeated compensate by over-controlling. Out of control of life, this couple overly controlled their yard and possessions. Children reacted negatively, the couple complained to the youths' parents, and misery recycled.

Life is not easy or lasting for any traveler. The hours that on some days seemed endless rapidly come to a close. We relentlessly journey toward our last days. And when the closing scene is reached, we will review the years of our lives and pass judgment on the quality of our journey. How did we handle our imperfections and the challenges that beset us? Did we retreat to safety, or did we become the heroes of our own great adventures?

THE FINAL DAYS OF THE HERO

And those whom you speak of Crito, naturally do so [avoid death]; for they think that they will be gainers by so doing . . . and I naturally shall not do so; for I think that I should gain nothing by drinking the poison a little later but my own contempt for so greedily saving up a life which is already spent.

Socrates

For it is not death or hardship that is a fearful thing, but the fear of death and hardship.

Epictetus

Most people share a similar vision for the final days of the people they love. They imagine them living at home surrounded by their loved ones. Conversations, rest, and silence flow naturally because a family understands the needs of each of its members. The elderly sojourner rests in his or her own bed and peers through familiar windows as the sun follows, as humans do, a faithful path, rising and setting in the sky. Memories of the great adventures, final farewells, messages of hope, and encouragement are shared. And when an elderly relative or friend senses that the time to depart is at hand, the spirit is released.

However, as advances in medical technology allowed doctors to extend the dying process, the nature of death and, therefore, of life changed. No longer are older adults who made thousands of courageous decisions in life given the right to die as they wish. That power has been assumed by the Sheriffs of death and it will be their philosophy that governs each of our final days. For the Sheriffs, death is not the natural conclusion of a life well lived, but the enemy, the stranger to be avoided. As an 8 year old religiously follows a rule even when situations demand flexibility, many in the medical profession maintain that their oath to preserve life overrides any personal beliefs that guided their patients during their lives. For the ill not fortunate enough to die on their own terms, the final days of life may be placed in the Sheriffs' hands. As a result, those who have conquered their fear of dying and death may be governed by those who have not.

Society's fear of death can now be measured by how long it prolongs a life already spent, even against the wishes of patients and their families. Chances are good that modern men and women will not die in their homes, but in a stark hospital room, their bodies invaded by tubes and supported by machines that prolong dying rather than living. At worse, hospital employees may require loved ones, particularly the very young, to wait outside the room, or to visit only briefly during the last days of their loved one's life. Therefore, strangers decide when silence, visiting, and final farewells are appropriate. As a result, the rhythm of life and death alters. What is lost in this modern scenario is much more than a relative. Surrendered is the final blessing a sojourner can share with those to be left behind.

Too frequently the voices of men and women who made difficult yet wise decisions time and again in life are largely muted by the clamor of opposing medical ethicists who are certain how all people must die and who claim the last days of the dying hero as a symbol of their cause. Although the individual's wishes are largely irrelevant to these professionals, the dying elder would understand their debate.

On one hand, many ethicists believe each individual should decide whether or not life support systems or extraordinary means should be used to prolong life, that the right to choose one's final passage is the most basic human freedom. Many even support an individual's right to voluntarily end by suicide a life besieged by Alzheimer's disease or other progressive, painful, irreversible illnesses.

But other voices are heard. Some worry that a general acceptance of passive or active euthanasia could endanger the lives of individuals devalued by society. Would life be prematurely terminated for the poor, mentally or physically disabled, or others who have no advocates and whose lives are not highly valued by those charged with their care? This debate is crucial in a society that protects the rights of individuals. But it is ironic that men and women who were admired for their autonomy, courage, and wisdom in life become in death objects manipulated and largely ignored by those involved in the debate.

Somewhere death picked up a dirty name in the Western world. Although death is the only certain event that each of us will share, it is the topic people are least likely to discuss. Perhaps the growing avoidance of the quest for truth and faith made death a mysterious outsider. For those individuals who have focused their energy on personal achievement and gratification, death ends the possibility of personal accomplishment, experience, and sensuality. To these travelers, death becomes an evil ending rather than a promised destination or even liberation.

How unnatural fear makes us. Couples often avoid making their wills or planning for the family's future in the event of the early death of one or both parents. The funeral industry continues to make millions by taking advantage of a nation's fear. Corpses are decorated and shaped to look as lifelike as possible, then placed in expensive coffins guaranteed for centuries against intrusion by the elements. Despite their loss of a spouse, parent, or child, grieving family members are admired when they refuse to shed tears or to display openly their sense of loss. Left alone and without support in the months that follow, those who failed to grieve at funerals may face increased depression and despair. Death has become the single syllable with the power to end the most animated conversations abruptly. It is as if much of the public lives with a terrible secret (the coming of death), one that everyone knows about but has collectively agreed to ignore. Nevertheless, death comes despite public or private denials or flights toward youthful obsessions. Even in death, the dragons roar. The elderly and their families can face together these final trials, just as other life challenges were met. For life's adventurers to avoid uncomfortable discussions of death and dying could eventually place a family in a prolonged state of agony and confusion, trying to be faithful to an elder's unstated beliefs and wishes.

As in all confrontations with life's crises, courage, honesty, and direct communications become weapons of relief. For some, the hope of continued life and the belief in miracles or medical science makes the extension of life by any available means preferable. In addition, many will find doctors who focus on the quality of living rather than the prolongation of dying. To others, however, the continuation of life through the use of life support systems and other extraordinary means represents the greedy "saving up (of) a life which is already spent." In their final days, the dying may prefer to live in hospitals, hospices, or their homes. Yet to be honored, their desires must be known. The elderly should die as they will, not as others believe they should.

Of course, sharing one's preference for dying does not insure that it will be observed. Circumstances can transfer the power over those final days to someone else's judgment, but when a private belief becomes a public declaration, family members can become unified. Standing together they will celebrate the philosophy and beliefs of their relative, even if they lose control over the dying process. The final hope and will of the sojourner can guide, encourage, and

soothe the lives of those left behind and thus become the elderly's final affir-
mation of the goodness of life and the meaning of death.

Commenting on the final days of older adults, Erikson observed that our
elders who have the integrity not to fear death will have children who will not
fear life. Even in death, the dragons can be overcome and life for others transformed.

Chapter 9

POSTSCRIPT:
HEROES IN OUR PAST

> You may ask, "How did this tradition get started?" I'll tell you: "I don't know." But it's a tradition. And because of our traditions everyone of us knows who he is and what God expects him to do.
>
> Tevye, *Fiddler on the Roof*

Ponderings. *What special family traditions have been passed down through the generations? What stories are shared about individuals who influenced the lives of older family members? How did the past generations help each other during difficult times? What special strengths and history come from your ethnic background? For instance, what qualities allowed African Americans to survive slavery and struggle for equality? What traditions from the past are worth carrying into the future? Who are the people who have had the most positive influence? What lessons, beliefs, and values should be passed to the next generation?*

Those who long to hear stories of heroes and adventure, need only to look to the lives of their ancestors. Some came as immigrants; others came as slaves. It is all there for every family: dragons and trials, courage and timidity, faith and despair, love and loneliness, birth and death.

The Old Immigrants came to the shores of America with dreams for their family's future and little more. Most of them left a secure existence for a world that promised a more meaningful life. For them to venture into the new world required the courage to give up an easier road. Through dedicated work, and

197

with the support of strong immigrant communities, many immigrant parents created better lives for themselves and future generations.

As in the stories of Odysseus, early Americans lived in a distinct age, faced different dragons, and were governed by the customs and traditions of their day. Nevertheless, as in each generation, these heroes found passion and meaning in their love, work, sense of community, and spiritual expression. That many succeeded against overwhelming odds gives Americans today the courage to believe in themselves, that they too can become consummate heroes in a new age.

Times change. But in today's world, there are New Immigrants. Ironically, they are immigrants within their own country; families who dare to hear a call and, like many of their ancestors, leave the safety of a known world to pursue new, exciting dreams. To flourish as families, the New Immigrants must be as wise as the old generation of immigrants, but also must possess the courage to be different from others and to defy the dragons of this age. In some ways many of the new challenges of the era described in this book make the journeys of New Immigrants harder, but in some ways the challenges may be easier.

The impetus to write this chapter originated with my fascination for how two people, Rosel Hoffberger Schewel and Charles Catalano, came to be respected family members and admired leaders in their communities. One was of Jewish and the other of Italian heritage. The Hoffberger family owned the Baltimore Orioles from 1969 to 1980. Sports fans throughout the world followed two of their teams through exciting World Series play. Theirs is a story representative of the American dream: immigrants who achieved success in a new country. What first stirred my interest in the Catalanos was an unusual incident that displayed an extraordinary dedication to their extended family. On the 10th anniversary of Charles Catalano's medical practice in central Virginia, he rented a bus and instructed the driver to go to the residence of each of his relatives (most of whom lived in New York and New Jersey), to pick up those who could travel, and to bring them to a family celebration in Virginia. For indeed, his success was their success; his family's happiness was everyone's joy.

Initially I knew Rosel Hoffberger Schewel and Charles Catalano only as colleagues and friends whom I admired, but I wondered what adventures in the past led to their successes. So I traveled to Baltimore and Brooklyn to discover their heroes in the past. I was fascinated by what I learned.

As one ages, he or she begins to realize how important the past can be to the present generation. Indeed, in order to flourish, today's families must possess the courage, adventurousness, and wisdom of their ancestors. To discover special qualities of past family members gives each individual an appreciation for the human spirit that lies within. For adventure, excitement, and inspiration, one need only to recall the lives of those who made life today possible.

THE HOFFBERGERS OF BALTIMORE: A FAMILY OF FAMILIES

In 1882, Charles and Sarah Hoffberger gave up the familiar roads of life in their homeland (Galicia, a region in Central Europe) to create a new course for themselves and future generations in the United States. Seven children, all sons, survived infancy and carried forward their parents' vision (one child, the only girl, died in infancy). Actually, this story is not about a single family, but about a family of families who worked and lived in a supportive community.

Seventeen cousins make up the third generation of the Hoffberger family. My good fortune in working with one of the cousins, Professor Rosel Schewel, sparked my interest in interviewing several members of her immediate family. I found each interview to be fascinating and informative. I only wish that time allowed me to interview each member of the Hoffberger clan.

When Charles Hoffberger came to the United States, he collected driftwood on the shores of Chesapeake Bay and sold the wood for fuel. He opened a dairy store and created an ice business. If only Charles Hoffberger could have known that his early efforts would eventually lead his children and grandchildren to be recognized internationally for their philanthropy! In the 1950s, the Hoffbergers received the Freedom Medal of the State of Israel. Also, Mayor McKeldin of the city of Baltimore presented the family with a certificate in recognition of their exemplary service to the citizens of that city. During the ceremony that celebrated the Hoffbergers' generativity, a letter was read from Cardinal Sheehan that praised the Hoffbergers for their dedicated service to humanity. How did this family travel so far in just three generations?

Financial success for the Hoffbergers came originally from their business in ice, coal, and home heating oil. Charles Hoffberger bought a wagon to carry coal; his business flourished. More wagons were purchased and the business continued to grow. Hoffberger's death at the age of 50 in 1907 left the business in the hands of his seven sons: Abraham, Harry, Michael, Samuel, Jacob, Saul, and Joseph (Figure 9.1).

Figure 9.1.   Hoffberger Brothers. Courtesy of Professor Rosel Schewel.

As children, the seven sons set up the early pattern of working hard in the family business. Rena Hoffberger, wife of Saul Hoffberger, recalled the hard work that characterized her husband's youth: "When the boys came home from school, they helped their mother put milk in containers. Then they started the ice business. My husband used to carry blocks of ice on his shoulder to the top of tenements. That's the way they worked—on the shoulder, on the back—7 days a week."

They worked ferociously. They worked together as children and soon they were to live together as young adults.

Harry Hoffberger was perhaps the most unique and independent of all of the Hoffberger brothers. Early in his life, he amassed what was then a fortune (about $500,000), quit the Hoffberger business, and went into semi-retirement racing trotting horses. Tiring of this and being advised by his doctor to return to work, Harry rejoined the Hoffberger clan.

The Springdale Avenue Experience

Sarah Hoffberger bought houses for her children. The homes were located side by side on Springdale Avenue, and two of the other family houses stood within sight at opposite corners. Sarah Hoffberger tried to be fair in dealing with her seven sons. One of the sons, Samuel Hoffberger, had three children:

Jerry, Lois and Rosel. Lois Hoffberger Feinblatt, a psychotherapist in Baltimore, remembered:

> My grandmother was so determined that everyone would have things equal that the houses were all of equal size even though the families were not the same size. One family had five children; one family had two children. But the houses were of equal size. There was one backyard shared by the families. The whole thrust of the family was that everyone was equal and everyone did the same thing. In fact, my grandmother was so determined that everyone should be equal that if a tree grew too large and shaded one home unequally, she had it cut down. Then she planted a Japanese maple tree of equal size in the corner of each yard.

In this small area around Springdale Avenue, a close-knit society arose. Within a few blocks, a synagogue was on one corner and a public school across the street. Cousins played with cousins. Relatives encouraged one another. The Springdale Avenue experience provided a community that enriched each member of the Hoffberger families.

The Simplicity of Roles

The Hoffberger families lived in an era when men's and women's roles were divided simply. Rena Hoffberger (wife of Saul) recalled:

> The men worked long hours and nights. The women always understood. My husband told me, "The children are your responsibility. The house is your responsibility. My responsibility is to bring home the money." How the others felt I'm not sure, but I imagine it was the same, because the men all worked incredibly long hours.

As one would expect in ethnic homes at the turn of the century, male interests dominated family life. As one member of the third generation recalled,

> An interesting thing is that it was a very male-dominated household. My father had two friends who came over to the house every Friday night for supper. And they talked about the most boring things about business. It didn't matter that the children weren't a bit interested in that. It was nothing like the interest taken in children at today's supper tables—"What did you do in school today?" etc.

Despite the limited interactions between children and their fathers, the male influence proved to be powerful. Leroy Hoffberger, a lawyer in Baltimore and one of three sons born to Mildred and Jack Hoffberger, recalled his father's influence:

> My dad was a strong figure in my life—strong because it was a tendency of Jewish wives to build up their husbands, that they worshiped in the first instance, then wanted to have the kids see as they did, as some kind of superhuman figure. My dad worked 7 days per week and ran the family's ice business [Figure 9.2]. He went to work at 4 a.m. and never returned before 6 p.m. and much later in the summer. We didn't see a great deal of him, but his image was always there.

Because of their husbands' prolonged absences from home, women created their own supportive community composed of family, in-laws, and close friends. Lois Feinblatt observed:

> I think that this community gave them [the women] a circle of security. If any trouble did arise in any of the marriages—and we knew of none—then everyone was around to give their support. So there was less pressure on marital partners than there is today. Today we see a tremendous amount of dependence on the husband and wife for each other. If they don't satisfy each other, there isn't someone else to talk to or to beat it out with or to go to the shore with for the day.

Figure 9.2.   Hoffberger horse and cart. Courtesy of Professor Rosel Schewel.

Family routines became important. The routines offered stability and consistency. Rosel Hoffberger Schewel, a college professor in Virginia, recalled:

> Parents did not play with their children much. I never remember a father playing baseball with a son, for instance, but you spent your time with the family. You sat down for meals with the entire family. On Friday night, the Sabbath, we always had company, usually the same people.

For the most part, men and women seemed to delight in their roles. Their self-satisfaction became a blessing to their children. A cousin remembered:

> My mother was absolutely the perfect wife. She never complained. She had a wonderful sense of herself as a woman. She loved her role. And this was one of the greatest gifts to me. She wasn't a complaining, discontented woman. And the sense of the satisfaction which she got out of kids permeated the air.

Men also gained security in their roles, even into the third generation. The family business assured each of Charles Hoffberger's grandchildren a position of importance. No matter where, for how long, or how successfully a young Hoffberger might venture away from the family business, he could always return to find a significant place in the family's work. As Leroy Hoffberger explained:

> There were no males of my generation who did not work together. Every male was placed in a spot where my father's generation thought they might prosper. Each one of us was aware that the others were doing their bit for the family. For the male members of the family there was a continuous contact. . . . We met periodically to discuss business problems and to make plans. We tried to smooth over various ambitions. We worked hard to create a cooperative business.

Possibly when parents feel satisfied with their own work—whether in a career or in the home—their children reap the greatest benefits.

Children: Everyone Felt Special

None of the Hoffbergers could recall children who experienced serious emotional or behavioral problems. Occasional pranks or a mischievous teen experiment caused some consternation, but no "problem children" emerged. Or, at the least, no major problems were observed by those family members interviewed.

Several explanations might account for the Hoffberger children's success. Members in a close, responsive community might quickly call any signs of misbehavior to the attention of parents. Also, relatives or other adults in a tight community could comfortably respond to and derail potential misbehavior. As opposed to present society with its latchkey children, some familiar adult was always close by to watch over children in the Springdale Avenue community.

A primary contributor to the children's success came from the adults' attitudes toward and treatment of behaviors that might bring negative responses from today's busy parents. Professor Schewel explained:

> In a Jewish family, not a lot was considered to be misbehaving. There was a lot of attention focused on kids. Then you had a feeling that everyone thought that what you did was pretty great, that you were pretty cute. I know I felt like a favorite child, but I think that all of the Hoffberger children felt that way.

Children need to feel unique and valuable. The positive atmosphere in the Springdale Avenue community allowed children to build their self-confidence.

Parents' expectations were high for their children's success in school. A cousin recalled: "It was expected that you behave and that you do well in school. The teacher was always right. If the teacher said that you didn't do your homework, you didn't do it."

Leroy Hoffberger experienced similar expectations from his parents:

> We never had any doubt in our minds that we would stay in school and do well. That was made very clear. We brothers helped each other and created a friendly competition. As a result, two of us graduated from Princeton and another from Duke. It wasn't always so much a love of knowledge, but trying to satisfy your parents who said, "We don't want you to go through the struggle we experienced."

Of course, as in so many families, the Hoffberger's children possessed a variety of temperaments and attitudes. Some of these traits might cause serious problems in today's rushed homes and schools. However, the Hoffbergers relabeled potentially negative characteristics to give them a positive connotation. For example, a rebellious child was considered to be spirited and independent. Or, a child who engaged in frequent misbehavior was called mischievous. By not anchoring a child with a negative label, parents could work more cooperatively with their children. More important, children did not live up to their negative labels or reputations, a severe problem the school system today created and now faces.

Jerry Hoffberger's youth provides a perfect example. As he reflected about his early years, he recalled: "I wasn't a little rebellious; I was a lot rebellious. It was a rebellion against authority. For example, I was told not to play football, so I went out and played football."

When Jerry Hoffberger began to experience difficulties with authority figures in the public schools, his family searched for a private school that might provide more flexibility. Jerry recalled:

> It was a question of how to get this kid—who doesn't want to study and doesn't want to do much of anything—motivated, so I went to private school. . . . One of the reasons I wanted to go away to school was because it would be a different kind of authority. It wasn't parental. So if you told them to go to hell, it wasn't so bad.

A similar dilemma confronted the family when Jerry balked at attending the family synagogue, where Hebrew prayers were recited, which he could not understand. Instead of creating a war with him, the family began to attend a synagogue where the prayers were said in English. The family avoided debilitating battles and searched for mutually acceptable compromises. Although Jerry Hoffberger may not have enjoyed attending either his new school or the new synagogue, he did attend both. His participation must have brought with it some satisfaction for his parents.

In today's rushed world, Jerry might fall through the cracks. Professionals and parents today have little time to allow children to learn to use talents that fail to conform to a narrow standard of proper behavior and acceptable academic learning.

Children need time to find their places in the world. Too often independence and spirited behavior are falsely considered to be signs of learning disabilities or emotional problems. But with special handling, Jerry Hoffberger emerged to become one of the most successful of the Hoffberger businessmen. He also became well known to baseball fans around the nation. When the Hoffberger family owned the Baltimore Orioles from 1969 to 1980, Jerry was the Chairman of the Board.

Family Support of the Sick and the Elderly: Extended Community

If the character of a family can be evaluated by how it treats its elders, the Hoffbergers—like many immigrant families—provide excellent models. Jerry Hoffberger remembered: "The elderly were treated with great discretion and respect. . . . If you were older, you were bowed down to. It was a given. The older you got, the more venerated you became, whether you deserved it or not."

Rosel recalled that the family enjoyed the older family members:

> My mother's mother lived with one of her daughters. We visited her every Saturday night. No one thought of or indicated that having her live with them was a burden. My mom wanted to visit and did every day. My grandmother was always around. She was to be a person of great prestige at my wedding.

Not only were the elderly treated well, but so were any family members who had special needs. For example, Jerry recalled, "Uncle Harry, the elder statesman in the family, was sick for years. Everyone visited him. Not a day went by when people didn't visit." This interest in others was also shared with people outside the immediate family.

The Origins of Social Interest

The desire to serve others was passed down from generation to generation through modeling, requirement, and religious practice. Lois Feinblatt recalled:

> It was always a family of doing for other people. Always a tremendous sense of community, doing for your temple, school, and family. . . . For example, the first generations brought extended family over from Europe and had them live with them until the new immigrants could get a job and move off on their own. It did not occur to them not to share. I think our interest in giving to others came more from osmosis. My mother was not a very talkative woman, but my parents lived a certain way and we were observers of that. We didn't know there was any other way—other than a certain kind of service.

Children were required to participate in the world outside of their homes. Through these experiences, values developed. One cousin recalled:

> I don't remember any specific attempt to teach values. It was done by requiring certain things—participation in certain areas, like going to synagogue. Sometimes these requirements seemed negative, like belonging to the Boy Scouts whether or not you had interest in them. My dad used to work with many charities. He would take me along as a kid. Whether that led me to be active in community activities, I don't know.

Judaism provided an ethical and cultural foundation for the Springdale Avenue community. Each family created individual religious practices. Rena Hoffberger explained: "Not all of us went to the same temple. They all found their own niche when it came to religion. It never caused any ill feelings."

For the Hoffberger families, religious tradition included attending the synagogue, lighting the Friday candles, serving the synagogue through volunteer work, contributing to the Jewish National Fund, celebrating the Passover meal, and following a variety of Jewish rituals. What influenced most of the third generation of Hoffbergers were Jewish culture, ethics, and traditions. Theological discussions were rarely shared.

Leroy Hoffberger recalled:

> We were always aware that we were Jewish. I think much of my parents' sensitivity and values came rom Judaism, but not necessarily the religious part. . . . Much in Judaism talks of being a decent human being. This rubbed off on us. Charity in Judaism is called *tzedekah*, which means justice, doing justice to your fellow man. We were aware of that. I've spent much of my life trying to make this a better place to live. Although my parents' teachings were not always presented in a religious context, they displayed a great Jewish influence.

As one might expect, Charles Hoffberger's grandchildren grew up with a strong sense that their parents believed in God. Each child was left to create his or her own vision of the nature of God, but everyone shared a feeling for others that remains prominent in their lives and in the lives of their children.

THE CATALANOS FROM BROOKLYN: "NO ONE WAS ALLOWED TO FAIL"

When Charles Catalano left Brooklyn with his wife Marcia in 1971 to attend medical school in Italy, 50 family members flocked to the airport to bid him farewell. That emotional gathering of an Italian family must have been a sight even for the hallways of Kennedy International Airport. Charles Catalano's acceptance into medical school represented a family member's success that was made possible by three generations of hard work plus the nourishment of a supportive community.

The Catalano story differs from that of the Hoffberger's. The Catalanos owned no family business. Their financial success was modest. No standard existed for the children to strive for educational success. However, much of their story is familiar: Family members found meaning through their love, work, and religion. They created a community filled with social interest, with concern for future generations.

From Sicily to the United States

When Charles Catalano's grandfather, Joseph Catalano, journeyed to the United States from Sicily at the turn of the century, he had only a few dollars in his pocket. He began to work for the railroad, a job at which he labored for 30 years. Grandfather Catalano and his wife, Lena, had four children: Margaret, Anthony, Ann, and Charlie.

The youngest child, Charlie Catalano, married Rosalie Correnti in 1933. Rosalie gave birth to a daughter, Lee, and two sons, Joe and Charles. With no family business to step into, Charlie Catalano tried to create a career of his own. He opened a candy store, ran a coffee shop, worked as a traveling salesman, delivered interoffice mail, and worked for the Navy's shipyard. Although Charlie Catalano proved to be ambitious and industrious, his ventures into the business world failed. Several times he declared bankruptcy. To help the family, Rosalie Catalano held a job in what the family called a sweat shop. There she made piece goods and worked long hours. The family struggled financially.

Grandmother Correnti: The Great Encourager

Soon after Charles Catalano was born in 1948, his father became known as Ravioli Charlie. He made and sold ravioli to local businesses. Rosalie Catalano continued to work in the dress factory. To help raise the children, Rosalie's mother, Maria Correnti, moved into the family's three-bedroom home in Brooklyn. At night, Grandmother Correnti (Figure 9.3) shared a bedroom with her two grandsons.

With both parents working, the raising of young Charles became Grandmother Correnti's special responsibility. She encouraged him and made him feel important. Always young Charles felt her love, concern, and compassion. Grandmother Correnti encouraged Charles to become a success. She nourished in him a self-confidence that would last a lifetime. As Charles Catalano recalled: "She was a saint, the spiritual leader of our family. In her eyes, I was the only one."

Figure 9.3. Grandmother Correnti. Courtesy of Dr. Charles Catalano.

Charles Catalano's childhood experience proved to be similar to those of the Hoffberger children. The young felt special and competent. Their abilities, rather than their disabilities, drew the attention of adults.

Family encouragement was not limited to the home; everywhere in the community, the Catalanos found supportive relatives. Charles' aunt, Josie

Correnti, recalled: "On a single block one cousin owned a vegetable store, one owned a fish store, one ran a deli, and my father owned a grocery store. Also, we all went to the same church." Josie Correnti added with a smile, "It was hard to misbehave much."

Work played a central role in the Italian community. Men, and often other family members, worked 12 hours a day for at least 6 days of the week. Long hours of labor became a way of life. Everyone understood how much effort it required for grocery stores, delis, and fish stores to survive. Family life adjusted to the demands of work.

Another accepted institution in this Italian community was the Roman Catholic Church. Families attended mass and learned the catechism. Although theology rarely became a topic of family conversation, the ethics taught by the church contributed significantly to the children's values. Children grew up believing in a God that gave their lives a purpose beyond the present.

Whenever an individual experienced problems, the family would help. "No one was allowed to fail," one Italian immigrant's son told me. For example, if a child dropped out of school a relative would employ him. As Josie Correnti explained, "When a boy got tired of school, he quit. But they were lucky enough to fall into business." Luck played less of a role in young people's success than the spirit of caring for others.

This spirit of giving, as with the Hoffbergers, was striking in the family's treatment of the elderly or sick. Josie Correnti recalled:

> When a grandparent became ill, he or she simply chose which child they preferred to live with. We were, for example, quite crowded with a large family, but there was always room for Grandpa. The children respected him. He was Grandpa.

Each family found an opportunity to help other family members. When tragedy struck Josie Correnti's family, her relatives were there to help. Josie Correnti's husband became terminally ill in 1976, and his condition required constant supervision at home. However, Josie Correnti needed to keep her job, one that would prove invaluable in supporting her 11-year-old son after the death of her husband. Charles' mother, Rosalie, stayed with her brother from 9 until 5 every day for the rest of his life. Josie Correnti kept her job, and her husband died with confidence in the security of his family's future.

Charles Catalano's family loved and supported him. But the course of his life changed when a man from outside the family entered Charles' life.

Uncle Ettore: Giving to Others

On the way to interview members of the Catalano family, story after story was heard about Uncle Ettore and the crucial contributions he made to young Charles Catalano's life. Halfway through an interview with Uncle Ettore, I discovered that he was not a relative of the Catalanos, but as Charles put it: "He became a member of the family through my mother."

Ettore Vignone's wife, Jaynette, met Rosalie Correnti in the sweat shop before her marriage to the elder Charlie Catalano. They soon became good friends and later the two families spent weekends together at Coney Island and visited regularly in each others' homes.

Whenever Rosalie Catalano found the behavior of one of her sons to be too challenging, she would send him for a time to stay with Uncle Ettore. Of course, the Vignones had three children of their own, but they never minded adding to their family.

Ettore Vignone was the image of a hard-working optimist, a perfect model for the Catalano boys. Uncle Ettore believed that a person could reach any dream that he or she worked hard enough to achieve. His life seemed to prove the truth of his belief. When he arrived in America, he labored to earn a meager living. He recalled:

> I did anything to make a dollar. I was a gandy dancer (worked on the tracks for the railroad), dug ditches, shoveled, and carried coal. It was money my family needed as we grew. I painted, did carpentry work, roofing work—everything in the world. It was tough; I had a very understanding wife. She helped. She did beading—sewing beads on fancy clothes.

Eventually, Ettore Vignone rose through the ranks to become the Director of Housing for Jersey City.

Uncle Ettore's belief that through work dreams come true brought him closer to young Charles Catalano. What Charles needed was a belief in the tenet that he could succeed. Ettore Vignone recalled:

> Charles' parents were wonderful. We all tried to encourage our children. I would say to the Catalanos: "Take a position where you believe he will succeed. If they [your children] want something, they will get it." I encouraged Charles to do what he wanted to do, to try to succeed.

Charles' brother studied to be a pharmacist; so did Charles. But Charles wanted more; he wanted to become a doctor. The obstacles seemed overwhelming. No one from either the Catalano or Correnti family had graduated from college. To be able to attend medical school seemed to him like a fantasy.

To be accepted into medical school, Charles Catalano needed to take classes in New Jersey. Complications mounted. He had neither transportation nor housing. Young Charles turned to Uncle Ettore for help. Uncle Ettore opened his home once again. He told Charles Catalano: "You have a house, my house. You have a car, my car."

Soon Charles gained acceptance into a medical college in the family's home country, Italy. New obstacles mounted. His recent marriage brought another person's life into the decision of whether or not to go to medical school. The distance between Italy and Brooklyn would be great. He did not speak Italian fluently. And, after all, to become a pharmacist would be easier.

At the crossroads of a crucial life decision, Charles again asked for Uncle Ettore's advice. For the man who believed that you should follow your dreams, advice came easily: "Everyone encouraged Charles to be a pharmacist, but he wanted to be a doctor. He said to me, 'But I have to go to Italy to study.' I replied, 'So go to Italy and study.'" That was all Charles needed.

So it was that Charles and Marcia Catalano traveled to the airport with a caravan of 50 people, the community that allowed them to succeed. And the two special people who encouraged Charles Catalano to become everything that he dreamed he could be were there to see him off. Uncle Ettore said his farewells. Then Grandmother Correnti looked at Charlie and said, "Arrivederci." Although she was not ill, she said the words in the way that means, "I will never see you again." "She felt," explained Charles Catalano, "that she had done her job. She had raised me well." Two weeks later, with her grandson safely back in her home country, Grandmother Correnti, the great encourager, died.

Charles Catalano went to Italy with the goal of returning after 2 years to attend a medical school in the United States. With encouragement from everyone in his family, including Uncle Ettore, Charles succeeded. He was accepted by the University of Miami Medical School. On the occasion of his graduation, 30 relatives traveled by car, plane, train, or bus from Brooklyn to Miami to share the moment with him. For most, it was their first trip outside of Brooklyn. Ten years later, those healthy enough to travel boarded a bus once again, this time to visit the home of the young doctor's family in Virginia. The celebration was an expression of Charles Catalano's gratitude for his family's support.

More than this, the trip symbolized his family's emergence as New Immigrants. No longer did relatives own stores on each street corner. No longer was Uncle Ettore a short drive away. No longer did the community's children attend the Catholic church together. No longer were relatives around to absorb some of the challenges facing a young married couple. No longer would a proud grandmother help raise a Catalano child. Instead, the Catalanos joined the ranks of the New Immigrants.

THE NEW IMMIGRANTS

The New Immigrants will journey away from the shores of the contemporary world of The Rush to create a meaningful life for themselves and their families. Although times have changed, the modern travelers will choose as their own some of those same foundations that supported the lives of the Old Immigrants: love, work, community, and faith. Their choices will in many ways set them apart from others. The New Immigrants must be as tenacious and as wise as the Old Immigrants. Modern distractions will frequently threaten to destroy their opportunity to create meaningful lives. Therefore, this generation needs one another's support. One of the greatest threats that face individuals in this era is a lack of connection with others.

The Springdale Avenue Community Revisited

The Springdale Avenue community in Baltimore is no more. The old houses of the Hoffberger families still stand close together. The Japanese maple trees, planted by Sarah Hoffberger so long ago, shade each yard, but new people live in the homes. Most do not know the story of the Japanese maples or the family of families that once lived there.

The young people have the same twinkle in their eyes that young Jerry Hoffberger had years ago. I talked to a 5-year-old boy, apparently playing hookey for the day, who lives in Jerry Hoffberger's old home. When I told him that a man once lived in his house who was Chairman of the Board of the Baltimore Orioles, the youngster's eyes glistened with excitement. Then I asked, "Would you like to own the Orioles someday?" Quickly, the youngster responded, "No, I want to play for them." Maybe someday he will.

The world is a better place now that most people no longer must live in communities that are segregated because of race, religion, or nation of origin. The loss of the Springdale Avenue community should not be mourned. The breakdown of the old patriarchy freed women to develop their talents and to gain more individual freedoms. Men no longer must try to be superhuman, to bear the cares of the entire world on their shoulders. Husbands and fathers can freely display sensitive emotions. Most men can share more of their time with their families. A certain rigidity lessened with the end of the era of the Old Immigrants. More freedom for individuals emerged.

With the passing of communities similar to Springdale Avenue's, however, much was lost that enriched life. Most obviously, the sense of being closely connected to family, to traditions, to religious roots, and to community disappeared. With increased financial success and escalating mobility, many find themselves isolated and alone.

The first task of the New Immigrants will be to create a supportive community, their own Springdale Avenue. Where can they start to create a community that supports and nourishes its members? Most will begin by creating a strong marriage and family. Those who dedicate themselves to their marriages and children immediately defy many in this world who consider everyone and everything to be disposable when they do not promote individual ambition. This dedication to something more than one's own life requires a transformation toward inwardness described earlier.

Spouses and children require time, commitment, and dedication. In return, new immigrant families will gather the fruits of stability and love. More, they will contribute to the next generation in a meaningful rather than an incidental way. But something within the Springdale Avenue community will still be missing: the wider community. In that era, wives and husbands enjoyed a circle of security made up of other relatives, in-laws, and friends in their community. Families survive poorly in isolation; they need to feel connected.

The increased isolation of families may explain part of the new popularity that counselors are experiencing. According to Lois Hoffberger Feinblatt:

> I think that people's isolation makes counseling so popular today. Because people get a lot of reality from counselors—things that someone in another generation would have gotten from an aunt. They need someone to say, "No, the way your husband is acting is not right." There is no one for people to talk to.

Creating a circle of close friends helps. Friends may take on many of the functions of an extended family. Also, organizations can provide the support young families need. Most communities have support groups of men and women who face a variety of challenges. Also, there are political organizations, recreational teams, and other organizations that allow people to connect with others.

Churches in the modern era can play an increasing role in providing support for young families. The church enjoys enormous potential for reaching out to provide groups that sustain young couples and youthful parents. Not only could the church create groups that connect and enrich young families, but also they could tap their human and financial resources to provide innumerable aids to those in need, from child care to emergency professional services. Church buildings need to be filled with people during the weekdays.

Organizations that provide services for troubled families fight to receive adequate funding. They are immensely helpful. Most communities have homes and services for a variety of people from runaway children to unwed mothers. However, these services usually support the victims of this rushed world. Communities also need more groups and organizations that help prevent families from failing.

Grandmother Correnti

When a family's world becomes stressful, who tells children that they are the most special gifts on the face of this earth? More people like Grandmother Correnti are needed. Today, families drift too far away from older adults. This seems a waste of resources. Older people can make a critical difference in the lives of families.

Now that mobile families often live at a distance from grandparents, senior citizens may be the nation's most underused resource. Most older adults mature into loving, giving people. If tapped by individual families, churches, or communities, senior citizens could play a powerful role in reconstructing families. Every child will blossom with the love of a Grandmother Correnti. In each of our communities, senior citizens form an invaluable resource of unconditional love. If older people could only connect with the children who need them.

Uncle Ettores

Possibly the most tragic part of not being connected closely to a community is losing opportunities to give to others. Each of us can enrich someone's life. We need to find occasions when we, like Uncle Ettore, can say "You have a car, my car. You have a house, my house." Giving to others enriches their lives, but the life of the giver is equally enriched. With a lack of extended family nearby, the Uncle Ettores of this world will make a critical difference.

World Community

With nuclear weapons still casting a shadow over our fragile planet, citizens no longer can satisfy themselves with being a part of a small community. Our connection to the world community must be extended. Problems of war, poverty, disease, starvation, ignorance, and pollution must concern the New Immigrants. Until members of the world's nations and people in the inner cities of the United States feel like an extended family, future generations of all families will live in jeopardy. Work must be done to free the children of the future so that they may live meaningful lives.

CONCLUSION

After discussing many of the grave concerns that the older generation holds for the future of its children, Rena Hoffberger offered some optimistic advice: "I don't think that people who anticipate bringing children into the world should hesitate in any way. You just hope and pray that children follow in your path."

But what path will the children follow? Will it be the highway of The Rush that leads to chaos, or will it be a heroic journey through life's greatest adventures?

BIBLIOGRAPHY

Adler, A. (1973). *The practice and theory of individual psychology.* Patterson, New Jersey: Littlefield.

Bedell, G. (1972). *Kierkegaard and Faulkner: Modalities of existence.* Baton Rouge: Louisiana State University Press.

Campbell, J. (1968). *Hero with a thousand faces.* Princeton: Princeton University Press.

Campbell, J. (1970a). *The masks of God: Creative mythology.* New York: Penguin.

Campbell, J. (1970b). *The masks of God: Oriental mythology.* New York: Penguin.

Campbell, J. (1976a). *The masks of God: Occidental mythology.* New York: Penguin.

Campbell, J. (1976b). *The masks of God: Primitive mythology.* New York: Penguin.

Carmody, D., & Carmody, J. (1983). *Religion: The great questions.* New York: Harper and Row.

Coles, G. (1987). *The learning mystique.* New York: Pantheon.

Dreikurs, R., & Mosak, H. (1966). The tasks of life. I: Adler's three tasks. *The Individual Psychologist, 4,* 18–22.

Dreikurs, R., & Mosak, H. (1967). The tasks of life. II: The fourth task. *The Individual Psychologist, 4,* 51–55.

Dreikurs, R., & Soltz, V. (1964). *Children: The challenge.* New York: Meredith Press.

Eliade, M. (Ed.). (1986). *The encyclopedia of religion.* New York: Macmillan.

Erikson, E. (1968). *Identity: Youth and crisis.* New York: W.W. Norton.

Erikson, E., & Newton, H. (1973). *In search of common ground.* New York: W.W. Norton.

Erikson, E. (1982). *The life cycle completed: A review.* New York: W.W. Norton.

Erikson, E. H., Erikson, J. M., & Kivnick, H. Q. (1986). *Vital involvement in old age.* New York: W.W. Norton.

Fishman, C., & Minuchin, S. (1981). *Family therapy techniques.* Cambridge: Harvard University Press.

Fowler, J. (1976). Stages in faith: The structural developmental approach. In T. Hennessy (Ed.), *Values and moral development* (pp. 173–210). New York: Paulist Press.

Fowler, J. (1981). *Stages of faith.* New York: Harper & Row.

Fowler, J. (1991). *Weaving the new creation: Stages of faith & the public church.* San Francisco: Harper.

Fowler, J., & Nipkow, K. (1991). *Stages of faith & religious development: Implications for church, education & society.* New York: Crossroad Publishing Company.

Freud, S. (1962). *Totem and taboo.* (J. Strachey, Trans.). New York: W.W. Norton.

Freud, S. (1975). *Beyond the pleasure principle.* (J. Strachey, Trans.). New York: W.W. Norton.

Friedan, B. (1981). *The second stage.* New York: Summit Books.

Fromm, E. (1982). *Escape from freedom.* New York: Avon.

Gardner, H. (1983). *Frames of mind: The theory of multiple intelligences.* New York: Basic Books.

Gilligan, C. (1977). In a different voice: Women's conceptions of the self and of morality. *Harvard Educational Review, 47,* 481–517.

Gilligan, C., Lyons, N. P., & Hanmer, T. J. (1990). *Making connections: The relational worlds of adolescent girls at Emma Willard School.* Cambridge: Harvard University Press.

Gilligan, C., Ward, J., Taylor, J., & Bardigge, B. (1990). *Mapping the moral domain.* Cambridge: Harvard University Press.

Gould, R. (1978). *Transformations: Growth and change in adult life.* New York: Simon & Schuster.

Gould, R. (1980). Transformations during early and middle adult years. In N. J. Smelser & E. H. Erikson (Eds.), *Themes of work and love in adulthood* (pp. 213–237). Cambridge: Harvard University Press.

Hopkins, T. (1971). *The Hindu religious tradition.* Encino, CA: Dickenson.

Horney, K. (1950). *Neurosis and human growth: The struggle toward self-realization.* New York: W.W. Norton.

Johnson, W., & Robinson, R. (1977). *The Buddhist religion: A historical introduction.* Encino, CA: Dickenson.

Jung, C. (1969). *Man and his symbols.* New York: Doubleday.

Jung, C. (1955). *Modern man in search of a soul.* New York: Harcourt Brace Jovanovich.

Kagan, J. (1989). *Unstable ideas: Temperament, cognition and self.* Cambridge: Harvard University Press.

Keen, S. (1969). *An apology for wonder.* New York: Harper and Row.

Kohlberg, L. (1958). *The development of modes of moral thinking and choice in the years 10 to 16.* Unpublished doctoral dissertation, University of Chicago, Chicago, IL.

Kohlberg, L. (1966). A cognitive-developmental analysis of children's sex-role concepts and attitudes. In E.E. Maccoby (Ed.), *The development of sex differences* (pp. 82–172). Palo Alto, CA: Stanford University Press.

Kohlberg, L. (1969). Stage and sequence: The cognitive-developmental approach to socialization. In D.A. Goslin (Ed.), *Handbook of socialization theory and research* (pp. 347–480). Chicago: Rand McNally.

Kohlberg, L. (1976). Moral stages and moralization: The cognitive-development approach. In T. Lickona (Ed.), *Moral development and behavior* (pp. 31–53). New York: Holt, Rinehart, & Winston.

Kohlberg, L. (1981). *Essays on moral development: Vol. I. The philosophy of moral development.* San Francisco: Harper & Row.

Kohlberg, L. (1984). *Essays on moral development: Vol. II. The psychology of moral development.* San Francisco: Harper & Row.

Kohlberg, L. (1986). A correct statement on some theoretical issues. In S. Modgil & C. Modgil (Eds.), *Lawrence Kohlberg* (pp. 485–546). Philadelphia: Falmer Press.

Levenson, J. (1985). *Sinai and Zion.* New York: Harper & Row.

Martin, R. (1982). *Islam: A cultural perspective.* New York: Prentice Hall.

Maslow, A. (1983). *Religions, values and peak experiences.* Magnolia, MA: Peter Smith.

Napier, A., & Whitaker, C. (1978). *The family crucible.* New York: Bantam.

Noss, J., and Noss, D. (1983). *Man's religion.* New York: Macmillan.

Pahl, R. E. (1988). *On Work: Historical, comparative and theoretical approaches.* Oxford: Basil Blackwell.

Peck, S. (1987). *The different drum: Community making and peace.* New York: Simon and Schuster.

Peck, S. (1978). *The road less travelled.* New York: Touchstone.

Piaget, J. (1932). *The moral judgment of the child.* New York: Harcourt Brace Jovanovich.

Piaget, J. (1952). *The origins of intelligence in children.* New York: International Universities Press.

Piaget, J. (1954). *The construction of reality in the child.* New York: W.W. Norton.

Piaget, J. (1967). *The child's conception of the world.* Totowa, NJ: Littlefield, Adams.

Piaget, J., & Inhelder, B. (1969). *The child's conception of space.* (F. J. Langdon & J.L. Lunzer, Trans.). New York: W.W. Norton.

Piaget, J., & Inhelder, B. (1969). *The psychology of the child.* New York: Basic Books.

Rahman, F. (1979). *Islam* (2nd ed.). Chicago: University of Chicago Press.

Sartre, J. (1947). *The age of reason.* (E. Sutton, Trans.). New York: Vintage Books.

Sartre, J. (1956). *Being and nothingness: An essay on phenomenological ontology.* (H. Barnes, Trans.). New York: Philosophical Library.

Sartre, J. (1957). *Existentialism and human emotions.* New York: Philosophical Library.

Sartre, J. (1967). *Of human freedom.* (W. Baskin, Ed.). New York: Philosophical Library.

Seltzer, R. (1980). *Jewish people; Jewish thought.* New York: Macmillan.

Smart, N. (1988). *The world religions.* New York: Prentice Hall.

Tillich, P. (1952). *The courage to be.* New Haven: Yale University Press.

Vaillant, G. (1977). *Adaptation to life.* Boston: Little, Brown and Company.

West, G. K. (1986). Parenting without guilt: The predictable and situational misbehaviors of childhood. Springfield: Charles C. Thomas.

West, G. K. (1990). The 21 deadly myths of parenting and 21 creative alternatives. Tulsa, OK: Council Oak.

REFERENCES

Adler, A. (1958). *What life should mean to you.* New York: Capricorn.

Adler, A. (1964). *Superiority and social interest.* (H.L. Ansbacher & R.R. Ansbacher, Eds.). New York: The Viking Press.

Bishop, P., & Darton, M. (1987). *The encyclopedia of world faiths.* London: Macdonald & Co.

Bloom, A. (1987). *The closing of the American mind.* New York: Touchstone.

Buber, M. (1970). *I and Thou.* New York: Scribner.

Campbell, J., & Moyers, B. (1988). *The power of myth.* New York: Doubleday.

Concoran, M. (1978). Work experience, work interruption, and wages. In G. J. Duncan & J. N. Morgan (Eds.), *Five thousand American families—Patterns of economic progress.* Ann Arbor, MI: University of Michigan Institute for Social Research.

Cook, R. (1958). *One hundred and one famous poems.* Chicago: Reilly & Lee.

Corey, G. (1986). *Theory and practice of counseling and psychotherapy.* Pacific Grove, CA: Brooks/Cole.

Cuomo, M. (1986). The least of these. In S. Hewlett, A. Ilchman, & J. Sweeney (Eds.), *Family and work: Bridging the gap* (pp. 23–30). Cambridge: Ballinger.

Dickens, C. (1963). *A Christmas carol: In prose, being a ghost story of Christmas.* New York: Macmillan.

Dreikurs, R. (1971). *Social equality: The challenge of today.* Chicago: Regnery.

Elkind, D. (1981). *The hurried child.* Reading, PA: Addison-Wesley.

Elkind, D. (1984). *All grown up and no place to go.* Reading, PA: Addison-Wesley.

Erikson, E. (1964a). *Childhood and society.* New York: W.W. Norton.

Erikson, E. (1964b). *Insight and responsibility.* New York: W.W. Norton.

Erikson, E.H. (1988, June 14). Erikson, in his old age, expands his view of life. *New York Times,* C1 & C14.

Ford Foundation. (1989). *Work and family responsibilities: Achieving a balance.* New York: Author.

Friedan, B. (1963). *The feminine mystique.* New York: W.W. Norton.

Fromm, E. (1956). *The art of loving.* New York: Harper and Row.

Gardner, R. A. (1987). *Hyperactivity: The so-called attention-deficit disorders and the group of MBA Syndromes.* Cresskill, NJ: Creative Therapeutics.

Gilligan, C. (1982). *In a different voice: Psychological theory and women's development.* Cambridge: Harvard University Press.

Ginzberg, E. (1989). Progress so very slow. In S. Hewlett, A. Ilchman, & J. Sweeney (Eds.), *Family and work: Bridging the gap* (pp. 117–124). Cambridge: Ballinger.

Harper, L. (1960). *To kill a mockingbird.* Philadelphia: Lippincott.

Herzberg, F. (1966). *Work and the nature of man.* New York: World.

Kagan, J. (1984). *The nature of the child.* New York: Basic Books.

Kaufman, W. (1970). *Existentialism from Dostoevsky to Sartre.* New York: The World Publishing Company.

Kierkegaard, S. (1962). *The present age.* (A. Drug, Trans.). New York: Harper and Row.

Kierkegaard, S. (1968). *The sickness unto death.* (W. Lorie, Trans.). Princeton: Princeton University Press.

Kierkegaard, S. (1971). *Either/or, vol. 1.* (D. F. Swenson & L. M. Swenson, Trans.). Princeton: Princeton University Press.

Lerner, R. M. (Ed.). (1994). *Life-span development and behavior, vol. 9.* Hillsdale, NJ: Lawrence Erlbaum Associates.

Levinson, D. (1978). *The seasons of a man's life.* New York: Alfred A. Knopf.

Levinson, D. (1980). Toward a conception of the adult life course. In N. J. Smelser & E. H. Erikson (Eds.), *Themes of work and love in adulthood* (pp. 265–290). Cambridge: Harvard University Press.

Levinson, D. (1986). A conception of adult development. *American Psychologist, 41,* 3–13.

Macleish, A. (1958, December 22). Job and J.B. *Time Magazine,* 56.

Mandler, J. (1990, May/June). A new perspective on cognitive development in infancy. *American Scientist, 78*(3), 236–243.

Marcia, J. (1966). Identity six years after: A follow-up study. *Journal of Youth and Adolescence, 5,* 145–160.

Marcia, J. (1980). Identity in adolescence. In J. Adelson (Ed.), *Handbook of adolescent psychology* (pp. 159–187). New York: Wiley.

Marcia, J. (1991). Identity and self-development. In R. M. Lerner, A. C. Petersen, & J. Brooks-Gunn (Eds.), *Encyclopedia of adolescence* (vol. 1). New York: Garland.

Maslow, A. (1968). *Toward a psychology of being* (2nd ed.). New York: Van Nostrand Reinhold.

Maslow, A. (1971). *The farther reaches of human nature.* New York: Viking.

May, R. (1969). *Love and will.* New York: W.W. Norton.

May, R. (1981). *Freedom and destiny.* New York: W.W. Norton.

National Commission on Children. (1991). *Beyond rhetoric: A new American agenda for children and families.* Washington, DC: U.S. Government Printing Office.

Otto, R. (1958). *The idea of the holy: An inquiry into the non-rational factor in the idea of the divine and its relations to the creation.* Oxford: Oxford University Press.

O' Reilly, B. (1990a, January 1). Why grade "A" executives get an "F" as parents. *Fortune Magazine,* 36–46.

O' Reilly, B. (1990b, May 12). Is your company asking too much? *Fortune Magazine,* 38–46.

Postman, N. (1982). *The disappearance of childhood.* New York: Dell.

Rogers, C. (1951). *Client-centered therapy.* Boston: Houghton Mifflin.

Rogers, C. (1972). *On becoming a person.* Boston: Houghton Mifflin.

Rossi, P. (1989). *Down and out in America: The origins of homelessness.* Chicago: University of Chicago Press.

Roth, W. (1989). *Work and rewards: Redefining our work-life reality.* New York: Praeger.

Sekkaran, U. (1986). *Dual-career families: Contemporary organization and counseling issues.* San Francisco: Jossey-Bass.

Shakespeare, W. (1981). *Romeo and Juliet.* New York: Penguin.

Siegel, B. (1986). *Love, medicine and miracles.* New York: Harper & Row.

Shaw, G. (1955). *Man and Superman: A comedy and philosophy.* Baltimore: Penguin.

Slater, P. (1976). *The pursuit of loneliness: American culture at the breaking point.* Boston: Beacon Press.

Smart, N. (1984). *The religious experience of mankind.* New York: Macmillan.

Spenner, K.I. (1988). Occupations, work settings and the course of adult development: Tracing the implications of select historical changes. In P. B. Baltes, D. L. Featherman, & R. M. Lerner (Eds.), *Life-span development and behavior, vol. 9* (pp. 244–288). Hillsdale, NJ: Lawrence Erlbaum Associates.

Sternberg, R. (1986). A triangular theory of love. *Psychological Review, 93,* 119–135.

Sternberg, R. (1987). Liking versus loving: A comparative evaluation of theories. *Psychological Bulletin, 102,* 331–345.

White, B. (1975). *The first three years of life.* New York: Prentice Hall.

INDEX

ABOUT THE AUTHOR

Dr. Ken West teaches developmental psychology and graduate courses in marriage and family counseling at Lynchburg College in Virginia. Also, he writes a weekly column, entitled "Family Focus," for Lynchburg's News and Daily Advance. In addition, he is the author of numerous books and articles including *The Greatest Challenges in Human Development: Your Are the Hero, Parenting without Guilt, The 21 Deadly Myths of Parenting,* and *The Family: Live and In Concert.*

Dr. West has received awards for teaching excellence at the national, regional, and local levels. He became the second Lynchburg College professor to receive the prestigious, national honor, the T. A. Abbot Award for Teaching Excellence. Dr. West was the first recipient of Lynchburg College's Shirley

Rosser Award for Excellence in Teaching in 1989. In addition, he received the Distinguished Faculty Research Award in 1991 from his faculty colleagues. In 1993, he was selected as Educator of the Year by Phi Delta Kappa of Central Virginia.

Dr. West is the founder of the Lynchburg Parent Study Program, which is now sponsored by Randolph-Macon Woman's College, Lynchburg College and the Virginia Baptist Hospital.

Dr. West is married to Patty Leight West, a Ph.D. student (math education) at The University of Virginia. Ken and Patty have three children who attend the Lynchburg Public Schools: Patrick, Emily, and Dustin.

.